普通高等教育"十一五"国家级规划教材
PUTONG GAODENG JIAOYU SHIYIWU GUOJIAJI GUIHUA JIAOCAI

DIANQIGONGCHENG JIQI ZIDONGHUA ZHUANYE YINGYU

电气工程及其自动化专业英语

主编　苏小林　顾雪平
编写　王玲桃
主审　郑仰成　赵　萱

U0132216

中国电力出版社
http://jc.cepp.com.cn

内 容 提 要

本书为普通高等教育"十一五"国家级规划教材。

全书共分九章，主要内容包括电工基础、电子技术、电力电子技术、电机学、计算机、电力系统、继电保护、发电厂、自动化等。书中内容参考了原版专业教材、专业期刊等，经改编而成。书中介绍了专业英语和科技英语的阅读、翻译知识、特点、难点和技巧，常见专业文体的写作知识。每章节配有综合练习，分为单元选题、回答问题和英译汉三类。

本书主要作为普通高等学校电气工程及其自动化专业的本科专业英语教材，也可作为高职高专电力技术类专业的专业英语教材，还可作为相关工程技术人员学习专业英语的参考用书。

图书在版编目（CIP）数据

电气工程及其自动化专业英语/苏小林，顾雪平主编. —北京：中国电力出版社，2008

普通高等教育"十一五"国家级规划教材

ISBN 978-7-5083-7000-2

I. 电… II. ①苏… ②顾… III. ①电气工程-英语-高等学校-教材 ②自动化技术-英语-高等学校-教材 IV. H31

中国版本图书馆 CIP 数据核字（2008）第 045982 号

中国电力出版社出版、发行

（北京三里河路 6 号　100044　http://jc.cepp.com.cn）
北京丰源印刷厂印刷
各地新华书店经售

*

2008 年 5 月第一版　　2008 年 5 月北京第一次印刷
787 毫米×1092 毫米　16 开本 13.25 印张 318 千字
定价 **22.00** 元

敬 告 读 者

本书封面贴有防伪标签，加热后中心图案消失

本书如有印装质量问题，我社发行部负责退换

前　　言

　　电气工程及其自动化专业是一个宽口径专业，它包含了许多专业方向，涉及较多专业领域。各本科院校在人才培养中，注重培养学生基础扎实，知识面广，素质高，能力强。英语水平高低已成为社会及企事业单位衡量和评价学生能力的标准之一。加强英语教学，尤其是专业英语教学，已经引起各高校的重视。

　　专业英语着重于培养学生对英文专业资料、文献和信息的阅读能力，培养学生专业写作能力，同时兼顾培养学生的专业英文听说能力。通过专业英语的学习，达到扩充学生的专业词汇量，熟练掌握科技英语和专业英语特点的教学目的。

　　针对电气工程及其自动化宽口径的专业特点，在教材内容选材上，编者力求内容覆盖面广，其中包括电工基础、电子技术、电力电子技术、电机学、计算机、自动化、电力系统、继电保护、发电厂等。课文内容参考了原版专业教材、专业期刊文章等，经改编而成。

　　在教材的每一章节穿插介绍了专业英语和科技英语的阅读、翻译知识、特点、难点和技巧。同时还介绍了专业英语和科技英语中的常见文体的写作知识，如个人简历、商务信函、产品说明书、学术论文等。

　　在内容编排上，每章节由五大块组成：原文（课文），生词、术语、词汇，课文难点注释，翻译、写作等知识，综合练习。综合练习分为三类：根据课文选择正确答案、根据课文回答问题、英译汉。

　　本书共有九章，第一、二、三、四章由山西大学工程学院王玲桃编写，第六、七、八章由华北电力大学顾雪平编写，第五、九章和每章节的翻译、写作等知识由山西大学工程学院苏小林编写，全书由苏小林统稿。山西大学工程学院郑仰成、赵萱教授负责审阅本教材，并提出了许多建设性意见，在此表示衷心感谢，同时也感谢山西大学工程学院的郭晓红、张海荣给予的支持和帮助。

　　由于编者的水平有限，书中难免存在不妥或错误之处，殷切期望广大读者批评指正。请将您的宝贵意见和建议寄往：山西大学工程学院电力工程系（030013）。

编　者

2008 年 03 月

Contents

Chapter 1　Fundamentals of Electric Circuits

Section 1　Current and Voltage

Two variables $u(t)$ and $i(t)$ are the most basic concepts in an electric circuit, they characterize the various relationships in an electric circuit.

Charge and Current

The concept of electric charge is the underlying principle for explaining all electrical phenomena. Also, the most basic quantity in an electric circuit is the electric charge. Charge is an electrical property of the atomic particles of which matter consists, measured in coulombs (C).

We know from elementary physics that all matter is made of fundamental building blocks known as atoms and that each atom consists of electrons, protons, and neutrons. We also know that the charge e on an electron is negative and equal in magnitude to $1.60210 \times 10^{-19} \mathrm{C}$, while a proton carries a positive charge of the same magnitude as the electron. The presence of equal numbers of protons and electrons leaves an atom neutrally charged.

We consider the flow of electric charges. A unique feature of electric charge or electricity is the fact that it is mobile; that is, it can be transferred from one place to another, where it can be converted to another form of energy.

When a conducting wire is connected to a battery (a source of electromotive force), the charges are compelled to move; positive charges move in one direction while negative charges move in the opposite direction. This motion of charges creates electric current. It is conventional to take the current flow as the movement of positive charges, that is, opposite to the flow of negative charges, as Fig.1-1 illustrates. This convention was introduced by Benjamin Franklin (1706~1790), the American scientist and inventor. Although we now know that current in metallic conductors is due to negatively charged electrons, we will follow the universally accepted convention that current is the net flow of positive charges. Thus, Electric current is the time rate of charge, measured in amperes (A). Mathematically, the relationship among current i, charge q, and time t is

$$i = \frac{\mathrm{d}q}{\mathrm{d}t} \qquad (1\text{-}1)$$

The charge transferred between time t_0 and t is obtained by integrating both sides of Eq. (1-1). We obtain

$$q = \int_{t_0}^{t} i\,\mathrm{d}t \qquad (1\text{-}2)$$

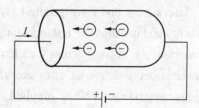

Fig.1-1　Electric current due to flow of electronic charge in a conductor

The way we define current as i in Eq. (1-1) suggests that current need not be a constant-valued function, charge can vary with time in several ways that may be represented by different kinds of mathematical functions.

Voltage, Energy, and Power

To move the electron in a conductor in a particular direction requires some work or energy transfer. This work is performed by an external electromotive force (emf), typically represented by the battery in Fig.1-1. This emf is also known as voltage or potential difference. The voltage u_{ab} between two points a and b in an electric circuit is the energy (or work) needed to move a unit charge from a to b; mathematically

$$u_{ab} = \frac{dw}{dq} \tag{1-3}$$

where w is energy in joules (J) and q is charge in coulombs (C). The voltage u_{ab} is measured in volts (V), named in honor of the Italian physicist Alessandro Antonio Volta (1745~1827), who invented the first voltaic battery. Thus, Voltage (or potential difference) is the energy required to move a unit charge through an element, measured in volts (V).

Fig.1-2 shows the voltage across an element (represented by a rectangular block) connected to

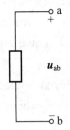

points **a** and **b**. The plus (+) and minus (−) signs are used to define reference direction or voltage polarity. The u_{ab} can be interpreted in two ways: ①point **a** is at a potential of u_{ab} volts higher than point **b**; ②the potential at point **a** with respect to point **b** is u_{ab}. It follows logically that in general

$$u_{ab} = -u_{ba} \tag{1-4}$$

Fig.1-2　Polarity of voltage u_{ab}

Although current and voltage are the two basic variables in an electric circuit, they are not sufficient by themselves. For practical purposes, we need to know *power* and energy. To relate power and energy to voltage and current, we recall from physics that power is the time rate of expending or absorbing energy, measured in watts (W). We write this relationship as

$$p = \frac{dw}{dt} \tag{1-5}$$

Where p is power in watts (W), w is energy in joules (J), and t is time in seconds (s). From Eq. (1-1), Eq. (1-3), and Eq. (1-5), it follows that

$$p = ui \tag{1-6}$$

Because u and i are generally function of time, the power p in Eq. (1-6) is a time-varying quantity and is called the instantaneous power. The power absorbed or supplied by an element is the product of the voltage across the element and the current through it. If the power has a plus sign, power is being delivered to or absorbed by the element. If, on the other hand, the power has a minus sign, power is being supplied by the element. But how do we know when the power has a negative or a positive sign?

Current direction and voltage polarity play a major role in determining the sign of power. It is therefore important that we pay attention to the relationship between current i and voltage u in Fig.1-3(a). The voltage polarity and current i direction must conform with those shown in Fig.1-3(a) in order for the power to have a positive sign. This is known as the passive sign convention. By the passive sign convention, current enters through the positive polarity of the voltage. In this case, $p = ui$ or $ui > 0$ implies that the element is absorbing power. However, if $p = {}^-ui$ or $ui < 0$, as in Fig.1-3(b), the element is releasing or supplying power.

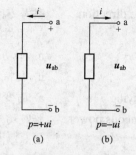

Fig.1-3   Reference polarities for power using the passive sign convention

(a) absorbing power;   (b) supplying power

In fact, the law of conservation of energy must be obeyed in any electric circuit. For this reason, the algebraic sum of power in a circuit, at any instant of time, must be zero

$$\sum p = 0 \qquad (1\text{-}7)$$

This again confirms the fact that the total power supplied to the circuit must balance the total power absorbed. From Eq. (1-7), the energy absorbed or supplied by an element from time t_0 to time t is

$$w = \int_{t_0}^{t} p\,\mathrm{d}t \qquad (1\text{-}8)$$

New Words and Expressions

current	n. 电流
voltage	n. 电压
variable	n. 变量
charge	n. 电荷；v. 充电，带电，起电
coulomb	n. 库仑（电荷的单位）
circuit	n. 电路
underlying	a. ①基本的，根本的　②潜在的，在下（面）的，下伏的
electron	n. 电子
positive charge	正电荷
negative charge	负电荷
magnitude	n. 大小，尺寸，数量，数值
electromotive	a. 电动的，起电的
electromotive force	电动势
ampere	n. 安，安培（电流的单位）
integrate	v. 积分，求积分
work	n. 功
potential difference	n. 电位差
rectangular	a. 矩形的，直角的，正交的
joule	n. 焦尔（能量、热量、功的单位）
volt	n. 伏特（电压、电位、电势的单位）
voltaic battery	伏达电池
convention	n. 习惯，惯例，常规

reference direction	参考方向
polarity	n. 极性
power	n. ①功率，效率 ②动力，电力，能力，电源 ③乘方，幂
watt	n. 瓦特（功率的单位）
time-varying	a. 时变的
instantaneous power	瞬时功率
passive	a. ①无源的 ②消极的，被动的；n. 无源
algebraic	a. 代数的
instant	n. 瞬间，瞬时，即刻，时，时刻

Notes

1. Charge is an electrical property of the atomic particles of which matter consists, measured in coulombs.

电荷是构成物质的原子的电气属性，其量纲为库仑。

2. The presence of equal numbers of protons and electrons leaves an atom neutrally charged.

质子和电子数量相同使得原子呈现电中性。leave 在此作"使，让"讲。

3. The voltage u_{ab} between two points a and b in an electric circuit is the energy (or work) needed to move a unit charge from a to b.

电路中 a、b 两点间电压 u_{ab} 等于从 a 到 b 移动单位电荷所需能量（或所需做的功）。

专 业 英 语 概 述

随着科学技术的发展、社会的进步，各国之间技术信息、学术交流和专业技术情报传播日益广泛。我国加入 WTO 后，与世界各国在电气工程及其自动化领域的技术合作、交流、竞争日益频繁，各类英文技术情报资料、专业技术文献、工程设备文档资料等大量涌现。因此，电气工程及其自动化专业领域的工作者必须具备良好的基础英语能力和专业英语能力，才能高效、快速、准确地吸收最新技术情报和开展国际科学技术交流，才能跟上该专业领域的技术发展。

电气工程及其自动化专业英语是英语在电气工程及其自动化专业领域的应用，因此专业英语是以基础英语作为基础。为了体现科学技术资料的客观、科学、精确和准确，专业英语与基础英语有着很大的差别，其文章的结构具有如下特点：

（1）长句多，有时甚至一个段落只有一个句子；

（2）大量使用被动语态和非谓语动词；

（3）介词短语多；

（4）名词性词组多；

（5）使用虚拟语气的句子多；

（6）专业术语、合成新词及半技术词汇多。

专业英语以其独特的语体，明确地表达作者在其专业方面的见解，表达方式直截了当，具有准确、精练、正式、逻辑性强的特点，注重客观事实和真理。专业英语属于科技英语的范畴，具有科技英语的特点，与专业内容联系紧密，专业性强。例如，同一个词在不同学科的专业英语中，其涵义可能不同。不同学科的专业英语有着各自的特点。

通过专业英语的学习，不仅要扩充、掌握大量的专业词汇，还要熟悉专业英语的词法、句法的特点，提高专业英语的阅读理解能力、翻译能力和写作能力。

要正确地理解专业英语文献资料，并准确地用汉语表达，除了要求我们熟练地运用汉语表达方式外，还要具有一定的专业知识和专业水平，注重与专业内容联系，使用规范的专业术语。

Exercises

I. Choose the best answer into the blank

1. It is conventional to take the current flow as the movement of _____.
   A. negative charges　　B. positive charges　　　C. any charge　　　D. protons
2. Electric current is the time rate of charge, measured in _____.
   A. watts　　　　　　B. volts　　　　　　　C. joules　　　　　D. amperes
3. The energy required to move a unit charge through an element is _____.
   A. current　　　　　B. power　　　　　　C. voltage　　　　　D. potential
4. The plus (+) and minus (−) signs in an electric circuit diagram are used to define _____.
   A. voltage polarity　B. current direction　　C. power flow　　　D. absorbed power
5. According to the passive sign convention, if the power has a plus sign, power is _____ by the element.
   A. supplied　　　　　B. absorbed　　　　　C. generated　　　D. transferred

II. Answer the following questions according to the text

1. Is current in any electric circuit always a constant-valued function? Why?
2. How does current change when the time rate of charges is greater?
3. How to interpret the $u_{ab} = -1$ volt in two ways?
4. What relation is between power and energy?
5. Why do current direction and voltage polarity play a major role in determining the characteristics of power?

Section 2　Circuit Elements

An electric circuit is simply an interconnection of the elements. There are two types of elements found in electric circuits: passive elements and active elements. An active element is capable of generating energy while a passive element is not. Examples of passive elements are resistors, capacitors, and inductors. The most important active elements are voltage or current sources that generally deliver power to the circuit connected to them.

Independent sources

An ideal independent source is an active element that provides a specified voltage or current that is completely independent of other circuit variables.

An independent voltage source is a two-terminal element, such as a battery or a generator, which maintains a specified voltage between its terminals. The voltage is completely independent of the current through the element. The symbol for a voltage source having u volts across its terminals is shown in Fig.1-4(a). The polarity is as shown, indicating that terminal a is u volts above terminal b. Thus if $u > 0$, then terminal a is at a higher potential than terminal b. The opposite is true, of course, if $u < 0$.

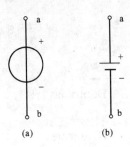

Fig.1-4　Symbols for independent voltage sources
(a) used for constant or time-varying voltage;
(b) used for constant voltage (dc)

In Fig.1-4(a), the voltage u may be time varying, or it may be constant, in which case we would probably label it U. Another symbol that is often used for a constant voltage source, such as a battery with U volts across its terminals, is shown in Fig.1-4(b). In the case of constant sources we shall use Fig.1-4(a) and 1-4(b) interchangeably.

We might observe at this point that the polarity marks on Fig.1-4(b) are redundant since the polarity could be defined by the positions of the longer and shorter lines.

An independent current source is a two-terminal element through which a specified current flows. The current is completely independent of the voltage across the element. The symbol for an independent current source is shown in Fig.1-5, where i is the specified current. The direction of the current is indicated by the arrow.

Independent sources are usually meant to deliver power to the external circuit and not to absorb it. Thus if u is the voltage across the source and its current i is directed out of the positive terminal, then the source is delivering power, given by $p = ui$, to the external circuit. Otherwise it is absorbing power. For example, in Fig.1-6 (a) the battery is delivering 24 W to the external circuit. In Fig.1-6(b) the battery is absorbing 24 W, as would be the case when it is being charged.

Fig.1-5　Symbols for independent current sources

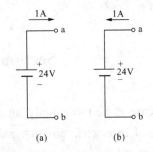

Fig.1-6　Symbols for independent sources
(a) A source delivering power; (b) A source absorbing power

Dependent sources

An ideal dependent (or controlled) source is an active element in which the source quantity is controlled by another voltage or current.

Dependent sources are usually designated by diamond-shaped symbols, as shown in Fig.1-7. Since the control of the dependent source is achieved by a voltage or current of some other element in the circuit, and the source can be voltage or current, it follows that there are four possible types of dependent sources, namely:

（1）A voltage-controlled voltage source (VCVS).

（2）A current-controlled voltage source (CCVS).

（3）A voltage-controlled current source (VCCS).

（4）A current-controlled current source (CCCS).

Dependent sources are useful in modeling elements such as transistors, operational amplifiers and integrated circuits.

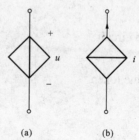

(a)   (b)

Fig.1-7   Symbols for dependent sources

(a) Dependent voltage source; (b) Dependent current source

It should be noted that an ideal voltage source (dependent or independent) will produce any current required to ensure that the terminal voltage is as stated, whereas an ideal current source will produce the necessary voltage to ensure the stated current flow. Thus an ideal source could in theory supply an infinite amount of energy. It should also be noted that not only do sources supply power to a circuit, but they can absorb power from a circuit too. For a voltage source, we know the voltage but not the current supplied or drawn by it. By the same token, we know the current supplied by a current source but not the voltage across it.

New Words and Expressions

active	a. ①有源的，有功的，有效的 ② 活动的，主动的，积极的 ③活性的，放射的，激励的
active element	有源元件
resistor	n. 电阻，电阻器
capacitor	n. 电容器
inductor	n. 电感器
source	n. 电源，（光，能，动力，信号，辐射，根，来，起）源
ideal independent source	理想独立源
generator	n. ①发电机 ②（脉冲，信号，气体）发生器，振荡器，加速器
constant voltage source	恒定电压源
independent source	独立源
dependent source	受控源
controlled source	受控源
diamond-shaped	a. 菱形的
voltage-controlled voltage source	电压控制电压源
current-controlled voltage source	电流控制电压源
voltage-controlled current source	电压控制电流源

current-controlled current source	电流控制电流源
transistor	n. 晶体管，半导体管
operational	a. ①运算的，计算的 ②操作的，工作的，业务的，运转的
amplifier	n. 放大器
integrated circuit	集成电路
token	n. ①标记，象征，记号 ②特征，证明
by the same token	同理，同样；另外，还有

Notes

1. In Fig.1-6(b) the battery is absorbing 24 W, as would the case when it is being charged.

   图 1-6 中，电池就像充电情况，吸收功率 24W。

2. It should be noted that an ideal voltage source (dependent or independent) will produce any current required to ensure that the terminal voltage is as stated, whereas an ideal current source will produce the necessary voltage to ensure the stated current flow.

   应该注意：一个理想电压源（独立或受控）可向电路提供任意电流以保证其端电压为规定值，而电流源可向电路提供任意电压以保证其规定电流。

翻 译 标 准

　　翻译既与阅读有关，又有很大不同。阅读专业外文资料，只要自己能看懂，正确理解其内容即可，不涉及用一种语言文字表达的问题。而翻译的任务是要把一种语言表达的内容，完整而正确地用另一种语言表达出来。由于英语和汉语在语言规则和习惯上各不相同，各有特点，在词汇和语法上也有着很大差异。在翻译过程中，要做到使原文的内容准确而通顺地表达清楚，在用词造句上就必须符合汉语的表达规则和习惯。

　　专业英语翻译是对原文的一种再创作过程，译者不仅需要有较好的相关专业知识，还需要不断探索和掌握翻译的内在规律，才能做好这项工作。对于专业英语翻译，应达到"准确明白"、"通顺严密"、"简练全面"这三项标准。

　　（1）准确明白，一是指要准确无误地表达原文的含义，不得有错误和遗漏之处，在技术内容上要忠实原文；二是要清楚明白地表达原文的意思，不得有模糊不清、模棱两可之处。要达到这一标准，首先要深刻地、正确地理解原文，其次在组织译文时要注意避免歧义。

　　（2）通顺严密，是指译文应当合乎中文的语法要求，语句流畅，使读者阅读易懂；同时又应严密，不能因通顺而牺牲了原文的严密性，损害了原文的内容。要达到这一标准，一是选词造句正确，二是语气表达正确。

　　（3）简练全面，是指译文要尽可能简短、精练，没有冗词费字，同时不要有任何遗漏。要达到这一标准，需在翻译时不受原文结构的限制，利用适当的转换译法，力求译文简洁明快、精练流畅。

　　专业英语翻译人员为达到以上三条标准，需做到以下几点要求：

　　（1）掌握英语语法知识。包括词法、句法和各种习惯用法。在翻译过程中，通过英语语法分析，有利于正确地理解原文。所以，需要不断地学习和掌握英语语法，提高英语水平。

（2）具有一定深度的专业知识和较为广博的科学知识。只有较为深入地掌握了专业知识，才能在翻译过程中，正确地理解原文的专业技术内容，并能使用正确的专业术语。由于学科之间的联系越来越紧密，交叉内容也越来越多，因此，还需要广泛了解其他有关学科的一般常识。

（3）有较高的汉语修养。即能较为熟练地运用汉语的语法修辞手段来准确地表达原文的技术内容。

（4）掌握翻译方法和技巧。即熟悉英语各种常见句型、短语、词汇的不同翻译方法和技巧，在翻译过程中才能较为得心应手地进行翻译。

Exercises

I. Choose the best answer into the blank

1. An independent voltage source is a _____, which maintains a specified voltage between its terminals.

    A. one-terminal element   B. two-terminal element

    C. three-terminal element   D. four-terminal element

2. Resistors are _____ elements.

    A. passive   B. active

    C. independent source   D. dependent source

3. An ideal dependent source is an _____ element in which the source quantity is controlled by another voltage or current.

    A. passive   B. active

    C. independent   D. inductive

4. There are _____ possible types of dependent sources.

    A. two   B. three

    C. four   D. five

5. For a voltage source, its terminal voltage is known but its _____ must be determined by the external circuit connecting with it.

    A. electromotive force   B. current

    C. control coefficient   D. polarity

II. Answer the following questions according to the text

1. What difference is there between an independent source and a dependent source?

2. What element is an ideal independent source?

3. Is the voltage of an independent voltage source dependent of the current through the element? How to find the current through it?

4. What are four possible types of dependent sources?

5. Is the terminal voltage of independent voltage source always constant?

III. Translate the following into Chinese

    All the simple circuit elements that will be considered in the work that follows can be classified according to the relationship of the current through the element to the voltage across the element. For instance, if the voltage across the element is directly proportional to the current through it, or $u = ki$, we shall call the element a resistor. Other types of simple circuit elements have a terminal voltage which is proportional to the time derivative or the integral with respect to time of the current. There are also elements in which the voltage is completely independent of the current or the current is completely independent of the voltage; these are the independent sources. Furthermore, we shall need to define special kinds of sources in which the source voltage or current depends upon a current or voltage elsewhere in the circuit; such sources will be termed dependent sources or controlled sources.

Section 3　Ohm's Law

The circuit element used to model the current-resisting behavior of a material is the resistor. The resistor is the simplest passive element.

Georg Simon Ohm (1787~1854), a German physicist, is credited with formulating the current-voltage relationship for a resistor based on experiments performed in 1826.This relationship is known as Ohm's Law.

Ohm's Law states that the voltage across a resistor is directly proportional to the current flowing through the resistor. The constant of proportionality is the resistance value of the resistor in ohms. The circuit symbol for the resistor is shown in Fig.1-8. For the current and voltage shown, Ohm's law is

$$u(t) = Ri(t) \tag{1-9}$$

where $R \geqslant 0$ is the resistance in ohms.

Rearranging Eq. (1-9) into the form $R = u(t) / i(t)$, we see that

$$1\ \text{ohm} = 1\ \text{V/A}$$

The symbol used to represent the ohm is the capital Greek omega (Ω)

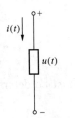

Fig.1-8　Circuit symbol for the resistor

Since R is constant, Eq.(1-9) is the equation of a straight line. For this reason, the resistor is called a linear resistor. A graph of $u(t)$ versus $i(t)$ is shown in Fig.1-9, which is a line passing through the origin with a slope of R. Obviously, a straight line is the only graph possible for which the ratio of $u(t)$ to $i(t)$ is constant for all $i(t)$.

Resistors whose resistances do not remain constant for different terminal currents are known as nonlinear resistors. For such a resistor, the resistance is a function of the current flowing in the device. A simple example of a nonlinear resistor is an incandescent lamp. A typical voltage-current characteristic for this device is shown in Fig.1-10, where we see that the graph is no longer a straight line. Since R is not a constant, the analysis of a circuit containing nonlinear resistor is more difficult.

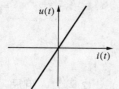

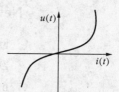

Fig.1-9   Voltage-current characteristic   Fig.1-10   Typical voltage-current characteristic

for a linear resistor   for a nonlinear resistor

In reality, all practical resistors are nonlinear because the electrical characteristics of all conductors are affected by environmental factors such as temperature. Many materials, however, closely approximate an ideal linear resistor over a desired operating region. We shall concentrate on these types of elements and simply refer to them as resistors.

Since the value of R can range from zero to infinity, it is important that we consider the two extreme possible values of R. An element with $R = 0$ is called a *short circuit*, as shown in Fig.1-11 (a). For a short circuit

$$u = iR = 0 \tag{1-10}$$

showing that the voltage is zero but the current could be anything. In practice, a short circuit is usually a connecting wire assumed to be a perfect conductor. Thus, a short circuit is a circuit element with resistance approaching zero.

Similarly, an element with $R = \infty$ is known as an *open circuit*, as shown in Fig.1-11 (b). For an open circuit

$$i = \lim_{R \to \infty} \frac{u}{R} = 0 \tag{1-11}$$

indicating that the current is zero though the voltage could be anything. Thus, an open circuit is a circuit element with resistance approaching infinity.

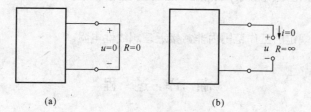

(a)   (b)

Fig.1-11

(a) Short circuit ($R = 0$);   (b) Open circuit ($R = \infty$)

Another important quantity which is useful in circuit analysis is known as conductance, defined by

$$G = \frac{1}{R} = \frac{i}{u} \tag{1-12}$$

The conductance is a measure of how well an element will conduct electric current. The unit of conductance is the siemens (S).

New Words and Expressions

Ohm	欧姆（电阻，电抗，阻抗的单位）
Ohm's Law	欧姆定律
resistance	n. ①电阻，电阻器（件，装置） ②阻力，阻尼 ③抵抗，抵制，反对
rearrange	v. 重新整理（安排，布置，排列），调整
linear	a. ①线性的，一次的 ②（直）线的，直线型的，线状的
linear resistor	线性电阻
nonlinear	a. 非线性的，非直线的
nonlinear resistor	非线性电阻
incandescent	a. 白炽（热）的，炽热的
incandescent lamp	白炽灯
voltage-current characteristic	伏安特性
short circuit	短路
open circuit	开路
conductance	n. ①电导，导电性，导纳 ②传导（性，率，系数）
siemens	n. 西门子（电导单位）

Notes

1. Georg Simon Ohm (1787~1854), a German physicist, is credited with formulating the current-voltage relationship for a resistor based on experiments performed in 1826.

   德国物理学家乔治西蒙欧姆（1787~1854），1826 年通过实验提出了电阻的电流电压关系，为此而享誉世界。

2. Many materials, however, closely approximate an ideal linear resistor over a desired operating region.

   不过，许多材料在规定的工作范围内非常接近理想线性电阻。

翻 译 过 程

要高质量地完成翻译任务，必须从深刻理解原文入手，力求确切表达原文。翻译需经历三个过程：理解阶段，表达阶段，校核阶段。

（1）理解阶段，主要是通过辨明词义，弄清各种语法成分及其相互关系，即单词、短语、从句的确切含义和句子所叙述的专业内容，并把前后句子贯串起来理解，形成对原文的完整印象，真正掌握原文的内容和实质。

（2）表达阶段，是在理解的基础上，以忠实于原意为前提，灵活地运用各种翻译方法和技巧，写出符合汉语规范、表达习惯以及翻译标准的译文。为此，需做到准确选词，即选择汉语中最恰当的词来翻译原文中有关的词；恰当造句，即在尽可能忠实于原文风格的前提下，力求按照汉语的规范恰当地组织每一句译文，避免歧义，力求简练。

（3）校核阶段，是理解与表达的进一步深化，是对原文内容进一步核实，对译文语言进一步推敲，进行必要的润色和修改，使译文符合标准规范。校核通常又要经历初校、复校和定稿三个步骤。

为了达到翻译标准，需要利用各种翻译的方法和技巧。概括起来有词序的变更、词性的转换、词义的引申、用词的增删、句型的改造等。相关内容在后面章节分别介绍。

Exercises

I. Choose the best answer into the blank

1. The circuit element used to model the current-resisting behavior of a material is _____.

    A. the capacitor   B. the inductor   C. the resistor   D. the dependent source

2. Ohm's Law states that the voltage across a resistor is _____ the current flowing through the resistor.

    A. equal to   B. directly proportional to

    C. inversely proportional to   D. different from

3. A resistor whose resistances vary with its current is known as _____.

    A. a linear resistor

    B. a constant resistor

    C. a nonlinear resistor

    D. a time-varying resistor

4. _____ is a circuit element with resistance approaching infinity.

    A. An open circuit

    B. A short circuit

    C. A resistive circuit

    D. An inductive circuit

5. An electric heater draws 10 A from a 120V line. The resistance of the heater is _____.

    A. 1200 Ω   B. 120 Ω   C. 12 Ω   D. 1.2 Ω

II. Answer the following questions according to the text

1. What is Ohm's law?

2. Does the resistance value of a linear resistor vary with the current through it?

3. What feature of the voltage-current characteristic curve is for a linear resistor?

4. What is a short circuit?

5. What relationship between resistance and conductance is there?

III. Translate the following into Chinese

It must be emphasized that the linear resistor is an idealized circuit element; it is a mathematical model of a physical device. "Resistors" may be easily purchased or manu- factured, but it is soon found that the voltage-current ratio of this physical device is reasonably constant only within certain ranges of current, voltage, or power and depends also on temperature and other environmental factors. We shall usually refer to a linear resistor as simply a resistor, using the longer term only when the linear nature of the element needs emphasis. Any resistor that is nonlinear will always be described as such. Nonlinear resistors should not necessarily be considered as undesirable elements.

Section 4   Kirchhoff's Laws

The network variables may have many interrelationships among themselves. Some of these relationships are due to the nature of the variables. A different class of relationship occurs because of the restriction that some specific type of network element places on the variables. Still another class of relationship is one between several variables of the same type which occurs as the result of the network configuration, i.e., the manner in which the various element of the network are interconnected. Such a relation is said to be based on the topology of the network. Kirchhoff's Current and Voltage Laws are laws that are based on the connective features of a network. These laws say nothing about the elements themselves.

Kirchhoff's Current Law

Kirchhoff's Current Law is based on the law of conservation of charge, which requires that the algebraic sum of charges within a system can not change.

Kirchhoff's Current Law (KCL) states that the algebraic sum of currents entering a node   (or a closed boundary) is zero. Mathematically, KCL implies that

$$\sum_{n=1}^{N} i_n = 0 \tag{1-13}$$

where N is the number of branches connected to the node and i_n is the nth current entering (or leaving) the node. By this law, currents entering a node may be regarded as +, while currents leaving the node may be taken as $-$.

Consider the node in Fig.1-12. Applying KCL gives

$$i_1 + (-i_2) + i_3 + i_4 + (-i_5) = 0 \tag{1-14}$$

Since current i_1, i_3, i_4 are entering the node, while currents i_2, and i_5 are leaving it. By rearranging the Eq.(1-14), we get

$$i_1 + i_3 + i_4 = i_2 + i_5 \tag{1-15}$$

An alternative form of KCL: **The sum of the currents entering a node is equal to the sum of the currents leaving the node.**

Note that KCL also applies to a closed boundary. This may be regarded as a generalized case, because a node may be regarded as a closed surface shrunk to a point. In two dimensions, a closed boundary is the same as a closed path. As typically illustrated in the circuit of Fig.1-13, the total current entering the closed surface is equal to the total current leaving the surface.

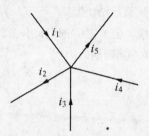

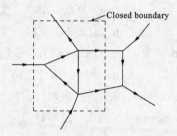

Fig.1-12　Current at a node illustrating KCL　　　Fig.1-13　Applying KCL to a closed boundary

Kirchhoff's Voltage Law (KVL)

Kirchhoff's voltage law is based on the principle of conservation of energy.

Kirchhoff's Voltage Law (KVL) states that the algebraic sum of all voltages around a closed path (or loop) is zero. Expressed mathematically, KVL states that

$$\sum_{m=1}^{M} u_m = 0 \tag{1-16}$$

where M is the number of voltages in the loop and u_m is the mth voltage.

To illustrate KVL, consider the circuit in Fig.1-14. The sign on each voltage is the polarity of the terminal encountered first as we travel around the loop. We can start with any branch and go around the loop either clockwise or counterclockwise. Suppose we start with the voltage source and go clockwise around the loop as shown;

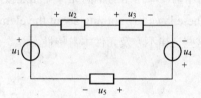

Fig.1-14　A single-loop circuit illustrating KVL

then voltages would be $-u_1$, $+u_2$, $+u_3$, $-u_4$, and $+u_5$, in that order. For example, as we reach branch 3, the positive terminal is met first; hence we have $+u_3$. For branch 4, we reach the negative terminal first; hence, $-u_4$. Thus, KVL yields

$$-u_1 + u_2 + u_3 - u_4 + u_5 = 0 \tag{1-17}$$

Rearranging terms gives

$$u_2 + u_3 + u_5 = u_1 + u_4 \tag{1-18}$$

Which may be interpreted as

Sum of voltage drops = Sum of voltage rises

This is an alternative form of KVL. Notice that if we had traveled counterclockwise, the result would have been u_1, $-u_5$, $+u_4$, $-u_3$, and $-u_2$, which is the same as before except that the signs are reversed. Hence, Eq. (1-16) and Eq. (1-18) remain the same.

New Words and Expressions

network	n.	网络，电路，电网
configuration	n.	结构，构造
topology	n.	拓扑，拓扑学，拓扑结构

node	n. ①节点，结点，交点，叉点　②（波）节，结，节
branch	n. ①支路，支线，支脉　②分支（路，线，流）　③部门，分部，分行
dimension	n. ①维（数），度（数）　②尺寸，线度　③量纲，因次
loop	n. 回路，闭合电路，环路，循环，环
clockwise	a.; ad.　顺时针方向（的）
counterclockwise	a.; ad.　逆时针方向（的）

Notes

1. Kirchhoff's Current and Voltage Laws
   基尔荷夫电流、电压定律
2. A different class of relationship occurs because of the restriction that some specific type of network element places on the variables. Still another class of relationship is one between several variables of the same type which occurs as the result of the network configuration, i.e., the manner in which the various element of the network are interconnected.
   一种不同类型的关系是由于网络元件的某种特定类型的连接对变量的约束。另一类关系由于网络结构，即网络的不同元件互相连接的方式所产生的相同形式的一些变量间的关系。
3. These laws say nothing about the elements themselves.
   这些定律不涉及元件本身特性。

专业英语的语法特点

专业文献是专业技术人员进行科学技术交流、思想交流的载体，所以专业英语要求客观、真实、明确、严密、简洁地表达有关的科技实质。这些决定了专业英语有其独特的语法特点、文体和表达风格。

（1）惯用时态。专业英语中多用动词的现在时，尤其是多用一般现在时，来叙述事实或真理，客观地表述定义、定律、定理、方程式、公式、图表等。用一般过去时来介绍实验情况或叙述事物的历史发展经过等。用一般将来时叙述计划要做的工作和预期获得的结果等。

（2）大量使用被动语态。专业英语更注重对事实、方法、性能和特性做出客观表述。采用被动语态能更为客观，有助于将读者的注意力集中在描述的事物、事实、现象或过程上。

（3）大量使用非限定动词。在专业英语中，为了描述的明确、简练，多采用不定式短语、分词短语和动名词短语，特别是分词短语应用较多。

（4）大量使用名词及介词短语。同样是为了达到明确和简练的要求，在专业英语中多采用名词和介词短语。

（5）条件句较多。专业文献中常需提出假设和推理，因而条件句使用较多。

（6）长句较多。由于专业英语的作用是陈述事理、描述过程，它所给出的定义、定理、定律或描述的概念及工艺过程，都必须严谨、准确。由此必然带有许多修饰、限定和附加成分，使专业英语中出现了包含有许多子句的复杂句。因此，与日常英语相比，使用的长句较多。有时一个长句就是一个较长的段落。

Exercises

I. Choose the best answer into the blank

1. Kirchhoff's Laws are laws that are based on the _____.

   A. nature of the network element

   B. topology of the network

   C. nonlinear or linear elements

   D. types of network elements

2. Kirchhoff's Current Law can be stated in _____.

   A. only a way   B. two ways

   C. three ways   D. four ways

3. Kirchhoff's Current Law is based on _____.

   A. Ohm's Law   B. the law of conservation of charge

   C. the law of conservation of energy D. the Coulomb's law

4. Kirchhoff's Voltage Law is based on _____.

   A. Ohm's Law   B. the law of conservation of charge

   C. the law of conservation of energy D. the Coulomb's law

5. The algebraic sum of all voltages around a loop is _____.

   A. zero   B. indefinite value

   C. sum of voltage rises   D. sum of voltage drops

II. Answer the following questions according to the text

1. Are Kirchhoff's Laws valid in a nonlinear circuit?

2. How does Kirchhoff's Voltage Law state in two ways?

3. If currents leaving a node are regarded as +, what sign must current entering the node be taken as?

4. Widely speaking, can a closed boundary be regarded as a node for KCL?

5. Is the sign of each voltage in KVL equation related to going around a loop clockwise or counterclockwise?

III. Translate the following into Chinese

If a circuit has two or more independent sources, one way to determine the value of a specific variable (voltage or current) is to use nodal or mesh analysis. Another way is to determine the contribution of each independent source to the variable and then add them up. The latter approach is known as the superposition. The superposition principle states that the voltage across (or current through) an element in a linear circuit is the algebraic sum of the voltages across (or currents through) that element due to each independent source acting alone.

Section 5　Basic Analysis Methods

Having understood the fundamental laws of circuit theory (Ohm's law and Kirchhoff's laws), we are now prepared to apply these laws to develop two powerful techniques for circuit analysis: nodal analysis, which is based on a systematic application of Kirchhoff's current law (KCL), and mesh analysis, which is based on a systematic application of Kirchhoff's voltage law (KCL). With the two techniques to be developed in this section, we can analyze almost any circuit by obtaining a set of simultaneous equations that are then solved to obtain the required values of current or voltage. One method of solving simultaneous equations involves Cramer's rule, which allows us to calculate circuit variables as a quotient of determinants.

Nodal Analysis

A convenient choice of voltages for many networks is the set of node voltages. Since a voltage is defined as existing between two nodes, it is convenient to select one node in the network to be a reference node or datum node and then associate a voltage or a potential with each of the other nodes. The voltage of each of the non-reference nodes with respect to the reference node is defined to be a node voltage. It is common practice to select polarities so that the node voltages are positive relative to the reference node. For a circuit containing N nodes, there will be $N-1$ node voltages, some of which may be known, of course, if voltage sources are present.

Frequently the reference node is chosen to be the node to which the largest number of branches are connected. Many practical circuits are built on a metallic base or chassis, and usually there are a number of elements connected to the chassis, which is often then connected to the earth. The chassis may then be called ground, and it becomes the logical choice for the reference node. For this reason, the reference node is frequently referred to as ground. The reference node is thus at ground potential or zero potential, and the other nodes may be considered to be at some potential above zero.

The application of KCL results in an equation relating node voltages. Clearly, simplification in writing the resulting equations is possible when the reference node is chosen to be a node with a large number of elements connected to it. As we shall see, however, this is not the only criterion for selecting the reference node, but it is frequently the overriding one.

In the network shown in Fig.1-15, there are three nodes, numbered as shown. Since there are four branches connected to node 3, we selected it as reference nodes, identifying it by the ground connection shown.

The voltage between node 1 and the reference node 3 is identified as u_1, and u_2 is defined between node 2 and the reference. These two voltages are sufficient, and the voltage between any other pair of

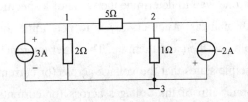

Fig.1-15　A given three-node circuit

nodes may be found in terms of them. For example, the voltage of node 1 with respect to node 2 is $(u_1 - u_2)$.

We must now apply Kirchhoff's current law to nodes 1 and 2. We do this by equating the total current leaving the node through the several conductances to the total source current entering the node. Thus,

$$0.5\, u_1 + 0.2(u_1 - u_2) = 3$$

or
$$0.7\, u_1 - 0.2u_2 = 3 \qquad\qquad (1\text{-}19)$$

At node 2 we obtain

$$u_2 + 0.2(u_2 - u_1) = 2$$

or
$$-0.2\, u_1 + 1.2\, u_2 = 2 \qquad\qquad (1\text{-}20)$$

Solve the Eq.(1-19) and Eq. (1-20) to obtain the unknown node voltage u_1 and u_2, then any current or power in the circuit may now be found.

Steps to nodal analysis:

(1) Select a node as the reference node. Assign voltages u_1, u_2, ...,u_{n-1} to the remaining $n-1$ node.

(2) Apply KCL to each of the $n-1$ non-reference nodes. Use Ohm's law to express the branch currents in terms of node voltages.

(3) Solve the resulting simultaneous equations to obtain the unknown node voltages, then solve the other required variables.

Mesh Analysis

Mesh analysis provides another general procedure for analyzing circuits, using mesh currents as the circuit variables. Using mesh currents instead of element currents as circuit variables is convenient and reduces the number of equations that must be solved simultaneously. Recall that a loop is a closed path with no node passed more than once. A mesh is a loop that dose not contain any other loop within it.

Nodal analysis applies KCL to find unknown voltages in a given circuit, while mesh analysis applies KVL to find unknown currents. Mesh analysis is not quite as general as nodal analysis because it is only applicable to a circuit that is planar. A planar circuit that is planar. A planar circuit is one that can be drawn in a plane with no branches crossing one another; otherwise it is nonplanar. A circuit may have crossing branches and still be planar if it can be redrawn such that it has no crossing branches. A mesh is a loop that does not contain any other loops within it.

In Fig.1-16, for example, there are two meshes in this circuit. The current through a mesh is known as mesh currents in a given circuit. If we label the left–hand mesh of our problem as mesh 1,then we establish a mesh current i_1 flowing in a clockwise direction about this mesh. A mesh current is indicated by a curved arrow that almost closes on itself and is drawn inside the appropriate mesh, as shown in Fig.1-16. The mesh current i_2 is established in the remaining mesh, again in a clockwise direction.

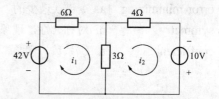

Fig.1-16 A circuit with two meshes

Although the direction is arbitrary, we shall always choose clockwise mesh currents because a certain error-minimizing symmetry then results in the equations.

One of the greatest advantages in the use of mesh currents is the fact that Kirchhoff's current law is automatically satisfied. If a mesh current flows into a given node, it obviously flows out of the node also.

Applying KVL to each mesh , we obtain

$$-42 + 6\,i_1 + 3\,(\,i_1 - i_2) = 0$$
$$3\,(\,i_2 - i_1) + 4\,i_2 - 10 = 0$$

or

$$9i_1 - 3i_2 = 42 \tag{1-21}$$
$$-3\,i_1 + 7\,i_2 = 10 \tag{1-22}$$

Note in Eq. (1-21) that the coefficient of i_1 is the sum of the resistances in the mesh 1, while the coefficient i_2 is the negative of the resistance common to meshes 1 and 2. Now observe that the same is true in Eq. (1-22).

Notice that the branch currents are different from the mesh currents unless the mesh is isolated.

Steps to mesh analysis:

（1）Assign mesh current $i_1, i_2, \ldots, i_n$ to the n meshes.

（2）Apply KVL to each of the n meshes. Use Ohm's law to express the voltages in terms of the mesh currents.

（3）Solve the resulting n simultaneous equations to the mesh currents, and then solve the other required variables.

New Words and Expressions

nodal	a. 节点的，结点的，交点的，节的，结的
nodal analysis	节点分析
mesh	n. 网孔，网格，网眼，网状
mesh analysis	网孔分析
simultaneous	a. ①联立（方程）的　②同时（存在，发生）的，一起的，同步的
quotient	n. ①商（数），系数　②份额，应分得的部分
determinant	n. ①行列式　②决定因素，遗传素
datum	n. ① 基准（点，线，面），基标　②数据，资料，信息
chassis	n. 底盘，底（盘）架，底板（座）
planar	a. ①平面的，平的　②二维的，二度的
error-minimizing	a. 令错误最少的
symmetry	n. 对称（性，现象），均称，调和
coefficient	n. ①系数，因数，常数，率　②折算率

Notes

1. Cramer's rule   克莱姆定则

2. Mesh analysis is not quite as general as nodal analysis because it is only applicable to a circuit that is planar.

由于网孔分析法仅适用于平面电路，故网孔分析法不像节点分析法那样通用。

专业英语的词汇特点 I

专业英语中大量使用专业词汇和半专业词汇。专业词汇是指仅用于某一学科或专业的词汇或术语；半专业词汇是指各学科通用的词汇或术语。如果不懂得某一特定领域内的专业术语或词汇，就不可能正确阅读和理解该领域的专业技术文献。

专业词汇的产生有两个主要来源，一是来自英语日常词汇，二是来自拉丁语和希腊语词根及词缀的词汇。对于来源于英语日常词汇的专业词汇，虽词形一样，但却有着不同的词义。大部分专业词汇，尤其是名词术语则是由拉丁语和希腊语的词根和词缀构成，这些词根和词缀都有着特定的意思。掌握英语构词特点，能扩大词汇量，便于我们记忆和理解这些专业词汇，提高阅读能力。

半专业词汇用在不同学科中虽然基本含义不变，但其确切含义则存在较大差别。例如：power一词在日常英语中表示"力量，权力"等意思，用于机械专业表示"动力"，用于电力专业表示"电力，功率"。

构词方式多种多样，下面介绍一些专业英语中常见的词缀。

一、前缀（prefixes）

1. anti-/counter- 反，抗，防，逆，耐

   antivirus 防病毒；anti-interference 抗干扰；anti-phase 反相；counterclockwise 逆时针方向的（地）；countercurrent 反向电流。

2. auto- 自动、自

   autotransformer 自耦变压器；autocoder 自动编码器；automoduation 自调制；automobile 自动车。

3. bi- 双，重

   bipolar relay 双极继电器；bilateral 两边的，双边的；bimetal 双金属。

4. co- 共，同，一起，相互

   coaxial cable 同轴电缆；cosine 余弦。

5. de- 表示相反动作

   demodulator 解调器；deform 变形。

6. deci- 表示十分之一，分

   decimal 十进制；decibel 分贝；decimeter 分米。

7. di- 双，偶，两

   diode 二极管；dipole 偶极子；dioxide 二氧化物。

8. dis- 表示相对单词的反义词

   displace 位移；disconnect 解开，断开。

9. equi- 同等，均

equipartition 均分；equilibrium 均衡，平衡。

10. hydro- 水，氢化

　　hydrodynamic 水力的，水压的，流体动力学的；hydroelectric 水力发电的。

11. hyper- 高，超，重，极度

12. in- 表示否定

　　inaccurate 不精确的；invariable 不变的。

13. inter- 相互，际间

　　internet 互联网；interchange 互换；interface 界面；intercity train 城际列车。

14. mal- 不，失

　　malfunction 失灵，故障；malformation 畸形；maltreat 滥用，乱用。

15. mega- 兆，百万

　　megawatt 兆瓦；megaton 百万吨级。

16. micro- 微观，微型，百万分之一

　　microelectronics 微电子学；microcomputer 微型计算机；microfilm 微缩胶卷；micrometer 微米；microwave 微波。

17. mini- 小

　　minicomputer 小型计算机；minbus 微型公共汽车。

18. multi- 多

　　multi-frequency 多频率。

19. over- 过，超，太

　　overfrequency 超频；overcharge 过度充电。

20. photo- 光，光电，光敏

　　photocell 光电池；photohead 光电传感头；photoreceptor 感光器。

21. post- 后

　　postfault 故障后。

22. pre- 在前，预先

　　preheat 预热；precondition 前提，先决条件。

23. semi- 半

　　semiconductor 半导体。

24. sub- 子，亚，低，次，副

　　subsystem 子系统，分系统；substation 变电站；subcode 子码。

25. tele- 远，电

　　telemetry 遥测术；telecommunication 电信；teleswitch 遥控开关；telecontrol 遥控。

26. thermo- 热

　　thermostat 恒温器；thermoelectric 热电的；thermo-fuse 热熔丝。

27. tri- 三

　　triangle 三角形。

28. ultra- 超，过

　　ultra-high-frequency 超高频；ultrasonic 超声波。

29. un- 表示相反的意思

　　unequal 不等；unvarying 不变的。

Exercises

I. Choose the best answer into the blank

1. Nodal analysis is based on a systematic application of _____, and satisfies automatically _____.

　　A. KCL, KCL　　B. KCL, KVL　　　　C. KVL, KVL　　　　　D. KVL, KCL

2._____ method is choosing node voltages as circuit variables.

　　A. Nodal analysis　　　　　　　　　B. Mesh analysis

　　C. Loop analysis　　　　　　　　　　D. The superposition principle

3. For a circuit containing N nodes and M branches, there will be _____ independent voltages.

　　A. N　　　　　　B. $N-1$　　　　　　C. $M-N-1$　　　　　D. $N-2$

4. The potential at reference node or datum node is _____ in nodal analysis.

　　A. zero　　　　　B. indefinite value　　　C. arbitrary value　　　D. one

5. Mesh analysis applies _____ to find unknown currents which are _____ currents.

　　A. KCL, mesh　　B. KVL, mesh　　　　C. KCL, branch　　　　D. KVL, branch

II. Answer the following questions according to the text

1. What are unknown variables in applying nodal analysis method to analyze a circuit?

2. What law is applied to each mesh in a planar circuit in mesh analysis?

3. What law is applied to each node in nodal analysis?

4. How many steps to nodal analysis?

5. Why is mesh analysis not as general as nodal analysis?

III. Translate the following into Chinese

　　The ratio of the phasor voltage to the phasor current is the impedance of a circuit, symbolized by the letter Z. The impedance is a complex quantity having the dimensions of ohms. Impedance is not a phasor and cannot be transformed to the time domain by multiplying by $e^{j\omega t}$ and taking the real part. Instead, we think of an inductor L as being represented in the time domain by its inductance L and in the frequency domain by its impedance $j\omega L$. A capacitor in the time domain is a capacitance C and an impedance $1/j\omega C$ in the frequency domain. Impedance is a part of the frequency domain and not a concept which is a part of the time domain.

Section 6　Sinusoidal AC Circuit Analysis
and Three-Phase circuits

Phasor relationships for circuit elements

　　We can proceed to our simplification of sinusoidal steady-state analysis by establishing the relationship between the phasor voltage and phasor current for each of the three passive elements.

The resistor provides the simplest case. In the time domain, as indicated by Fig.1-17(a), if the current through a resistor R is $i = I_m \cos(\omega t + \phi)$, the voltage across it is given by Ohm's law as

$$u(t) = Ri(t) = RI_m \cos(\omega t + \phi) \qquad (1\text{-}23)$$

The phasor form of this voltage is

$$\dot{U}_m = RI_m \angle \phi = R\dot{I}_m \qquad \dot{U} = R\dot{I} \qquad (1\text{-}24)$$

Fig.1-17(b) shows that the voltage-current relation for the resistor in the phasor domain continues to be Ohm' law, as in the time domain. We should note from Eq. (1-24) that the voltage and current relation is in phasor, as illustrated in the phasor diagram in Fig.1-18.

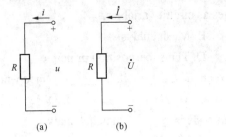

Fig.1-17   voltage-current relation for the resistor in the   Fig.1-18   phasor diagram for the resistor

(a) time domain;   (b) frequency domain

For the inductor L, assume the current through it is $i = I_m \cos(\omega t + \phi)$. The voltage across the inductor is

$$u = L\frac{di}{dt} = -\omega LI_m \sin(\omega t + \phi) \qquad (1\text{-}25)$$

The voltage is written to

$$u = \omega LI_m \cos(\omega t + \phi + 90°) \qquad (1\text{-}26)$$

which transforms to the phasor

$$\dot{U} = \omega LI_m e^{j(\phi+90°)} = \omega LI_m e^{j\phi} e^{j90°} = \omega LI_m \angle \phi e^{j90°} \qquad (1\text{-}27)$$

But $I_m \angle \phi = \dot{I}$, $e^{j90°} = j$. Thus,

$$\dot{U} = j\omega L\dot{I} \qquad (1\text{-}28)$$

showing that the voltage has a magnitude of ωLI_m and a phase of $\phi + 90°$. The voltage and current are 90° out of phase. Specifically, the current lags the voltage by 90°. Fig.1-19 shows the voltage-current relations for the inductor. Fig.1-20 shows the phasor diagram.

For the capacitor C, assume the voltage across it is $u = U_m \cos(\omega t + \phi)$. The current through the capacitor is

$$i = C\frac{du}{dt} \qquad (1\text{-}29)$$

By following the same steps as we took for the inductor, we obtain

$$\dot{I} = j\omega C\dot{U} \qquad (1\text{-}30)$$

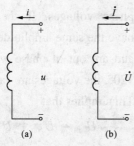

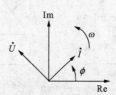

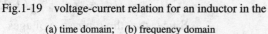

Fig.1-19   voltage-current relation for an inductor in the   Fig.1-20   phasor diagram for the inductor

(a) time domain;   (b) frequency domain

showing that the current and voltage are 90° out of phase. To be specific, the current leads the voltage by 90°. Fig.1-21 shows the voltage-current relations for the capacitor, Fig.1-22 gives the phasor diagram.

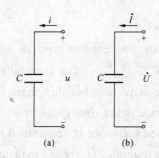

Fig.1-21   voltage-current relation for the capacitor in the   Fig.1-22   phasor diagram for the capacitor

(a) time domain;   (b) frequency domain

Sinusoidal AC Circuit Analysis

We also know that Ohm's Law and kirchhoff's Law are applicable to AC circuits. The methods of simplifying circuit analysis (such as nodal analysis, mesh analysis, Thevenin's theorem and so on) are applied in analyzing AC circuits. Since these techniques were already introduced for DC circuits, our major effort here will be to introduce the steps of analyzing AC circuit.

Analyzing AC circuit usually requires three steps.

（1）Transform the circuit to the phasor or frequency domain.

（2）Solve the problem using circuits techniques (nodal analysis, mesh analysis, super- position theorem etc.).

（3）Transform the resulting phasor to the time domain.

Balanced Three-Phase Voltages

A typical three-phase system consists of three voltage sources connected to loads by three or four wires(or transmission lines). A three-phase system is equivalent to three single-phase circuits. The voltage sources can be either wye-connected as shown in Fig.1-23(a) or delta-connected as in Fig.1-23(b).

Let us consider the wye-connected voltages in Fig.1-23(a) for now. The voltages $\dot{U}_{an}$, $\dot{U}_{bn}$, and $\dot{U}_{cn}$ are respectively between lines a, b, c, and the neutral lines n. These voltages are called

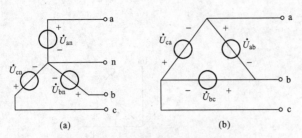

(a)　　　　　　　　　　　　(b)

Fig.1-23　Three-phase voltage sources

(a) Y-connected source;　(b) △-connected source

phase voltages. If the voltage sources have the same amplitude and frequency ω and are out of phase with each other by $120°$, the voltages are said to be balanced. This implies that

$$\dot{U}_{an} + \dot{U}_{bn} + \dot{U}_{cn} = 0 \quad （1\text{-}31）$$

$$|\dot{U}_{an}| = |\dot{U}_{bn}| = |\dot{U}_{cn}| \quad （1\text{-}32）$$

Since the three-phase voltages are $120°$ out of phase with each other, there are two possible combinations. One possibility is shown in Fig.1-24(a) and expressed mathematically as

$$\dot{U}_{an} = U_p\angle 0°$$
$$\dot{U}_{bn} = U_p\angle -120°$$
$$\dot{U}_{cn} = U_p\angle -240° = U_p\angle +120°$$

where U_p is the effective value. This is known as the abc sequence or positive sequence. In this phase sequence, $\dot{U}_{an}$ leads $\dot{U}_{bn}$, which in turn leads $\dot{U}_{cn}$. The other possibility is shown in Fig.1-24(b). This is called the acb sequence or negative sequence. For this phase sequence, $\dot{U}_{an}$ leads $\dot{U}_{cn}$, which in turn leads $\dot{U}_{bn}$. The phase sequence is the time order in which the voltage pass through their respective maximum values. The phase sequence is determined by the order in which the phasors pass through a fixed point in the phase diagram. The phase sequence is important in three-phase power distribution. It determines the direction of the rotation of a motor connected to the power source.

Like the generator connections, a three-phase load can be either wye-connected or delta-connected, depending on the end application. Fig.1-25(a) shows a wye-connected load, and Fig.1-25(b) shows a delta-connected load. The neutral line in Fig.1-25(a) may not be there, depending on whether the system is four-wire or three-wire. (And, of course, a neutral connection is topologically impossible for a delta connection.) A wye- or delta-connected load is said to be unbalanced if the impedances are not equal in magnitude or phase. A balanced load is one in which the phase impedances are equal in magnitude and in phase.

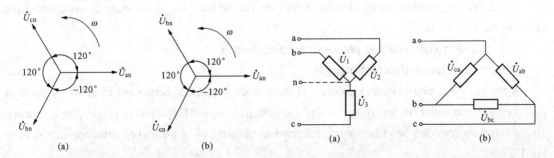

(a)　　　　　　　　　　　(b)　　　　　　　　　　(a)　　　　　　　　　(b)

Fig.1-24　Phase sequences

(a) abc or positive sequence;　(b) acb or negative sequence

Fig.1-25　Two possible three-phase load configurations

(a) a Y-connected load;　(b) a △-connected load

Since both the three-phase source and the three-phase load can be either wye- or delta-connected, we have four possible connections: Y-Y connection (i.e. Y-connected source with a Y-connected load); Y-△ connection; △-△ connection; △-Y connection.

It is appropriate to mention here that a balanced delta-connected load is more common than a balanced wye-connected load. This is due to the ease with which loads may be added or removed from each phase of a delta—connected load. This is very difficult with a wye-connected load because the neutral may not be accessible. On the other hand, delta-connected sources are not common in practice because of the circulating current that will result in the delta-mesh if the three-phase voltage are slightly unbalanced.

New Words and Expressions

phasor	n. 相量，相图，相位复（数）矢量
sinusoidal	a. 正弦（波，式，形，曲线）的
steady-state	a. 稳态的
domain	n. ①（定义）域，区（领）域，定义范围　②区，范围，界　③支配，所有权，统治权
time domain	时域
phasor diagram	相量图
frequency domain	频域
transform	v.; n. ①变换，改变，转换，换（折）算　②变换式，反式
magnitude	n. ①大小，幅值，幅度，量，数量，尺寸，（数）值　②等级，（数）量级
phase	n. ①相（位）　②（发展）阶段，时期，局面　③方（侧）面
lag	n.; v. 滞后，落后，迟（时）滞
lead	v. 超前，提前，领先
AC = alternating current	交流电流，交流电，交流
theorem	n. 定理，原理（则），命题，法则
DC = direct current	直流电流，直流电，直流
superposition	n. 叠加，重叠
superposition theorem	叠加定理
three-phase	三相
transmission	n. 输电，传（输，递，送，播，导）
equivalent	a. 等效的，等值的，等同的
phase voltage	相电压
amplitude	n. 振幅，幅度，波幅
(be) out of phase	异相（的）
effective	a. 有效的，等效的，生效的，能行的，有作用的，有影响的
sequence	n. 顺序，次序，时序，序列，系列
positive sequence	正序

phase sequence	相序
negative sequence	负序，反序
load	n. 负荷，负载
topologically	ad. 在拓扑结构上，从拓扑结构
impedance	n. 阻抗

Notes

1. Thevenin's theorem	戴维南定理
2. wye-connected	Y 形连接的，即星形连接
3. delta-connected	△形连接的，即三角形连接
4. be 120° out of phase	相位相差 120°

5. On the other hand, delta-connected sources are not common in practice because of the circulating current that will result in the delta-mesh if the three-phase voltage are slightly unbalanced.

另一方面，如果三相电压稍有不平衡就会在三角形连接的网孔中产生循环电流，因此实际情况中三角形连接的电源并不常用。

专业英语的词汇特点 II

二、后缀（suffixes）

1. -able 形容词的词尾，表示"……的"
   stable 稳定的；reliable 可靠的；comparable 可比较的。
2. -al 形容词词尾，表示"……的"
   digital 数字的；functional 功能的，函数的。
3. -ance/-ence 名词词尾
   capacitance 电容；resistance 电阻；reactance 电抗；existence 存在。
4. -ary 形容词词尾，表示"……"
   elementary 初步的；momentary 瞬息的。
5. -en 一般是形容词+en 构成，表示"使……"
   soften 软化；harden 使……变硬。
6. -er/-or 表示"机器、设备、物件等"
   air-oil booster 气-液增压器；air compressor 空气压缩机。
7. -free 形容词词尾，表示"无……的"，"免于……的"
   loss-free 无损耗的；dust-free 无尘的。
8. -ics 名词词尾，表示学科名称
   physics 物理学；mathematics 数学；electronics 电子学。
9. -ity 构成抽象名词，表示"性，度"
   stability 稳定性；reliability 可靠性；feasibility 可行性。
10. -ive 形容词词尾，表示"……的"
    conductive 导电的；active 有源的；passive 无源的；inductive 感性的。

11. -less 形容词词尾，表示"无……"

     wireless 无线的。

12. -meter 表，计

     speedmeter 速度计；ohmmeter 电阻表。

13. -proof 形容词词尾，表示"防……的"

     fire-proof 放火的；lightningproof 防雷的。

14. -tion/-sion 名词词尾

     generation 发电；motion 运动；transmission 传输，发射。

15. -or/-er 名词词尾，表示"器、物或人"

     generator 发电机；motor 电动机；transmitter 发射机。

16. -ist/-ician 名词词尾，表示从事某方面工作的人，……家

     specialist 专家；mathematician   数学家。

Exercises

I. Choose the best answer into the blank

1. The voltage across an inductor leads the current through it by _____.

     A. 0°   B. 90°   C. −90°   D. 180°

2. The voltage across an capacitor lags the current through it by _____.

     A. 0°   B. 90°   C. −90°   D. 180°

3. If in an acb phase sequence, $\dot{U}_{an} = 100\angle{-20°}$, then $\dot{U}_{bn}$ is _____.

     A. $100\angle{-140°}$ B. $100\angle{100°}$

     C. $100\angle{-50°}$ D. $100\angle{+50°}$

4. The three-phase source and the three-phase load have _____ possible connections.

     A. one   B. two   C. three   D. four

5. The three voltages that have the same amplitude and frequency ω and are out of phase with each other by 120° are said to be _____.

     A. balanced three-phase voltages

     B. unbalanced three-phase voltages

     C. unsymmetrical three-phase voltages

     D. positive sequence three-phase voltages

II. Answer the following questions according to the text

1. What relation is there between voltage across a resistor and current through it in phase?

2. Which steps to analyze any ac steady-state circuit?

3. What is phasor sum of three-phase voltages in a symmetrical three-phase system?

4. What is the phase sequence of the three-phase electric circuits?

5. Which ways can three loads be connected with each other in to form a three-phase load?

III. Translate the following into Chinese

   Both wye and delta source connections have important practical applications. The wye source connection is used for long distance transmission of electric power, where resistive losses (I^2R) should be minimal. This is due to the fact that the wye connection gives a line voltage that is $\sqrt{3}$ greater than the delta connection; hence, for the same power, the line current is $\sqrt{3}$ smaller. The delta source connection is used when three single-phase circuits are desired from a three-phase source. This conversions from three-phase to single-phase is required in residential wiring because household lighting and appliances use single-phase power. Three-phase power is used in industrial wiring where a large power is required. In some applications, it is immaterial whether the load is wye- or delta- connected.

Chapter 2　Electronics

Section 1　Introduction

To say that we live in an age of electronics is an understatement. From the omnipresent integrated circuit to the equally omnipresent digital computer, we encounter electronic devices and systems on a daily basis. In every aspect of our increasingly technological society— whether it is science, engineering, medicine, music, maintenance, or even espionage—the role of electronics is large, and it is growing.

In general, all of the tasks with which we shall be concerned can be classified as "signal-processing" tasks. Let us explore the meaning of this term.

Signal

A signal is any physical variable whose magnitude or variation with time contains information. This information might involve speech and music, as in radio broadcasting, a physical quantity such as the temperature of the air in a room, or numerical data, such as the record of stock market transactions. The physical variables that can carry information in an electrical system are voltage and current. When we speak of "signals", therefore, we refer implicitly to voltages or currents. However, most of the concepts we discuss can be applied directly to systems with different information-carrying variables. Thus, the behavior of a mechanical system (in which force and velocity are the variables) or a hydraulic system (in which pressure and flow rate are the variables) can often be modeled or represented by an equivalent electrical system. An understanding of the behavior of electrical systems, therefore, provides a basis for understanding a much broader range of phenomena.

Analog and Digital signals

A signal can carry information in two different forms. In an analog signal the continuous variation of the voltage or current with time carries the information. An example, in Fig.2-1, is the voltage produced by a thermocouple pair when the two junctions are at different temperatures. As the temperature difference between the two junctions varies, the magnitude of the voltage across the thermocouple pair also varies. The voltage thus provides an analog representation of the temperature difference.

The other kind of signal is a digital signal. A digital signal is one that can take on values within two discrete ranges. Such signals are used to represent ON-OFF or YES-NO information. An ordinary household thermostat delivers a digital signal to control the furnace. When the room temperature drops below a preset value, the thermostat switch closes turning on the furnace. Once the room temperature rises high enough, the switch opens turning off the furnace. The current through the switch provides a digital representation of the temperature variation: ON equals "too cold" while OFF equals "not too cold".

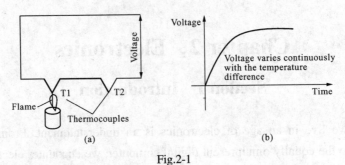

Fig.2-1

(a) An example of an analog signal; (b) Voltage-time characteristic

Signal-Processing Systems

A signal-processing system is an interconnection of components and devices that can accept an input signal or a group of input signals, operate on the signals in some fashion either to extract or improve the quality of the information, and present the information as an output in the proper form at the proper time.

Fig.2-2 illustrates the components in such a system. The central circles represent the two types of signal processing (digital and analog), while the block between the two signal- processing blocks represents the conversion of an analog signal to equivalent digital form (A/D=Analog-to-Digital) and the reverse conversion of a digital signal to the corresponding analog form (D/A=Digital-to-Analog). The remaining blocks involve inputs and outputs— getting signals into and out of the processing system.

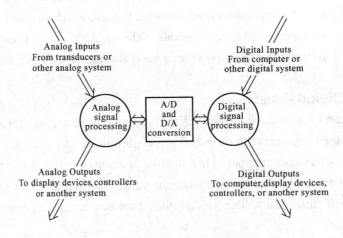

Fig.2-2 Components of a signal system

Many electrical signals derived from physical systems are obtained from devices called transducers. We have already encountered an example of an analog transducer, the thermocouple pair. It converts temperature difference (the physical variable) to a voltage (the electrical variable). Generally, a transducer is a device that converts a physical or mechanical variable to an equivalent voltage or current signal. Unlike the thermocouple example, however, most transducers require some form of electrical excitation to operate.

The output from a system can be in many forms, depending on the use to be made of the information contained in the input signals. One can seek to display the information, either in analog form (using a meter, for example, in which the needle position indicates the size of the variable of interest) or in digital form (using a set of digital display elements that are lit up with a number corresponding to the variable of interest). Other possibilities are to convert the output to sound energy (with a loudspeaker), or to use the output as an input signal to another system, or to use the output as a control signal to initiate some action.

New Words and Expressions

electronics	n. 电子学，电子仪器，电子设备，电子线路
understatement	n. 轻描淡写，有节制的表达
omnipresent	a. 无处不在的，普遍存在的
electronic	a. 电子（学）的
transaction	n. ①交易，业务 ②办理，处理，执行，记录
digital	a. 数字的，数字式的，计数的
espionage	n. 谍报，间谍活动，密探，监视
signal-processing	a. 信号处理的
analog	n. ①模拟（量，装置，设备，系统） ②类似，类比，比拟
velocity	n. 速度，速率
thermocouple	n. 热电偶
discrete	a. 离散的，不连续的，分散的
household	a.; n. 家用的，普通的，一般用途的，家庭，家，户
thermostat	n. 恒温器，定温器，温度自动调节器
preset	v.; a. ①预定，预置，（预先）调整 ②安装程序，按预定程序扎制，给定程序的
switch	n. 开关；v. 接通或关断，转变，换接
A/D = Analog-to-Digital	模数转换，模数变换
D/A = Digital-to-Analog	数模转换，数模变换
transducer	n. 传感器，变送器，发射器，换能器，换流器
excitation	n. ①激励，激发，激磁 ②刺激，干扰
display	v. 显示，显像，表现，陈列，展览；n. 显示，指示，表现

Notes

1. This information might involve speech and music, as in radio broadcasting, a physical quantity such as the temperature of the air in a room, or numerical data, such as the record of stock market transactions.

   这种信息或许像无线广播的演讲和音乐，或许是像室内温度的物理量，或许像股市交易记录的数字数据。

2. The other kind of signal is a digital signal. A digital signal is one that can take on values within

two discrete ranges. Such signals are used to represent ON-OFF or YES-NO information.

另一种信号是数字信号。数字信号是在两个离散的范围内能够呈现一定数值的信号。这种信号常用以表示开—关或是—不是信息。

专业英语的词汇特点 III

随着科学技术、社会经济和各学科专业的发展，新的专业词汇也不断出现。其构词方法除了加词根和词缀的方法外，还有合成法、混成法、截短法、缩略法、转化法几种。

（1）合成法，两个或两个以上的词结合成一个新词。专业英语中的合成词有合写式（无连字符）和分写式（有连字符）两种。例如，hardware 硬件；software 软件；pulse-scaler 脉冲标定器。

（2）混成法，两个词中在拼写或读音上比较适合的部分以"前一词去尾、后一词去首"的方式，加以叠合混成新词，而混成的新词兼具有两个旧词的形和义。例如，telex = teleprinter+exchange 电传；transistor = transfer + resistor 晶体管。

（3）截短法，删除某一词中的一个或多个音节形成新词，其词义不变。例如，auto = automobile 汽车；lab = laboratory 实验室；amp = ampere 安培。

（4）缩略法，将某一词组中主要的词的第一个字母组成新词。例如，radar = radio detecting and ranging 雷达；UPS = uninterrupted power supply 不间断电源；DC = direct current 直流电；AC= 交流电；CAD = computer assisted design 计算机辅助设计。

（5）转化法，不通过任何词形上变化，直接转化为另一个词。在转化过程中，词性有所改变而词义则与转化前的原义仍保留若干联系。例如，Xerox 用静电复印法复印。

Exercises

I. Choose the best answer into the blank

1. The voltage produced by a thermocouple pair is ＿＿＿＿ signal.

    A. a digital   B. an analog   C. a discrete   D. a control

2. ON-OFF information can be represented by ＿＿＿＿ signal.

    A. a digital   B. an analog   C. a continuous   D. a control

3. A device that can convert an analog signal to the corresponding digital form is called ＿＿＿＿ for short.

    A. A/D   B. D/A   C. D/D   D. A/A

4. The thermocouple pair converts temperature difference to a ＿＿＿＿.

    A. current   B. voltage   C. power   D. energy

5. A D/A is a device that can convert a digital signal to the equivalent ＿＿＿＿.

    A. digital form   B. numerical form

    C. binary form   D. analog form

II. Answer the following questions according to the text

1. What is a signal?

2. Which forms can a signal carry information in?

3. What basic components does a signal-processing system consist of ?

4. What role does a transducer play in a signal-processing system?

5. What does the output form of a system depend on?

III. Translate the following into Chinese

Analog electronics pertains to those systems in which the electrical voltage and electrical current are analogous to physical quantities and vary continuously. Electronic circuits that reproduce music must have voltages and currents that are proportional to the sound. A high fidelity amplifying system attempts to keep the analogy as true as possible. Analog electronic circuits are carefully designed to make the electrical voltages and currents follow the input signal. If an input signal doubles in amplitude, the output voltage or current also should double; this is possible because the circuit elements are made to operate within limits that preserve the linearity.

Section 2   Boolean Algebra for Digital Systems

Introduction

The mathematics of computers and other digital electronic devices have been developed from the decisive work of George Boole (1815~1864) and many others, who expanded and improved on his work. The body of thought that is known collectively as symbolic logic established the principles for deriving mathematical proofs and singularly modified our understanding and the scope of mathematics.

Only a portion of this powerful system is required for our use. Boole and others were interested in developing a systematic means of deciding whether a proposition in logic or mathematics was true or false, but we shall be concerned only with the validity of the output of digital devices. True and false can be equated with one and zero, high and low, or on and off. These are the only two states of electrical voltage from a digital element. Thus, in this remarkable algebra performed by logic gates, there are only two values, one and zero; any algebraic combination or manipulation can yield only these two values. Zero and one are the only symbols in binary arithmetic.

The various logic gates and their interconnections can be made to perform all the essential functions required for computing and decision-making. In developing digital systems the easiest procedure is to put together conceptually the gates and connections to perform the assigned task in the most direct way. Boolean algebra is then used to reduce the complexity of the system, if possible, while retaining the same function. The equivalent simplified combination of gates will probably be much less expensive and less difficult to assemble.

Rules of Boolean algebra for digital devices

Boolean algebra has three rules of combination, as any algebra must have: the associative, the commutative, and the distributive rules. To show the features of the algebra we use the variables A,

B, C, and so on. To write relations between variables each one of which may take the value 0 or 1, we use $\overline{A}$ to mean "not A", so if A = 1, then $\overline{A} = 0$. The complement of every variable is expressed by placing a bar over the variable; the complement of $B = \overline{B}$ = "not B". Two fixed quantities also exist. The first is identity, **I** = 1; the other is null, null = 0.

Boolean algebra applies to the arithmetic of three basic types of gates: an OR-gate, an AND-gate and the inverter. The symbol and the truth tables for the logic gates are shown in Fig.2-3, the truth table illustrate that the AND-gate corresponds to multiplication, the OR-gate corresponds to addition, and the inverter yield the complement of its input variable.

We have already found that

$$AB = \text{"A AND B"}$$

for the AND-gate and

$$A + B = \text{"A OR B"}$$

for the OR-gate.

The AND, or conjunctive, algebraic form and the OR, or disjunctive, algebraic form must each obey the three rules of algebraic combination. In the equations that follow, the reader may use the two possible values 0 and 1 for the variables A, B, and C to verify the correctness of each expression.

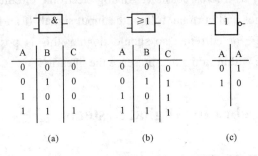

Fig.2-3   Logic symbols and truth tables for AND, OR, NOT

(a) AND;   (b) OR;   (c) NOT

Use A = 0, B = 0, C = 0; A = 1, B = 0, C = 0; and so on, in each expression. The associative rules state how variables may be grouped.

For   AND   (AB)C = A(BC) = (AC)B,

and for   OR   (A + B) + C = A + (B + C) = (A + C) + B

the rules indicate that different groupings of variables may be used without altering the validity of the algebraic expression.

The commutative rules state the order of variables.

For   AND   AB = BA,

and for   OR   A+B = B+A

the rules indicate that the operations can be grouped and expanded as shown.

Before we show the remaining rules of Boolean algebra for digital devices, let us confirm the distributive rule for AND by writing the truth table, Table 2-1. We will discover soon how we knew that we could write AB + C = (A + C)(B + C), which is proved by the truth table to be a proper expansion.

The more complex expression and its simpler form yield identical values. Because binary logic is dominated by an algebra in which a sum of ones equals one, the truth table permits us to identify the equivalence among algebraic expressions. A truth table may be used to find a simpler equivalent to a more complex relation among variables, if such an equivalent exists. We will see shortly how the reduction of complexity may be achieved in a systematic manner with truth tables and other techniques.

Table 2-1　Truth table for the AND-distribution rule

A	B	C	AB + C =Value		(A + C)(B + C) = Value	
0	0	0	0 + 0	0	0×0	0
0	0	1	0 + 1	1	1×1	1
0	1	0	0 + 0	0	0×1	0
0	1	1	0 + 1	1	1×1	1
1	0	0	0 + 0	0	1×0	0
1	0	1	0 + 1	1	1×1	1
1	1	0	1 + 0	1	1×1	1
1	1	1	1 + 1	1	1×1	1

Some additional relations in the algebra, which use identity and null, are worth nothing. Here we illustrate properties of the AND and OR operations that use the distributive rules and the fact that I is always 1 and null is always 0.

AND	$AI = A$ or	$A1 = A$
OR	$A+ \text{null} = A$	$A + 0 = A$
AND	$A\overline{A} = \text{null}$	$A\overline{A} = 0$
OR	$A + \overline{A} = I$	$A + \overline{A} = 1$
AND	$A \, \text{null} = \text{null}$	$A0 = 0$
OR	$A + I = I$	$A + 1 = 1$
AND	$AA = A$	
OR	$A + A = A$	

The relation $A + \overline{A} = I$ points out an important fact, that is, that I, the identity, is the universal set. Null is called the empty set.

We have considered several logical relations. For the two-value Boolean algebra of digital electronics, the choice of the technique depends upon the nature of the function whose reduction is desired. Some simple functions may be easily reduced by examining their truth table; others require the manipulation of Boolean algebra to reveal the relationship. When we consider the circuit for adding binary numbers, we see that Boolean algebra is required to discover a simplification in that particular application.

New Words and Expressions

Boolean	布尔的
symbolic	a. 符号的，记号的，象征（性）的
proof	n. 证明，证实，证据；v. 检验，试验；a. 试验过的，合乎标准的，防……的
singularly	ad. 非凡地，特殊地，奇异地，单独地
logic gate	逻辑门
manipulation	n. 处理，计算，操作，控制，管理
binary	n.; a. ①二进制的，二进位的，二元的，二成分的　②二，双，复

arithmetic	n. 算术，计算，运算；a. 算术的，计算的，运算的
associative	a. 结合的，联合的，相关的，
commutative	a. 交换的，换向的，代替的，相互的
distributive	a. 分配的，分布的，个别的
truth table	真值表
multiplication	n. ①乘法，相乘　②增加，增多，增殖，倍增
addition	n. ①加法　②增加，附加，相加
conjunctive	a. ①合取的，逻辑乘的　②连接的，连系的
disjunctive	a. 析取的，分离的，转折的
identity	n. 单位，同一，完全相同，一致，恒等，身份
null	n.；a. ①零的，空的，无　②不存在的，没有的
complement	n.；a. ①补码，补数，余的，补的　②补充，互补

Notes

1. George Boole (1815～1864)　乔治·布尔
2. Boolean algebra has three rules of combination, as any algebra must have: the associative, the commutative, and the distributive rules.

   布尔代数与任何代数一样具有结合律、交换律和分配律。

词义的确定——词义选择

英语语言中有一词多类、一词多义的现象。翻译时，不可避免地要确定词义。词义的确定涉及词义的选择和引申两个方面。

1. 根据专业选择词义

在英汉两种语言中，同一个词在不同的学科领域或不同的专业往往具有不同的词义。因此，在选择词义时，应考虑到阐述内容所涉及的概念是属于何种学科、何种专业。例如，power 一词含有"权力；电力；功率；能力；倍数；幂；化合价"等意思。

（1）Knowledge is *power*.

知识就是力量。（译成"力量"）

（2）Assume that the input voltage from the *power* supply remains constant.

假定由电源输入的电压保持不变。（译成"电源"）

（3）The third *power* of 2 is 8.

2 的三次方是 8。（译成"方"）

（4）By *power* we mean the rate of doing work.

所谓功率，指的是作功的速率。（译成"功率"）

（5）The combining *power* of one element in the compound must equal the combining power of the other element.

化合物中一种元素的化合价必须等于另一元素的化合价。（译成"化合价"）

（6）Energy is the *power* to do work.

能量是做功的能力。（译成"能力"）

（7）Electric *power* can be transmitted over long distance to users.

电力可通过远距离传输到用户。（译成"电力"）

（8）Basically, all *power* is with the people.

归根到底，一切权力属于人民。（译成"权力"）

2. 根据词类选择词

根据句法结构判明词在原句中应属于何种词类，再进一步确定词义。下面以 like 为例：

（1）*Like* charges repel, unlike charges attract.

同性电荷相斥，异性电荷相吸。（形容词，作"相同的"解）

（2）He *likes* power electronics.

他喜欢电力电子学。（动词，作"喜欢"解）

（3）In the sunbeam passing through the window there are fine grains of dust shining *like* gold.

在射入窗内的阳光里，细微的尘埃像金子一般在闪闪发亮。（介词，作"像"解）

（4）It is the atoms that make up iron, water, oxygen and the *like*.

正是原子构成了铁、水、氧等类物质。（名词，作"相同之物"解）

（5）Waves in water move *like* the waveform moves along a rope.

波在水中移动就像波形沿着绳子移动一样。（连词，作"像、如"解）

3. 据上下文选择词义

在确定某一词所属词类的基础上，根据上下文逻辑关系和语气连贯性来选择词义。科技文章具有较强的科学性、逻辑性，词与词之间、段与段之间总是互相依存，相互制约的。不能孤立、片面、静止地去理解一个词的词义。选择词义时应该词不离句，结合上下文进行推敲。例如：

（1）The transformer *works* properly.

这台变压器运转正常。

（2）The motor is *not working*.

电动机故障了。

（3）The threads of the screw *work* hard.

这螺丝的螺纹太涩了。

（4）In order to meet the *critical* service requirements, scientists are still looking for better materials.

为满足使用的紧迫要求，科学家们仍在寻找更好的材料。

（5）We can heat the steel again to a temperature below the *critical* temperature, then cool it slowly.

我们可以把钢材再次加热到临界温度以下的某一温度，然后再让它慢慢地冷却。

4. 根据搭配习惯选择词义

同一词在不同的搭配情况下词义不同，在翻译时应注意根据搭配习惯来正确选择译文词义。例如：heavy 一词：heavy current 强大电流；heavy industry 重工业；heavy line 粗线；heavy traffic 交通拥挤。

Exercises

I. Choose the best answer into the blank

1. Any algebraic combination or manipulation can yield only _____ values in Boolean algebra.

    A. one　　　　　B. two　　　　　C. three　　　　　D. four

2. According to the text, the AND-gate corresponds to _____, the OR-gate corresponds to _____.

    A. multiplication, subtraction　　　　　B. multiplication, division

    C. multiplication, addition　　　　　D. addition, subtraction

3. The commutative rule is used for the AND algebraic operation to alter _____ of variables.

    A. the order　　　B. the value　　　C. the validity　　　D. the result

4. The associative rule indicates that different groupings of variables do not alter _____ of the algebraic expression.

    A. the order　　　B. the operational order　　C. the validity　　　D. the form

5. The relation $A + \overline{A}$ results in _____.

    A. null　　　　　B. identity　　　C. indefinite value　　　D. zero

II. Answer the following questions according to the text

1. Which symbols are there in binary arithmetic? What are they?

2. What are the rules of combination about Boolean algebra?

3. What are the three basic gates in digital circuits?

4. What functions does a truth table have?

5. How many rules of Boolean algebra do you know? Say out these rules as many as possible.

III. Translate the following into Chinese

    There are many different ways to build electronic circuits with input-output charac- teristics that correspond to the various digital operations. Several of these circuit types are manufactured in integrated circuit form. The collection of integrated circuit logic functions that share a common circuit type is called a logic family. Within each family, the wiring diagram for the logic inputs and outputs is identical to the logic flow diagram (only the power supply and ground connections must be added). Therefore, one generally selects a single logic family with which to implement all the digital circuits in a particular application. Occasionally, one must make connections between digital circuits constructed from logic families with input and output voltage ranges that are not compatible with one another. In these cases, it is necessary to construct additional circuits that interface one family with another.

Section 3　Analog—Digital Conversion

    Many quantities have continuous values, including temperature, pressure, displacement, rotation, voltage, current, and intensity of light and sound. The digital representation of the values is important for digital processing and analysis, for regulation and control, and for recording and transmitting the data that quantize them. The task of quantizing the continuous values into a binary scale is called analog-to-digital conversion (ADC).

Digital-to-analog conversion (DAC) is the inverse process, in which data in discrete values, are converted or restored to a continuously variable form. The clarity and fidelity of laser-read digital recordings of music and speech and the freedom of these recordings from background noise are recent advancements, but the human ear cannot convert binary data recorded on a disc to music or speech. The electronic conversion of binary data to analog signals is necessary.

Some ways of sampling analog signals cannot be considered analog-to-digital conversion because the amplitude of the signal, an important aspect of the information content, is not expressed in binary form. In the straightforward sampling of a sine wave, the amplitude is an essential part of the information content. In contrast, the conversion from an analog signal to a digital signal results in a binary number at each sampling point.

The transducer is the name of the device that produces a voltage or a current proportional to the physical phenomenon to which it responds. A temperature transducer, for example, can generate a voltage related to the temperature. In some cases the voltage is derived from the sensitive element in an electrical circuit, as when a temperature sensitive resistor and a constant resistance form a voltage divider whose voltage is related directly to the temperature. Some transducers generate voltages directly, such as photoelectric elements and piezoelectric devices. Many voltage sources require voltage amplification to facilitate conversion from their analog values to binary numbers.

Analog-to-digital conversion

Only two basic techniques exist for analog-to-digital conversion (ADC). One is to compare the analog voltage amplitude to a binary voltage scale in which the match yield the binary number that corresponds to the amplitude. The other technique is to integrate the analog signal and to use the measured time (a given number of clock pulses) for the amplitude of the integral to reach a value to establish an equivalent binary number. Each of the systems discussed below uses one or the other of these techniques.

Two important parameters must be considered in selecting a conversion technique or a variation of a conversion technique. One is the precision required in the analog-to-digital conversion; the other is the speed or the time interval allowed for the conversion. These two parameters are essentially incompatible because high-precision and high-speed conversions are difficult to achieve concurrently. High-speed or fast analog-to-digital conversion is a relative term, but in the context of digital computer conversion of binary data from analog to digital, "high-speed" sampling intervals are about ten computer clock cycles rather than tens of thousands. Conversion in the interval of one microsecond is moderately fast but not limiting.

Because many analog-to-digital conversions need not be made quickly, a high degree of precision is possible. The complexity and cost of attaining high precision, however, may modify the goal. The application intended for the conversion of the analog variable may determine what degree of digital precision is required.

The precision of analog-to-digital conversion is established by the number of binary bits, which correspond to maximum or full-scale analog value. Four bits allow the quantization in 0 to 15 equal intervals. For the binary representation of the amplitude to change by one bit, an analog amplitude must change by 6.25 percent. A byte (eight bits) allows a precision of 0.4 percent; seven bits of binary code correspond to approximately 1 percent encoding accuracy.

Digital-to-analog conversion

To convert a digital signal to analog, it is necessary to treat each bit in this weighted manner. A block diagram of such a device is shown in Fig.2-4. The reference voltage source feeds a precisely regulated voltage to the voltage switches. Upon receipt of a convert signal, binary data is clocked into the register, with each bit assigned a weighted value of current or voltage. These binary signals from the input register next feed voltage switches which provide one of two possible outputs. Thus, they are equivalent to an ordinary SPDT switch controlled by the binary signal from the register. The switches feed a resistive summing network which converts each bit into its weighted current value and sums them for a total current. This total value is then fed the amplifier, which performs two functions, current to voltage conversion and scaling, so that the output voltage of the D/A converter will be the proper value.

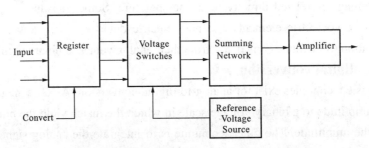

Fig.2-4　Block diagram of digital to analog converter

The input register is a parallel-in, parallel-out device. The converter signal is used to clock the input data into the register where it is stored until the next converter signal is received.

Both A/D and D/A converters have specifications of resolution, accuracy, speed, and gain; the A/D also has the problem of drift.

New Words and Expressions

displacement　　　n. ①位移，变位，移动，平移，偏移　②排（水，汽，气，液）量

intensity　　　　　n. ①强度，密度，亮度，光强　②强烈，紧张

regulation　　　　 n. ①调整，校准，控制　②规则，规章，规程，章程，条例，细则

quantize　　　　　v. ①量化，分层，取离散值　②（使）量子化

clarity　　　　　　n. 清晰，清晰度，透明，透明度

fidelity　　　　　　n. 保真，保真度，逼真，逼真度

disc	n. 盘，圆片，唱片
sample	v. 采样，取样，抽样； n. 采样，样品，标本，模型，实例
straightforward	a. ①直接的，明确的，坦率的 ②简单的，易懂的 ③顺向的，流水作业的
sine	n. 正弦
sensitive	a. 敏感的，灵敏的，易感光的；n. 对……敏感的材料
sensitive element	敏感元件
voltage divider	分压器
photoelectric	a. 光电的
piezoelectric	a. 压电的
amplification	n. 放大（率，系数，倍数，作用），加强，增强
pulse	n. 脉冲，脉动
integral	a. 积分的，累积的，整数的，整体的，总体的；n. 积分，整数，整体
parameter	n. 参数，参量，系数
precision	n. 精度，精密，精确； a. 精确的，精密的
incompatible	a 不相容的，不一致的
concurrently	ad. 同时
microsecond	n. 微秒
bit	n. 位，比特，二进制数
full-scale	a. ①满刻度的，满标度的，满量程的 ②完全的，全面的
quantization	n. 量化，分层，把连续量转换为数字
byte	n. 字节
code	n. 编码，密码，符号； v. 编码，译码
encode	v. 编码，译码，把……译成电码
weighted	a. ①加权的，权重的，加重的 ②受力的，负载的
receipt	n. 收到，接收，收据
amplifier	n. 放大器
register	n. ①寄存器，②记录，登记，注册，挂号；v. ①登记，注册，挂号 ②记数，存储
parallel-in	并联输入的
parallel-out	并联输出的
resolution	n. 分辨率，鉴别力
gain	n. 增益，放大系数，放大率，增量
drift	n. 漂移，偏移

Notes

1. analog-to-digital conversion（ADC）   模数转换
2. Digital-to-analog conversion（DAC）   数模转换
3. For the binary representation of the amplitude to change by one bit, an analog amplitude must change by 6.25 percent.

二进制表示改变一位，对应的模拟量大小就一定改变了 6.25%。

4. The switches feed a resistive summing network which converts each bit into its weighted current value and sums them for a total current.

通过开关供给一个电阻性的加法电路，加法电路把每一位转变为对应的加权负载电流值并求出总电流。

词义的确定——词义的引申

1. 专业化引申

基于基本词义，根据所涉及专业引申出其专业化语义，以符合技术语言规范和习惯。例如：

The running of such automated establishments remains only a matter of *reading* various meters mounted on panels. 管理这种自动化工厂只不过要求查看一下控制台上的各种仪表而已。

These experiments have *produced* some valuable data. 这些试验得出了某些有价值的数据。

2. 具体化引申

将原语句中含义较为笼统或抽象的词，引申为意思较为具体或形象化的汉语词语，避免译文概念不清或不符汉语表达习惯。例如：

At present coal is the most common *food* of a steam power plant. 目前，煤仍然是凝汽式电厂最常用的能源。

All *the wit and learning* in this field are to be present at the symposium. 这一领域里的全部学者们将出席这个科学讨论会。

Space technique has made great progress in the course of *this single generation*. 空间技术在近 30 年内取得了巨大的进展。

High voltage current is usually carried by overhead wire system so as to prevent *living things* being electrocuted. 为防止人畜触电，高压电一般采用架空线输送。

This nuclear power plant which is computer-controlled will *serve* the entire city. 这座由电子计算机控制的核电站将向全市供电。

3. 抽象化引申

将原句中含义较为具体或形象化的词语，引申为意思较为概括或抽象的汉语词语，以符合汉语的表达习惯。例如：

VLSI is still in its *infancy*. 超大规模集成电路仍处于发展初期。（不能翻译成"婴儿"）

There are three steps which must be taken before we *graduate from* the integrated circuit technology. 我们要完全掌握集成电路，还必须经过三个阶段。（不能翻译成"毕业于"）

In the modern world salt has many uses beyond the *dining table*. 在现代世界上，盐除供食用外，还有许多其他用途。

Electricity and electronics are really indivisible, *each* forming part of *the other*. 电学与电子学实际上是难以分开的，二者相互渗透、相互关联。

The *major contributors* in component technology have been in the semiconductor components. 元件技术中起主要作用的是半导体元件。

Exercises

I. Choose the best answer into the blank

1. The process of quantizing the continuous values into a binary scale is called _____.
   A. digital-to-analog conversion   B. digital-to-digital conversion
   C. analog-to-digital conversion   D. analog-to-analog conversion

2. _____ is a device that produces a voltage or a current proportional to the actual temperature.
   A. A temperature transducer   B. A pressure transducer
   C. A displacement transducer   D. A velocity transducer

3. The precision and the speed of an ADC are essentially _____.
   A. compatible   B. incompatible   C. equal   D. equivalent

4. The precision of ADC is determined by _____.
   A. its speed   B. its gain
   C. the accuracy of the reference voltage D. the number of binary bits

5. In Fig.2-4 the amplifier performs _____ functions.
   A. two   B. three   C. four   D. five

II. Answer the following questions according to the text

1. Why is it necessary that an analog quantity should be converted to a corresponding digital value in a computer control system?
2. Can the process of sampling analog signals be considered as analog-to-digital conversion? Why?
3. How many basic techniques are there for analog-to-digital conversion? What are they?
4. What parameters should be considered in selecting a conversion technique?
5. What specifications do both A/D and D/A converters have?

III. Translate the following into Chinese

The bipolar inverter is the basic circuit from which most bipolar saturated logic circuit are developed, including diode-transistor logic (DTL) and transistor-transistor logic (TTL). However, the basic bipolar inverter suffers from loading effects. Diode-transistor logic combines diode logic and the bipolar inverter to minimize loading effects. Transistor-transistor logic, which evolved directly from DTL, provides reduced propagation delay times, as we will show.

In DTL and TTL circuits, bipolar transistors are driven between cutoff and saturation. Since the transistor is being used essentially as a switch, the current gain is not as important as in amplifier circuits. Typically, for transistors used in these circuits, the current gain is assumed to be in the range of 25 to 50. These transistor need not be fabricated to as tight a tolerance as that of high-gain amplifier transistors.

Section 4   Operational Amplifiers

Introduction

Operational amplifiers are high-gain difference amplifiers, which were perfected during World

War II. They became the foundation of analog computers, at one time analog computers were called "differential analyzers" because they are used to solve differential equations. Operational amplifiers are also the basis of many important instruments.

The analog amplifier consists of a basic difference amplifier, implemented by feedback and other compensating amplifying circuits to give linear response, stability, freedom from drift, and other desirable properties. The complexity is required because operational amplifiers amplify dc as well as ac signals, capacitive coupling between amplifying stages is not permitted. Thus it is more difficult to isolate the long-term changes that arise from variations in temperature and power-supply voltage and from other effects that cause the output voltage to drift.

After the invention of the transistor, solid-state operational amplifiers were introduced as integrated circuits. Now operational amplifiers are used to make high-quality, low-power analog amplifier, and it is possible to avoid designing individual transistor amplifier stages for many application. For most amplifying purposes and for many measuring and control applications, simple arrangements of operational amplifiers with feedback circuits will meet the designer's needs. The availability of operational amplifiers as integrated circuits in the form of dual in-line packages (DIPs) or in other compact forms makes the solution of analog signal problems analogous in many respects to the solution of digital logic problems, that is, through the interconnection of integrated circuits.

Operational Amplifier

Fig.2-5 shows the symbol for an operational amplifier. There are two inputs: the one marked with a plus sign is the noninverting input, and the one marked with a minus sign is the inverting input. The voltage amplified by the operational amplifier is the voltage difference between the two inputs. The open-circuit gain is so large, 10^5 to 10^6, that a voltage difference of only a few microvolts will give an appreciable output. Because the operational amplifier is a difference amplifier, connections must always be made to both input terminals for proper operation.

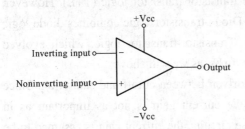

Fig.2-5 A symbol for an operational amplifier

If two different positive voltages are applied separately to the two inputs, the output of the operational amplifier will be at the maximum (saturated) value if the voltage at the noninverting input is larger than the voltage at the inverting input. If the voltages exchange their relative values—that is, if the inverting input exceeds the noninverting input—the operational amplifier will switch to a minimum output, which is the saturated negative voltage. The switching occurs very quickly whenever the relative values of the voltages change. We will see that an operational amplifier is an excellent voltage comparator because it produces a large voltage swing at the instant of crossing, when an earlier relation in voltage magnitudes is reversed by only a few microvolts.

If the operational amplifier is to operate in its linear range, a very small voltage difference must exist between the inverting and the noninverting inputs. In analyzing operational amplifying circuits, we assume, because of the large open-circuit gain, that the voltage difference across the inputs is negligible. In some cases we will set the voltage to zero. When a portion of the output signal is returned to the input as negative feedback, the voltage difference cannot grow large because the output changes to minimize the voltage difference between the inputs.

Two additional properties are present in operational amplifiers. They are a very high input impedance, approximately $10^6 \Omega$, and a low output impedance, approximately 100Ω. These properties contribute to the usefulness of operational amplifiers by allowing signal sources with small current capabilities to drive operational amplifiers directly. In turn, operational amplifiers may drive devices that have severe signal requirements.

To summarize, a good operational amplifier is characterized by a very large open-circuit gain of a million or so, an extremely small difference voltage between the inverting and the noninverting input terminals, a very high input impedance, and a small output impedance. An ideal operational amplifier, however, would have an infinite gain, a zero difference voltage between inputs, an infinite input impedance, and a zero output impedance.

Many operational amplifiers require two equal but opposite supply voltages, one positive and one negative. Typical values are $\pm 12V$ or $\pm 15V$. Other operational amplifiers may be operated with a single-ended power source, such as +15V. The useful range of the output voltage in an operational amplifier is approximately 80 percent of the supply voltages. With a two-sided power supply of ± 15 V, the output signal is restricted to about $\pm 12V$.

Many operational amplifiers have limitations, two of which need to be mentioned. One is that the gain decreases rapidly as the frequency increases. At small frequencies—as low as 10 Hz—the voltage gain begins to drop. (Power begins to drop at -20 dB Per decade.) The gain-versus-frequency limitation is offset by the use of negative feedback to expand the frequency band. The other limitation is the rate at which most operational amplifiers can respond to a step change in the input signal. Compared to digital gates, operational amplifiers are poor in this respect; common operational amplifiers change at a rate of approximately 1 V/μs. A TTL digital gate changes from one state to the other nearly 500 times faster.

The importance of operational amplifiers lies in the advantages of using negative feedback networks. Operational amplifiers and digital logic gates used together allow data to be processed and analyzed with the greatest advantages of both technologies.

New Words and Expressions

operational amplifier	运算放大器
difference amplifier	差动放大器
differential	a. 微分的，差动的，差分的，差别的；n. 微分，差动，差分，差别
feedback	n. 反馈，回复，反应
stability	n. ①稳定性，稳定度，安定性，复原性　②耐……性，耐久性
capacitive	a. 电容性的，电容的，容性的
coupling	n. 耦合，偶合，连接；a. 耦合的，连接的

long-term	a. 长期的，远期的
power-supply	n. 电源
solid-state	a. 固态的
microvolt	n. 微伏
saturate	v. 使饱和；a. 饱和的，浸透的
comparator	n. 比较器
swing	v.; n. 摇摆，摆动
single-ended	a. 单端的
two-sided	a. 双边的，双侧的，两边的，两方面的
frequency band	频带

Notes

| 1. World War II | 第二次世界大战 |
| 2. dual in-line packages (DIPs) | 双列直插式封装，双列直插式组件 |

长句的翻译

翻译长句子时，必须分析清楚原文的结构关系，在理解原文内容的基础上，分清主次，按照时间概念和逻辑顺序重新按汉语习惯加以组合处理，译出的句子既要准确地表达原文，又要符合汉语的习惯。常用的译法有顺译法、倒译法、分译法。

1. 顺译法

顺译法是指基本上保留原文的语法结构，依照原文顺序译出。一般地，当原文的语法结构和时间顺序与汉语相同时，可采用顺译法。在翻译过程中，根据具体情况，可增加或省略有关连接词。例如：

No such limitation is placed on an alternating-current machine; here the only requirement is relative motion, and since a stationary armature and a rotating field system have numerous advantages, this arrangement is standard practice for all synchronous machines rated above a few kilovolt-amperes.

交流机不受这种限制，惟一的要求是相对移动，而且由于固定电枢及旋转磁场系统具有许多优点，这种安排是所有容量超过几千伏安的同步机的标准做法。

For large motors, therefore, a phase-wound rotor is used, with the winding connected at one end to each other and at the other end to slip-rings, thus enabling the resistance of the rotor to be varied at will, providing a greater starting torque and some speed control.

因此，对于大型电机来说，一般采用相绕组转子，其绕线的一端互相连接，而另一端接于轴的滑环上。这样，可随意改变转子的电阻，从而可提供更大的起动转矩，并可适当控制的速度。

2. 倒译法

当原文的结构层次与汉语相反时，要从英语原文的后面译起，自下而上，逆着原文的顺序翻译，称为倒译法。例如：

The resistance of any length of a conducting wire is easily measured by finding the potential difference in volts between its ends when a known current is flowing.

已知导线中的电流，只要求出导线两端电位差的伏特数，就不难测出任何长度的导线的电阻。

Various machine parts can be washed very clean and will be as clean as new ones when they are treated by ultrasonics, no matter how dirty and irregularly shaped they may be.

各种机器零件无论多么脏，形状多么不规则，当它们用超声波处理后，可以被洗得非常干净，甚至干净得像新零件一样。

3. 分译法

为了汉语表述的方便，可将原文的长句拆开来分别译出。当长句中的主句与从句或介词短语及分词短语等多修饰的词与词之间的关系不是很密切，并且各自具有相对的独立意义时，可分解成几个部分或意思层，然后再按时间顺序、逻辑顺序有机地组合在一起，还可增减适当的词语以便短句之间的衔接。例如，可添加或利用原文中的总括性词语作为引语，而后分述各个部分；或先将某一短语和从句分出去单独译出，再利用总括性词语把它和主句联系到一起；或先译出原文的主要之点，再将次要部分作为补充说明译在后面。例如：

Pure science has been subdivided into the physical science, which deals with the facts and relations of the physical world, and the biological sciences, which investigate the history and working of life on this planet.

理论科学分为自然科学和生物科学。前者研究自然界的各种事物和其相互关系，而后者则探讨地球上生物的发展历史和活动。

The reason that a neutral body is attracted by a charged body is that, although the neutral body is neutral within itself, it is not neutral with respect to the charged body, and the two bodies act as if oppositely charged when brought near each other.

虽然中性物体本身是不带电的，但对于带电体来说，它并非中性，当这两个物体彼此接近时，就会产生极性相反的电荷作用。这就是中性物体被带电体吸引的原因。

Exercises

I. Choose the best answer into the blank

1. At one time, _____ were called "differential analyzers" because they are used to solve differential equations.
   A. digital computer   B. minicomputer
   C. analog computers   D. microcomputer

2. After the invention of the transistor, _____ operational amplifiers were introduced as integrated circuits.
   A. solid-state   B. liquid-state   C. ideal   D. inverting

3. If the operational amplifier is to operate in its linear range, _____ must exist between the inverting and the noninverting inputs.
   A. a very small current difference   B. a very small voltage difference
   C. a very large voltage difference   D. a very large current difference

4. The wide application of operational amplifiers lies in the advantage of using _____.

　　A. positive feedback networks　　　　B. large open- circuit gain

　　C. negative feedback networks　　　　D. small output impedance

5. The useful range of the output voltage in an operational amplifier is approximately ___ percent of the supply voltages.

　　A. 60　　　　　　B. 70　　　　　　C. 80　　　　　　D. 90

II. Answer the following questions according to the text

1. What characteristics has a good operational amplifier?

2. Why is it more difficult for operational amplifiers to isolate the long-term changes?

3. What factors limit the use of operational amplifiers according to the context?

4. Do many operational amplifiers commonly require power supply sources? What are the typical values?

5. How many inputs and outputs has a operational amplifier? What are their names?

III. Translate the following into Chinese

　　1. An operational amplifier (op-amp) is an integrated circuit that amplifies the difference between two input voltages and produces a single output. The op-amp is prevalent in analog electronics, and can be thought of as another electronics device, in much the same way as the bipolar or field-effect transistor. The term operational amplifier comes from the original application of the device in the early 1960s. Op-amps, in conjunction with resistors and capacitors, were used in analog computer to perform mathematical operation to solve differential and integral equations. The application of op-amp has expanded significantly since those early days.

　　2. The input transistor of the TTL circuit is driven between saturation and the inverse active mode. This transistor reduces the switching time by quickly pulling charge out of the base of a saturation transistor. The totem—pole output stage was introduced in order to increase the switching speed of the output stage. The maximum output was determined by specifying that the output transistor was saturation region and also by specifying a maximum collector current in the output transistor. Maximum output is also a function of the specified propagation delay time.

Chapter 3　Power Electronic Technology

Section 1　Semiconductor Switches

Semiconductor switches are very important and crucial components in power electronic systems. These switches are meant to be the substitutions of the mechanical switches, but they are severely limited by the properties of the semiconductor materials and the process of manufacturing.

Switching losses

Power losses in the power electronic converters are comprised of ①the switching losses and ②the parasitic losses. The parasitic losses account for the losses due to the winding resistances of the inductors and transformers, the dielectric losses of capacitors, the eddy and the hysteresis losses. The switching losses are significant and can be managed. They can be further divided into three components: (a) the on-state losses, (b) the off-state losses and ③the losses in the transition states.

On-State Losses

The electrical switches conduct heavy current and have nonzero voltage across the switch in the on-state. The on-state power losses are given by

$$P_{on} = u_{son}i_f \qquad (3\text{-}1)$$

The u_{son} and i_f are respectively the switch voltage in the on-state and the forward current through the switch. For example, the typical power diodes and the power transistors have nearly 0.5 to 1 volt across them in the on-state. The forward currents can be hundreds to thousands of amperes. The on-state power losses are very significant.

Off-State Losses

The electrical switches withstand high voltages and have nonzero leakage current through the switch in the off-state. The off-state power losses are given by

$$P_{off} = u_{soff}i_r \qquad (3\text{-}2)$$

The u_{soff} and i_r are respectively the reverse bias voltage in the off-state and the reverse current through the switch. For example, the typical power diodes and the power transistors have high reverse voltages in hundreds to thousands of volts and microamps to milliamps through them in the off state.

Transition-State Losses

The practical switching devices have limited capabilities of rate of voltage transition and the rate of current steering. These nonabrupt transition rates give rise to power losses in the switching devices. We will examine these switching losses in two cases separately: the inductive and capacitive loads.

Switching with Inductive Load

The inductor is assumed to be large so that the current through it in steady state is nearly constant I_o. Assume that initially the switch is off. The inductor current is $+I_o$ and freewheels through diode **V1**. When the switch is turned on, the current through the switch begins to build up linearly (an assumption) to **+I_o** while the diode **V1** is still on. The on diode has zero voltage across it (an ideal diode), hence, the voltage on the switch is held constant at **+U_S**. When the current buildup is over, the diode **V1** ceases to conduct and the voltage on the switch ramps linearly (again an assumption) down to zero.

When the switch is turned off, the voltage begins to build up linearly to **+U_S** while the diode **V1** is off. While the diode is off the current through the switch equals the inductor current, which is constant **I_o**. After the switch voltage reaches zero, the current through the switch begins to decrease below **I_o**, as the remaining current is now steered through the diode **V1**, which has now turned on. The current through the switch ramps down to zero ultimately. Switching waveforms with inductive load are shown in Fig.3-1.

The switching losses are given by

$$P_{Sw} = \frac{1}{2} U_s I_o [t_{on1} + t_{on2} + t_{off1} + t_{off2}] f_s \quad (3\text{-}3)$$

The switching power losses increase linearly with the switching frequency like in the resistive case but about six times more. The upper bound on the switching frequency is also about half.

$$f_{Smax} = \frac{1}{t_{on1} + t_{on2} + t_{off1} + t_{off2}} \quad (3\text{-}4)$$

Switching with capacitive load

The capacitor is assumed to be large so that the voltage through it in steady state is nearly constant U_o. Assume that initially the switch is on, hence, the current through the switch is **I_S**. The capacitor voltage is **U_o**, the voltage across the switch is zero and the diode **V1** is reverse biased. When the switch

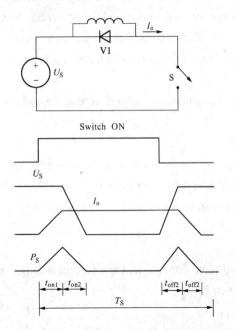

Fig.3-1　Switching waveforms with inductive load

is turned off, the switch voltage begins to ramp up to **+ U_o** while the diode **V1** is still off. During this buildup, the current through the switch is held constant at **I_S**. When the voltage buildup is over, the diode **V1** begins to conduct and the voltage on the switch is clamped at **U_o**, and the current through the switch ramps linearly (again an assumption) down to zero.

When the switch is closed, the current begins to build up linearly to **I_S** while the diode **V1** is still on. The voltage on the switch remains clamped at **U_o**. After the switch current reaches **I_S**, the diode turns off and the voltage on the switch begins to ramp down to zero.

The switching power losses in the case of capacitive load also have similar dependence as in the case of inductive loads.

The switching losses can be usually minimized in two ways: ①divert the energy from the switch to a loss or non-loss circuit or ②switch at either zero current or at zero voltage. The first is called snubbering and the later is known as zero-voltage and zero-current switching.

New Words and Expressions

semiconductor	n. 半导体	
power electronic	n. 电力电子	
loss	n. 损耗，损失	
parasitic	a. 寄生的，附加的	
winding	n. ①绕组，线圈　②一圈，一转	
transformer	n 变压器，变换器，变量器	
dielectric	n. 介质，电介质，绝缘材料；a. 绝缘的，介电的，介质的，不导电的	
eddy	n. 涡流，旋涡；　a. 涡流的，涡旋的；v. 涡流，起旋涡	
hysteresis	n. 磁滞，滞后，迟滞	
on-state	a. 通态的，接通的，开态	
off-state	a. 关态的，断开的，断态的	
microamp	n. 微安	
milliamp	n. 毫安	
steering	n. 转向，操纵，控制，调整	
buildup	n. ①形成，产生，出现　②增加，增大，上升　③建造，建起	
ramp	v. 斜变，倾斜，直线上升	
waveform	n. 波形	
clamp	v. 箝位，定位，使固定	
snubbering	n. 缓冲	

Notes

1. zero-voltage   电压过零的
2. zero-current   电流过零的
3. The practical switching devices have limited capabilities of rate of voltage transition and the rate of current steering. These nonabrupt transition rates give rise to power losses in the switching devices.

   实际开关装置限制了电压变换速率和电流换向速率。非突变引起了开关装置的功率损失。
4. The capacitor is assumed to be large so that the voltage through it in steady state is nearly constant U_o. Assume that initially the switch is on, hence, the current through the switch is I_S. The capacitor voltage is U_o, the voltage across the switch is zero and the diode **V1** is reverse biased.

   假设电容器很大，致使在稳态状态下其两端的电压接近为常数 U_o。假使开关开始处于闭合状态，则通过开关的电流为 I_S。电容器的电压为 U_o，开关两端的电压为零，二极管 **V1** 反向偏置。

词 类 的 转 换（一）

英语和汉语属于不同的语系，在词汇方面和语法方面有很大的差别。就词类来说，同一意思在两种语言中可以用不同的词类表达。因此，在翻译过程中，很多情况下需要进行词类转换。所谓词类转换，是指把原文语言中的某一词类转译为汉语的另一词类，如原文中的名词译成汉语的动词；原文中的动词译成汉语后变成副词等。掌握词类转换译法，可使我们脱离原文词类的限制，用汉语的适当词类予以表达。

一、转换成汉语动词

英语和汉语相比，英语的句法一般要求一个句子里只能有一个谓语动词，而其他动词都是非谓语形式，作主语、定语、状语等使用。然而在汉语中动词的使用比较灵活，一个句子中可以有几个动词。因此，英语中不少词类在翻译时需转译成动词。

1. 名词转换成动词

英语中表达动作概念的动名词、具有动作意义的抽象名词、由动词派生出来的名词、动词加名词构成的固定短语、介词加名词构成的固定短语等，往往可以根据具体情况译成汉语动词，例如：

The *application* of electronic computers makes for a tremendous rise in labor productivity. 使用电子计算机可以大大提高劳动生产率。

Computers can provide *analyses* of every operation in a factory. 计算机能对工厂的每道工序进行分析。

Primary forces have certain *valuations* that must be considered in any design. 在任何设计中，对于数值能确切计算的主要作用力都必须加以考虑。

Integrated circuits are fairly recent *development*. 集成电路是近年来发展起来的。

2. 形容词转换成动词

英语中某些由动词转换来的形容词、同介词搭配构成句子表语或定语的形容词、与连系动词一起构成复合谓语的形容词，通常可译成汉语中的动词，例如：

Copper wire is *flexible*. 铜线容易弯曲。

Television is *different* from radio in that it sends and receives pictures. 电视不同于无线电在于能发送并接收图像。

If extremely low-cost power were ever to become *available* from large nuclear power plants, electrolytic hydrogen would become competitive. 如能从大型核电站获得成本极低的电力，电解氢的竞争能力就会增强。

Heat is a form of energy into which all other forms are *convertible*. 热是能的一种形式，其他一切能的形式都能转化为热能。

3. 介词转换成动词

英语中的介词或介词短语在许多情况下可以译成汉语的动词，尤其是当它们用作表语或状语时，例如：

The letter E is commonly used *for* electromotive force. 通常用字母 E 表示电动势。

Except for atomic energy, all forms of energy used by man are *from* the sun. 除原子能之外，

人类所利用的一切形式的能量都<u>来自</u>太阳。

So long as we have means of producing heat we can keep the steam engine *at* work. 只要能产生热，就能使蒸汽机<u>做</u>功。

4. 副词转换成动词

英语中有些作表语的副词或复合宾语中的副词，往往可译成汉语的动词，例如：

The electric current flows through the circuit with the switch *on*. 如果开关<u>接通</u>，电流就流过线路。

Open the valve to let air *in*. 打开阀门，让空气<u>进入</u>。

We are *through* with our test report. 我们的试验报告<u>写</u>完了。

Exercises

I. Choose the best answer into the blank

1. The switching losses are comprised of the on-state losses, _____ and the losses in the transition states.

　A. the parasitic losses　　　　　　　　B. the dielectric losses

　C. the off-state losses　　　　　　　　D. the hysteresis losses

2. The typical power transistors in the on-state have _____.

　A. 0.1 V　　　　　B. 0.7 V　　　　　C. 2V　　　　　D. 5V

3. The power transistors, as electrical switches, withstand _____ voltages in the off-state.

　A. low forward　　　B. high forward　　　C. low reverse　　　D. high reverse

4. The rate of voltage transition and the rate of current steering can produce _____ in the switching devices.

　A. the switching losses　　　　　　　　B. the parasitic losses

　C. power losses　　　　　　　　　　　D. the dielectric losses

II. Answer the following questions according to the text

1. Which losses are power losses in the power electronic converters comprised of?

2. How to determine the off-state power losses in the electrical switches?

3. How do the switching power losses change with the switching frequency?

4. How many ways to minimize the switching losses are there?

III. Translate the following into Chinese

　Diodes in power electronic applications carry high currents, withstand high reverse voltages and should possess fast switching characteristics. These requirements render power diodes very different than the ordinary signal diodes. It is also difficult to achieve all the above three characteristics in a single device. Hence, several types of power diodes are available suited for particular applications.

　The power diode is a high-current, high-voltage diode with medium fast switching characteristics. The Schottky Barrier diode uses a metal-semiconductor junction and has a lower on-state voltage than the p-i-n diodes. It has the high-current capability and fast switching characteristics but it is a low-voltage device and exhibits a much higher leakage current. These diodes are ideally suited for switch-mode power supplies. The on-state power losses, which are calculated by multiplying the on-state voltage drop by the on-state current, determine the package size of all diodes.

Section 2   The DC-DC Converters

Introduction

The DC-DC converter converts a DC power source to another DC source with different terminal specifications. The DC-DC converters change DC to AC first and than change AC back to DC. The DC source is often the uncontrolled DC voltage with ripple from AC to DC rectifier.

The DC-DC converters are widely used in the switch-mode power supplies and DC motor drive applications. Some of these converters, especially in power supplies, have an isolation transformer. The DC-DC converters are also used as interfaces between the DC systems of different voltage levels.

The step-down and step-up voltage converters are the two basic converter topologies. These are referred as the Buck and Boost converters respectively. It must, however, be kept in mind that a step-down voltage converter is also a step-up current converter and vice versa because the input power must equal the output power. The Buck-Boost converter does both stepping up and down action. The ČUK converter is a dual of the Buck-Boost converter. All these converters have single, two and four quadrant variations in topologies.

The voltage source driven DC-DC converts are more popular than the current driven converters, hence, this section will concentrate on the voltage driven converters. All converts use effective filtering on both the input and the output to reduce the ac components from going outside the converters.

Buck Converter

The Buck converter is a voltage step-down and current step-up converter. The topology is shown in Fig.3-2. The two-position switch is synthesized from a switch and a diode. The switch is turned on for a time τ periodically at a rate $1/T_S$.

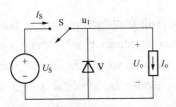

Fig.3-2   Buck converter topology

A prominent application of the Buck con- verter is a DC regulated power supply in which the output voltage is regulated against the variations in the load resistance and the input voltages. These power supplies are used in computers and portable instruments in the medical and communication field.

There are two modes of Buck converter operations in which the output current waveform is either continuous or discontinuous in time over a switching period.

Continuous conduction mode (CCM)

The ideal current sink in the output represents infinitely large inductor in series with the load resistance. This is a hypothetical circuit but its discussion provides a good understanding of the Buck converter operation.

The steady-state operation consists of two circuit modes, shown in Fig.3-3.

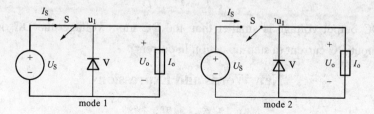

Fig.3-3   Circuit modes in steady-state operation

As the switch is turned on in mode 1, the diode is reverse biased and the current flows through inductor into the voltage sink. After a time τ, the switch is turned off. The inductor current then freewheels through the diode as shown in the circuit of mode 2. The second mode is terminated at T_S when the switch is turned on again. The current and voltage waveforms are shown in Fig.3-4.

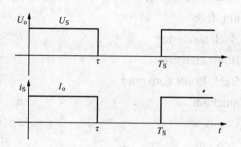

Fig.3-4   The current and voltage waveforms

The average output voltage is

$$\bar{U}_o = U_s \frac{\tau}{T_s} = DU_s$$

$$T_{vv} = \frac{\bar{U}_o}{U_S} = D \qquad\qquad (3\text{-}5)$$

or
$$T_{vv} = \tau f_S$$

D is called the duty ratio. The duty ratio D is also the turn ratio of the equivalent DC transformer. The turn ratio of the equivalent dc transformer can be controlled electronically in a range of $0\sim1$.

The DC output voltage is a linear function of the on-time of the switch, the pulse width, and the switching frequency (inverse function of the switching period T_S). The output voltage control using pulse width is known as the **PWM** control. The output voltage can also be controlled by switching frequency. The **PWM** control is more popular.

If the duty ratio D is made a linear function of $\boldsymbol{u}_C$, a control voltage

$$D = ku_C$$
$$\bar{U}_o = (kU_S)u_C \qquad\qquad (3\text{-}6)$$

The output voltage is then a linear function of the control voltage. This is also the principle of switch-mode linear amplifier. The gain of this amplifier is determined by the input dc source voltage.

Neglecting the power losses in the circuit elements, we could use the equation of the balance of power

$$U_S \overline{I}_S = \overline{U}_o I_o \tag{3-7}$$

where I_S is the average current from the DC source. Hence,

$$\frac{I_o}{\overline{I}_S} = \frac{U_S}{\overline{U}_o} = \frac{1}{D} \tag{3-8}$$

Although the DC output voltage is smaller than the DC input voltage, the DC output current is larger than the input DC current (a step-up action in current).

New Words and Expressions

ripple	n. 波纹，波度，微波
rectifier	n. 整流器
isolation transformer	隔离变压器
interface	n. 接口
Buck converter	降压式变换器，降压式斩波器
Boost converter	升压式变换器，升压式斩波器
Buck-Boost converter	升/降式变换器，升/降式斩波器
quadrant	n. 象限，四分之一圆周，九十度弧
step-down	a. 降压的，降低的
step-up	a. 升压的，升高的
dual	a. 二重的，对偶的
filter	n.; v. 滤波，过滤
periodically	ad. 周期地
portable	a. 手提的，轻便的，可携带的
sink	n. 换能器，变换器，散热器，汇点，收点，穴
hypothetical	a. 假设的，假定的，有前提的
duty ratio	功率比，能量比
turn ratio	匝数比
PWM　pulse width modulation	脉冲宽度调制

Notes

1. switch-mode power supplies　开关电源

2. All converts use effective filtering on both the input and the output to reduce the AC components from going outside the converters.
   所有的滤波器均对输入和输出采用有效的滤波，以减少从变换器输出的交流成分。

3. A prominent application of the Buck converter is a DC regulated power supply in which the output voltage is regulated against the variations in the load resistance and the input voltages.
   降压式变换器的一个著名应用是用于直流可调电源，调整其输出电压以补偿负荷电阻和输入电压的变化。

词类的转换（二）

二、转换为汉语名词

1. 动词转换成名词

英语中有些动词在翻译成汉语时很难找到相应的动词，这时可将其转译成汉语名词，例如：

The electronic computer is chiefly *characterized* by its accurate and rapid computations. 电子计算机的主要<u>特点</u>是计算准确而快速。

An electric current *varies* directly as the electromotive force and inversely as the resistance. 电流的<u>变化</u>与电动势成正比，与电阻成反比。

The design *aims* at automatic operation, easy regulation, simple maintenance and high productivity. 设计的<u>目的</u>在于自动操作，调节方便，维护简易，生产率高。

2. 形容词转换成名词

英语中有些形容词加上定冠词 the 表示某一类人或物，汉译时常译成名词。另外，英语中有些表示事物特征的形容词作表语时，往往可在其后加上"性"、"度"、"体"等词，译成名词，例如：

People are so much more *flexible* and *inventive* than robots. 人类比机器人更灵活而且更富有<u>创造性</u>。

Some people think tomorrow's computers will be *intelligent*. 有人认为未来的计算机就具有<u>智能</u>。

In fission processes the fission fragments are very *radioactive*. 在裂变过程中，裂变碎片具有强烈的<u>放射性</u>。

3. 代词转换成名词

英语中的代词译成汉语，有时为了使译文规范，须转换为名词，例如：

Radio waves are similar to light waves except that *their* wave-length is much greater. 无线电波与光波相似，只不过<u>无线电波</u>的波长更长一些。

The specific resistance of iron is not so small as *that* of copper. 铁的电阻系数不如铜的<u>电阻系数</u>那样小。

Electricity may be produced by a generator *which* is turned by a motor using any of the other forms of energy. 发电机可以发电，而<u>发电机</u>是由利用任何其他形式能量的原动机带动的。

4. 副词转换成名词

英语中有些副词，在句子中用作状语，译成汉语时可根据具体情况转换成汉语的名词，例如：

The quality of the operating system determines *how useful* the computer is. 操作系统的质量决定着计算机的<u>应用效能</u>。

Electromagnetic waves travel as *fast* as light. 电磁波传播的<u>速度</u>和光一样。

The instrument is used to determine *how fully* the batteries are charged. 这种仪表用来确定电池充电的<u>程度</u>。

The device is shown *schematically* in Figure 1. 图 1 所示为这种装置的<u>简图</u>。

Exercises

I. Choose the best answer into the blank

1. The DC-DC converter converts _____ input to _____ output.

　A. direct current , alternating current

　B. direct current, direct current

　C. alternating current, alternating current

　D. alternating current, alternating current

2. The Buck is a _____ converter.

　A. voltage step-up 　　　　　　　B. current step-down

　C. current step-up 　　　　　　　D. resistance

3. The PWM control that uses _____ to control the output voltage is more popular.

　A. switching frequency 　　　　　B. pulse width

　C. rise time 　　　　　　　　　　D. down time

4. The gain of switch-mode linear amplifier is determined by _____ voltage, and the output voltage is a linear function of _____.

　A. the output dc, the control voltage

　B. the input dc source , the control voltage

　C. the input dc source, the output voltage

　D. the input dc source, the control voltage

II. Answer the following questions according to the text

1. Which DC-DC converter is more popular, the current driven converter or the voltage driven converter?

2. What kind of converter is the Buck converter?

3. What is duty ratio?

4. How to control the dc output voltage of the Buck converter in continuous conductance mode?

III. Translate the following into Chinese

　　The boost converter is a voltage step-up and current step-down converter. The current source is synthesized from a DC voltage source by adding a large value inductor in series. In dc regulated power supply applications, the voltage sink represents a large value capacitor in parallel with the load resistance. In the application of the DC motor control, the voltage sink represents the back emf of the DC motor. The switching action produces a pulsating current. The capacitive filter smoothens the pulsating current and provides a DC voltage to the load.

Section 3　DC–AC Converters

Introduction

DC-AC converters are conventionally called the inverters. Such converters are very popular in the battery-operated power systems such as the uninterruptible power supplies (UPS) for hospitals, and AC motor drives. Low power level inverters are usually single-phase type and medium and high power inverters are three-phase type. We will look into the performance of DC-AC converters of several useful topologies. The focus will be on the inverter operation for low-frequency output voltages such as 50~60 Hz or 400 Hz in aircraft systems. Analyses of DC-AC converter circuits at low and high frequencies are very similar except that at high frequencies the parasitic capacitances and inductances, charge storage, and heat localizing problems in switching devices must be taken into account.

Controlled inversion

The DC to AC inverter system is shown in Fig.3-5(a). Input is from a DC source and the output is desired to be a sinusoidal voltage or current with zero DC component, single-phase or three-phase signal. The load is a *R-L-C* load, an AC voltage or an AC current sink. Control parameter may be, as shall be seen later, an angle, a pulse width, a voltage or a current signal. The converter consists of switches, reactive components such as *L, C*, transformers and resistances.

Switches including the diodes are assumed to be ideal and unidirectional, that is, they have zero on-state losses, zero off-state losses, zero switching losses and unrestricted voltage or current carrying capabilities. Switching devices in a practical design example must be selected with these desired characteristics in mind. Inductors, capacitors and transformers are assumed to be ideal.

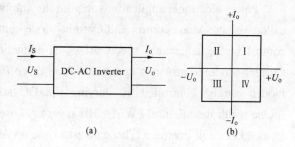

(a)

(b)

Fig.3-5

(a) A DC-AC inverter system; (b) operational quadrants
on the U_o-I_o plane

Electrical loads can be of three types: impedance load, AC voltage sink load or AC current sink load. Examples of impedance load are electromagnetic ac relays, electromagnetic pick up and lift equipments. The load comprises of a large value inductor. Examples of ac voltage sink are the constant speed drives for induction and synchronous motors. Examples of AC current sink are constant torque drives for the induction and synchronous motors.

Generally speaking, the input current is non-sinusoidal if the source is a DC voltage source and vice versa. The output voltage and the output current on the other hand, can be non-sinusoidal simultaneously. Hence, input and output low-pass filters are generally employed to reduce high frequency components of the non-sinusoidal signals on either side. A series inductor is a current smoother and a parallel capacitor is a voltage smoother.

Output current generally differs in phase with the output voltage. Hence, in a switching period, the polarities of current and voltage vary over all four quadrants, see Fig.3-6. Power flows from the converter to the load in the first and third quadrants and in the reverse direction in the second and fourth quadrants. A unidirectional switch in the inverters, therefore, has an inverse connected diode in parallel to allow bidirectional current flow.

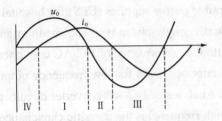

Fig.3-6　Output current and output voltage
waveform in an inverter

Inverters derived from voltage source (**VSI**) are ideally suited for supplying power to a resistive and inductive load and the applications that require constant torque operation of AC motors. Current Source Inverters (**CSI**) are ideally suited for supplying power to largely capacitive loads and AC voltage buses. Inverters can be further classified on the basis of the mode of control of the output variable: voltage or current.

Inverter control in practice concerns three aspects: fundamental frequency, amplitude, harmonic profile.

Fundamental frequency is either equal to the switching frequency of the inverter (square-wave and PWM inverters) or its simple fraction (1/3, 1/5, and so on) such as in Multiple PWM or sine PWM inverters.

Power electronic applications require the amplitude control of output voltage or output current, called Voltage-Mode control and Current-Mode control respectively. An example of Voltage-Mode control is the adjustable speed drives of induction and synchronous motors. An example of Current-Mode control is a constant torque drive for induction motors. Output amplitude in both modes can be controlled by varying the DC source voltage or by varying the pulse-width (pulse-width modulation, PWM). The inverters based on the control of DC source voltage are also termed DC-Link Inverters. These inverters use an AC to controlled DC converter on the input side. The inverter is square-wave controlled. This arrangement is expensive but exhibits a faster response time than PWM inverters. The control circuitry is also simpler.

Harmonic profiling is an extra feature added over the amplitude control. The objective of harmonic profiling is to bolster the amplitude of the fundamental component of the output voltage and the elimination or reduction of high order harmonics. One of the techniques involves the notching or adding step pulses to a base pulse. The other technique involves multiple pulses per cycle of the fundamental, each pulse-width modulated to achieve desired wave-shaping of the output waveform (Sine-**PWM**).

Inverter topologies

The DC-AC inverter can be thought of as a three-position switch as shown in Fig.3-7(a). The load is connected to the pole of the switch and the first two positions are connected to dc voltage or dc current sources of opposite polarities. The third position is connected to the zero terminal of the source. The pole of the switch stays in the first and second positions for equal amounts of time in a switching period. The output waveform for zero amount of time on the third position is a square wave. The output waveform for nonzero time is pulse wave.

The three-position switch may be synthesized by two unidirectional electronic switches as shown in Fig.3-7(b). The third position of the switch is simulated by turning both switches off in **VSI** topologies and on in **CSI** topologies. This is the basic bridge inverter topology. The two diodes provide the path for current flow from the load to the source as this may be required in an inverter operation involving more than one quadrant. Inverter supplying load to an ***R-L*** load operates in all four quadrants because the output voltage and current waveforms, for some segments in a switching period, have opposing polarities. A **MOSFET** has a built-in body diode that serves as the path for the current from the source to the drain. An **IGBT**, however, requires an external diode.

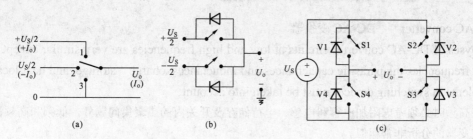

Fig.3-7

(a) The DC-AC inverter implemented by a 3-position switch; (b) the 3-position switch
synthesized from two 2-position switches; (c) full-bridge inverter topology

The 3-ϕ half-bridge inverter is made of three half-bridge inverters connected in parallel each switched 120° apart. This topology is capable of handling high power with minimum component stresses. The half-bridge topology of Fig.3-7(b) requires two separate voltage sources $U_S/2$. Fig.3-7(c) shows a full-bridge topology that requires a single voltage source.

New Words and Expressions

inverter	n. 逆变器
uninterruptible power supplies (UPS)	不间断电源
single-phase	a. 单相的
three-phase	a. 三相的
parameter	n. 参数
unidirectional	a. 单极性的，单向的
electromagnetic	a. 电磁的
relay	v. 中继，转播；n. 继电器
synchronous motor	同步电动机
torque	n. 转矩
non-sinusoidal	a. 非正弦的
low-pass	低通
smoother	n. 滤波器，整平器
polarity	n. 极性
bidirectional	a. 双向的
harmonics	n. 谐波
high order harmonics	高次谐波

induction	n. 感应
square-wave	方波
response time	响应时间
notching	n.; a. 阶梯式，下凹的，切口，开槽
step pulse	阶跃脉冲

Notes

1. DC-AC converter   DC-AC 变换器
2. Analyses of DC-AC converter circuits at low and high frequencies are very similar except that at high frequencies the parasitic capacitances and inductances, charge   storage, and heat localizing problems in switching devices must be taken into account.

   除在高频时必须考虑附加电容和电感、电荷储存及开关内的热聚集问题外，低频和高频情况下的逆变器的分析非常相似。
3. MOSFET metal-oxide-semiconductor field effect transistor   MOS 场效应晶体管
4. IGBT insutaled gate bipolar transistor   绝缘栅双极型晶体管

词 类 的 转 换（三）

三、转换成汉语形容词

1. 副词转换成形容词

Robotics is so *closely* associated with cybernetics that it is sometimes mistakenly considered to be synonymous. 机器人技术与控制论的联系如此密切，以致两者有时被错误地认为是同一回事。

Miniature gas detector is *chiefly* featured by small size, light weight, complete functions and long continuous working time. 袖珍式瓦斯检测器的主要特点是体积小、重量轻、功能齐全、连续工作时间长。

Gases and liquids are *perfectly* elastic. 气体和液体都是完全的弹性体。

2. 名词转换成形容词

The nuclear power system designed in China is of great *precision*. 中国设计的核动力系统十分精确。

Electronic computers and microprocessors are of great *importance* to us. 电子计算机和微处理器对我们来说十分重要。

Single crystals of high perfection are an absolute *necessity* for the fabrication of integrated circuits. 高度完整的单晶对于制造集成电路来说是绝对必要的。

四、转换成汉语副词

1. 形容词转换成副词

The engine has given a constantly *good* performance. 这台发动机一直运转良好。

The *same* principles of low internal resistance also apply to milliammeters. 低内阻的原理同样适用于毫安表。

A graph gives a *visual* representation of the relationship. 图表可以<u>直观地</u>显示要说明的关系。

2. 其他词类转换成副词

Rapid evaporation at the heating-surface *tends* to make the steam wet. 加热面上的迅速蒸发，<u>往往</u>使蒸汽的湿度加大。

The added device will ensure *accessibility* for part loading and unloading. 增添这种装置将保证工件装卸<u>方便</u>。

We shall develop the electric power industry *in a way*. 我们将<u>大规模</u>发展电力工业。

值得一提的是，上述介绍的种种词类转译法，在翻译过程中应灵活应用，以便将原文意思表达清楚，不可拘泥于原文的词类而使译文晦涩费解。

Exercises

I. Choose the best answer into the blank

1. High power inverters are usually _____.

    A. single-phase type   B. two-phase type

    C. three-phase type   D. DC-DC converters

2. The output of a inverter is desired to be a _____.

    A. dc voltage   B. sinusoidal voltage

    C. dc current   D. time-varying voltage

3. The constant speed drive for synchronous motors is the example of _____.

    A. impedance load   B. ac voltage sink load

    C. AC current sink load   D. DC load

4. Voltage source inverters are theoretically suited for supplying power to _____.

    A. capacitive loads   B. AC voltage buses

    C. inductive loads   D. dc motors

5. Output amplitude in Voltage-Mode control and Current-Mode control modes can be con- trolled by varying the DC source voltage or by varying the _____.

    A. dc source current   B. pulse-width

    C. pulse-amplitude   D. harmonic

II. Answer the following questions according to the text

1. What parameters may be used as control parameters in the DC-AC inverter system?

2. What does the DC-AC inverter consist of?

3. What characteristics do the ideal switches with the diode have?

4. What functions do low-pass filters have?

5. What aspects are concerned for inverter control in practical applications?

III. Translate the following into Chinese

    1. Reducing the harmonic content of the output voltage or current is one of the important tasks of the designers. Harmonics appear as the undesirable noise. Harmonics reduce the power factor. They may excite mechanical resonance at detrimental frequencies or generate acoustical noise in ac

motor drive systems. The ripple content (harmonics) is easily reduced by post-filtering after the converter. The post converter low-pass filter may be designed for cutoff frequencies that are several times lower than the switching frequency (usually in kilohertz). In the DC-AC inverters, however, the fundamental component of the output voltage or current is either the same as or a simple fraction of the switching frequency. Designing an effective low-pass filter with cutoff frequency between the fundamental frequency and the first undesired harmonic frequency is a difficult task. Hence, an active harmonic reduction strategy is often desirable.

2. Converter control refers to specifying the desired nominal operating condition and then regulating the converter so that it stays close to the nominal performance in the face of disturbances, noise and modeling errors. We can analyze the dynamic behavior of the power electronic converter (or local) of the steady-state operating point. The converter operation involves switching modes, therefore an overall converter model is a nonlinear model. The averaged model, localized to the steady-state operating point, is a linear model. The analytical techniques for linear systems are very well known.

Chapter 4　Electric Machinery

Section 1　Principle of Operation of an Inductive machine

The basic principle of operation of an induction machine is illustrated by the revolving horseshoe magnet and copper-disk experiment pictured in Fig.4-1. When the horseshoe magnet is rotated, the moving magnetic field passing across the copper disk induces eddy currents in the disk. These eddy currents are in such a direction as to cause the disk to follow the rotation of the horseshoe magnet. With the direction of rotation shown in the figure, the eddy currents will be as displayed in Fig.4-1 according to Fleming's right-hand rule.

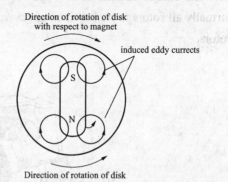

Fig.4-1　Rotation of a copper disk following the rotation of a permanent magnet

Fleming's right-hand rule: Place the thumb and the first and second fingers of the right hand so that all three are mutually perpendicular. With the hand in this position, the first finger is pointed in the direction of the field, the thumb is in the direction of motion of the relative motion of the conductor, and the second finger is the direction of the induced voltage. Note that the relative motion of the conductor is opposite to the rotation of the direction of rotation of the magnetic field.

By applying Fleming's right-hand rule, the force on the copper disk is determined to be in the direction of rotation of the magnet.

Fleming's left-hand rule: Place the thumb and the first and second finger of the left hand so that all three are mutually perpendicular to each other. With the first finger in the direction of the field and the second finger in the direction of the current, the thumb indicates the direction of the force.

Whereas the copper disk will rotate in the same direction as the rotating magnetic field, it will never reach the same speed as the rotating magnet, because if it did, there would be no relative motion between the two and therefore no current induced in the copper disk. The difference in speed between the rotating magnetic field and the copper disk is known as slip, which is essential to the operation of an induction motor. In induction motors the rotating magnetic field is set up by windings in the stator, and the induced currents are carried by conductors in the rotor. The rotating horseshoe magnet and copper disk are considerably different in structure from today's induction motor, but the basic principles of operation are the same.

The rotating magnetic field is essential to the functioning of an induction motor. In practical machines this rotating magnetic field is achieved by a combination of a space displacement of the windings and a time-phase displacement of the exciting voltage.

The rotor is formed from laminated electrical steel punching, and the rotor winding consists of bars contained in slots punched in the laminations. These bars are short-circuited at both ends by a short-circuiting ring. A bar-end ring structure, without the laminated core, is called a squirrel cage, as shown in the Fig.4-2. In small- and medium-horsepower sizes, rotors are made by casting aluminum into the rotor core. In the larger sizes of a-c motors, cast-aluminum rotor are not practical, and copper bars are inserted into the slots. These copper bars are short-circuited at both ends by a copper end ring, and the end ring is brazed or soldered onto the bars. Sometimes bronzes or other alloys are used to replace copper in making the cage and end ring. The sizes at which the transition between cast-aluminum and copper rotors takes place varies among rotor manufacturers, but virtually all rotors in motor sizes of several thousand horsepower and above are built with bar-type rotors.

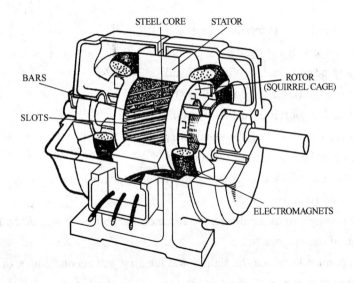

Fig.4-2　Squirrel-cage induction motors

Another construction feature dependent on motor size is the type of coil winding used. In small- and medium-size ac motors, most coils are random-wound. These coils are made with round wire, which is wound into the stator slots and assumes a diamond shape in the end turns; however, the wires are randomly located within a given coil, and hence the name "random-wound". For large ac motors and particularly for high-voltage motors, 2300V and above, form-wound coils are used. These coils are constructed from rectangular wire, which is bent into shape around forms and then taped. The coil is formed to the proper size so that the complete coil can be inserted into the stator slots at the time the stator is wound. Form-wound coils are used for high-voltage windings because it is relatively easy to add extra insulation on the individual coils before inserting them into the stator.

New Words and Expressions

induction machine	感应电机
horseshoe	n. ①马蹄形，U 形 ②马蹄铁
magnet	n. 磁铁，磁石，磁体
horseshoe magnet	马蹄形磁铁
eddy	n. 涡流，涡旋
permanent magnet	永久磁铁
perpendicular	a. ①（与……）垂直的 ②直立的；n. 垂直，正交，竖直
magnetic field	磁场
rotating magnetic field	旋转磁场
slip	n. 滑差（率），转差（率）
winding	n. 绕组
stator	n. 定子，静子，静片
rotor	n. 转子
exciting voltage	励磁电压
laminated	a. 叠片的，分层的，薄片的
punching	n. 冲压，穿孔
bar	n. ①线棒，导条 ②条，杆
slot	n. ①槽 ②隙缝
lamination	n. ①叠片，冲片 ②分层 ③薄片
braze	v. 铜焊，钎焊
solder	n. 焊料，接合物；v. 焊，焊接
short-circuiting	a. 使短路的
ring	n. 环
squirrel cage	鼠笼
core	n. ①铁芯 ②心，核心
coil	n. 线圈，绕组
random-wound	散绕
form-wound	模绕
insulation	n. 绝缘

Notes

1. Fleming's right-hand rule

2. In practical machines this rotating magnetic field is achieved by a combination of a space displacement of the windings and a time-phase displacement of the exciting voltage.

   在实际的电机中，旋转磁场是通过空间上交替布置的绕组和时间相位上相互交替的励磁电压来实现的。

3. These coils are constructed from rectangular wire, which is bent into shape around forms and then taped. The coil is formed to the proper size so that the complete coil can be inserted into the stator slots at the time the stator is wound.

这些线圈采用矩形截面的导线构成，将它们弯曲成型后缠上绝缘带。在制作定子绕组时，线圈被做成适当的尺寸，以便将整个线圈放置入定子槽内。

用 词 的 增 省（一）

所谓用词的增加和省略，是指在翻译过程中，必要时可添加一些原文中没有的词，或者省略一些原文中已有的词，使得译文在语法、语言形式上符合译文习惯，词语联想方面与原文一致起来。当然，这种用词的增省不是无中生有，而是对原文中的每一用词，经过仔细分析和体会其功用和含义后，按照翻译的标准来增省。用词增省可参照以下原则：

（1）使每句话的意思清楚明白；

（2）使每句话和上下文连贯；

（3）符合汉语科技文章的文体风格。

概括起来讲，用词的增省有三个方面的需要，即属于语法上的需要；属于汉语习惯行文表达的需要；属于技术上的需要。

1. 增加表示复数的词

在翻译过程中，可通过增加"一些"、"有些"、"各种"、"许多"和"几种"等词语把英语中表示名词复数的概念译出。例如：

There is enough coal to meet the world's needs for *centuries* to come. 有足够的煤来满足全世界未来几个世纪的需要。

In spite of the *difficulties*, our task was got over well. 虽然有各种困难，但我们的任务已顺利完成。

However, in spite of all this similarity between a voltmeter and an ammeter there are also important *differences*. 可是尽管电压表与电流表之间有这些类似之处，但还有若干重要的差。

2. 增加数词和量词

当具有几个成分并列时，可根据并列成分数量的多少，增译数、量词表示概括。在其他情况下，根据句子表示的意义，可按汉语习惯增添数、量词。例如：

The factors, *voltage, current and resistance,* are related to each other. 电压、电流和电阻这三个因素是相互关联的。

Based upon the relationship between *magnetism and electricity* are motors and generators. 电动机与发电机就是以磁和电这二者之间的关系为基础。

The revolution of the earth around the sun causes the changes of the *seasons*. 地球绕太阳旋转，引起四季的交替。

The starting and termination dates of the training shall be agreed upon between the *parties* in accordance with the stipulations of the Contract. 培训工作的起止日期应由双方根据合同的规定商定。

Exercises

I. Choose the best answer into the blank

1. The thumb is in the direction of _____ in Fleming's right-hand rule.

   A. the field

   B. rotation of the magnetic field

   C. the induced voltage

   D. the relative motion of conductor

2. In induction motors the speed of the rotating rotor _____ the speed of the rotating magnetic field.

   A. equals to   B. is much greater than   C. never reaches   D. keeps the same as

3. When the speed of the rotor is zero , the slip of induction machine is _____.

   A. 0.0   B. 0.1   C. 1.0   D. 0.3

4. Form-wound coils are widely used for _____ motors.

   A. small-size AC   B. medium-size AC   C. large AC   D. large DC

II. Answer the following questions according to the text

1. How to apply Fleming's right-hand rule to determine the direction of the induced voltage?

2. How to apply Fleming's left-hand rule to determine the direction of the force acting on a current-carrying conductor?

3. What does "slip" mean?

4. How does the induction machine work?

5. What characteristics does a squirrel cage have in construction?

III. Translate the following into Chinese

   Rotating electric machines take many forms and are known by many names — DC, synchronous, permanent-magnet, induction, hysteresis, etc. Although these machines appear to be quite dissimilar and require a variety of analytical techniques, the physical principles governing their behavior are quite similar, and in fact these machines can often be explained from the same physical picture. An induction machine, in spite of many fundamental differences, works on exactly the same principle; one can identify flux distributions associated with the rotor and stator, which rotate in synchronism and which are separated by some torque-producing angular displacement.

Section 2   Performance Characteristics of Induction Motors

   The rotating field travels around the air-gap at a speed of

$$r / s = f / (p/2) \tag{4-1}$$

Where r / s = revolutions per second of the rotating magnetic field; f = frequency of excitation, Hz; p = number of poles. The speed of rotation is more commonly expressed in revolutions per minute and is called synchronous r/min, where

$$\text{Synchronous r/min} = 120\,f/p \tag{4-2}$$

Fig.4-3 displays the speed-torque and speed-current curves for a polyphase induction motor and shows for these curves the three regions of major interest: Motoring, plugging, and generating.

Synchronous speed, defined in Eq.(4-2) and designated as N_S in Fig.4-3, is the speed at which the rotor is revolving in synchronism with the rotating magnetic field generated by the stator windings, and there is therefore no rotor current and no electrically generated torque.

Slip is the difference in speed between the rotor and the air-gap rotating magnetic field and is defined by

$$\text{Slip} = (\text{synchronous r/min} - \text{rotor r/min}) / \text{synchronous r/min} \tag{4-3}$$

Eq. (4-3) yields slip as a per-unit value, although it is often expressed as a percentage.

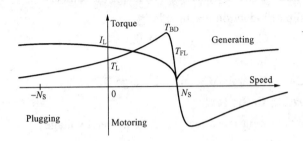

Fig.4-3　Speed-torque and speed-current curve for a polyphase induction motor

Breakdown torque is the maximum torque that the motor generates in the motoring region; it is shown at the point T_{BD} in Fig.4-3. The locked-rotor torque T_L in Fig.4-3 is the torque produced by the motor at zero speed and is important because this is the torque that must overcome any breakaway forces imposed by the load. Normally, a motor operates in the region between T_{BD} and synchronous speed, at the rated full-load torque indicated by T_{FL} on the curve. Slips in the region between zero speed and synchronous speed N_s range between 1.0 at zero speed and 0 at synchronous speed.

At speeds above synchronous speed the machine operates as induction generator, and this region of the speed-torque curve is labeled "Generating" in Fig.4-3. This region is also characterized by a maximum torque point, also called breakdown torque, and in general the breakdown torque in the generating region exceeds T_{BD} in the motoring region. Slip values for speeds above synchronous speed are negative, as is evident from Eq.(4-3). Operation in the generating region results from overhauling loads or from the motor being driven by a prime mover. For induction generating action to occur, the machine must have a source of leading exciting current. This leading excitation can be supplied from the power system if the motor is connected to such a system, or it can be provided by capacitors of appropriate value connected across the motor terminals. In recent years, induction generators have found application as wind-driven generators; they are connected to a power line and deliver power to the system whenever wind velocities reach a certain minimum value.

The third region of the speed-torque curve displayed in Fig.4-3 is the plugging region. A motor traverses this region when it is operating in one direction and then the direction of the rotating magnetic field is suddenly reversed. In Fig.4-3 the plugging region extends from minus N_s (slip = 2.0) to zero speed. Plugging is frequently used to accomplish fast speed reversal but is accompanied by high motor losses and large inrush currents.

New Words and Expressions

performance characteristics	工作特性
air-gap	气隙
polyphase	n.; a. 多相，多相的
motoring	n.; a. 电动机运行
plugging	反向制动，反相序制动控制
generating	n.; a. 发电机运行
Synchronous speed	同步速
breakdown torque	失步转矩，停转转矩
locked-rotor torque	止转转矩，起动转矩
breakaway	n. ①起步，起动　② 分离，脱离
breakaway force	起动力
rated	a. ①额定的，标称的　② 计算的，设计的
full-load	a. 满（负）载的
overhauling	a. 检修的，大修的
prime mover	原动机
induction generator	感应发电机，异步发电机
wind-driven generator	风力发电机
inrush current	涌流

Notes

1. Fig.4-2 displays the speed-torque and speed-current curves for a polyphase induction motor and shows for these curves the three regions of major interest: motoring, plugging, and generating.

   图 4-2 显示出多相感应电动机的转速力矩特性曲线和转速电流曲线，并示出这些曲线中最为有趣的三个区域，即电动机区、反向制动区和发电机区。

2. The locked-rotor torque T_L in Fig.4-2 is the torque produced by the motor at zero speed and is important because this is the torque that must overcome any breakaway forces imposed by the load.

   图 4-2 中的锁定转子转矩是电机在零转速时产生的，由于它必须克服由负载带来的任何起步阻力，因此非常重要。

3. Slips in the region between zero speed and synchronous speed Ns range between 1.0 at zero speed and 0 at synchronous speed.

   零转速时的转差率为 1.0，而在同步 Ns 时的转差率为 0。

用 词 的 增 省 （二）

3. 增加表示动词时态的词

汉语中动词没有时态变化，需要在译文中增加时间副词或助词来表示英语里的不同时态。

通常在翻译现在时，可增添"能"、"可"、"会"等字；译将来时可增添"将"、"要"、"会"等字；译过去时可增添"已"、"曾"、"过"、"了"、"以前"、"当时"、"过去"等词；译完成式可增添"已（经）"、"曾（经）"、"了"、"过"、"一直"等词；译进行时可增添"正（在）"、"在"等词。例如：

Scientists *are working* to develop new ways to make the semiconductor material used in computers and other modern electronic devices. 科学家们<u>正在</u>研究新的方法制造用于计算机和其他现代电子仪器中的半导体材料。

The gas discharge tube *converts* electric energy to light energy. 气体放电管<u>会将</u>电能转换成光能。

Recent research *has shown* a connection between smoking and cancer. 最近的研究<u>已经</u>证明了抽烟与癌症间的关系。

In developing Eq.(2) the assumption *was made* that the excitation system of the generator is inherently stable. 在推导方程（2）时，本文<u>曾</u>假定发电机励磁系统本身是稳定的。

4. 增加表达语气起连贯作用的词

为了使译文表达通顺，使词与词、句与句之间前后连贯，可增加一些起连贯作用的词。例如英语中的分词短语或从句作定语或状语，而含有明显的条件、时间、原因、让步等意义时，可分别增加连词"由于"，"如果"，"假使"，"只要"，"一旦"，"当……时"，"……时"，"虽然……"，"但……"等；对于陈述句可增添"的"，"了"，"哩"，"啦"等字。例如：

Using a transformer, power at low voltage can be transformed into power at high voltage. <u>如果</u>使用变压器，低电压的电力就能转换成高电压的电力。

Many persons learned to program with little understanding of computers or applications to which computers could or should be applied. 许多人<u>虽然</u>已经学会了编程序，但对计算机以及计算机能够或必备的种种用途所知甚少。

This question is really a circuit design rather than a layout problem. 这个问题是属于电路设计<u>方面的</u>，而不是布局<u>方面的</u>。

Do not leave dead batteries in the battery-box as this may cause malfunction. <u>注意</u>不要将废电池留在电池盒内，以免引起故障。

Exercises

I. Choose the best answer into the blank

1. When a induction motor with 10 poles is supplied by 50Hz three-phase ac power source, the synchronous revolutions per minute is _____.

   A. 1000　　　　　　B. 900　　　　　　C. 700　　　　　　D. 600

2. If the difference in speed between the rotor and the air-gap rotating magnetic field is smaller, the corresponding slip is _____.

   A. smaller　　　　　B. greater　　　　　C. equal　　　　　D. indefinite

3. The electric machine that operates at speeds above synchronous speed works in_____ region.

   A. motoring　　　　B. generating　　　　C. plugging　　　　D. stopping

4. The breakdown torque of a motor is the _____ torque that it generates?

   A. minimum   B. maximum   C. locked-rotor   D. synchronous

II. Answer the following questions according to the text

1. What relation is among revolutions per second of the rotating magnetic field, frequency of excitation, and number of poles?

2. What is the synchronous speed? How to determine it?

3. Is slip value for a machine operating in a motoring region positive or negative?

4. How can a induction machine operate as an induction generator?

III. Translate the following into Chinese

    The commonest form of AC motor is the polyphase induction motor. As its name suggests, the current in the rotor is derived from an external supply, as in the DC motor, but is induced by a moving magnetic field in the air-gap between the rotor and the stator. Excitation of the stator winding by a three-phase current causes a rotating magnetic field, as each of the electro-magnets in turn reaches its maximum strength. And this rotating magnetic field between the stator and the rotor induces a voltage in the rotor conductors.

Section 3　Synchronous machines

    A synchronous machine is an AC machine whose speed under steady-state conditions is proportional to the frequency of the current in its armature. Polyphase DC excited synchronous machines comprise a polyphase armature winding and a DC field winding. At synchronous speed, the rotating magnetic field created by the armature currents travels at the same speed as the field created by the field current, and a steady torque results. An elementary physical picture of how a synchronous machine works has already been given elsewhere, with emphasis on torque production in terms of the interactions among its magnetic fields.

    The purpose of this section is to develop a quantitative theory from which both the electrical and mechanical characteristics of synchronous motors and generators can be determined. The synchronous machine is idealized to the extent that the effects of salient poles and magnetic saturation are not included.

    Synchronous machines can be classified as cylindrical-rotor or salient-pole machines. The cylindrical-rotor construction is used in high-speed steam-turbine-driven generators. The armature windings consist of laminated conductors placed in the stator slots. They are usually 3-phase Y-connected windings, and voltages of above 13800 volts, line to line, are common in sizes above several thousand kilowatts. The rotor carries the DC field winding. Most of the turbine generators being built at present for 60-cps service are 2-pole 3600-rpm machines. Because of the economies of high-speed high-temperature high-pressure steam turbines, much study and some real pioneering work have been devoted to improvements in materials and design of both generators and turbines, and the maximum ratings for which 3600-rpm machines have been built have approximately doubled before the decade.

The advantages of large units are: somewhat increased efficiency, somewhat lower capital cost per kilowatt, and lower plant operating cost because of the greater ease of operating a generating station consisting of a relatively few large units as compared with one consisting of many smaller units.

The field windings are embedded in axial slots cut in the rotor and are held in place by metal wedges. They usually consist of concentric coils of insulated copper strap laid flat in the slots. The rotor coil ends and ends connections are firmly held in place by retaining rings shrunk on over the ends of the coils. The leads are connected to slip rings which make contact with carbon brushes through which the field current is introduced[7].

The mmf wave created by such a winding is shown by the step wave. The height of each step in the wave is proportional to the total current in the slot below it.

Because of the high rotational stresses, the rotors of turbine generators must be designed for as small a diameter as is consistent with other requirements. At the same time, limitations are imposed the axial length of the rotor by vibration considerations. Hence the design of the rotor is indeed a difficult problem, and the design of the whole machine is largely determined by it. Stresses are high, operating temperatures are high, and space is cramped. The insulation is subjected to severe rotational stresses, relatively high temperatures, and severe stresses caused by thermal expansion of the coils. These factors make a low-voltage rotor winding desirable. Turbine generators usually are designed for excitation at voltages of 125 to 375 volts. The field current usually is obtained from an exciter directly coupled to the shaft of the generator.

The air gaps of turbine generators usually are much longer than in other types of machines. A long air gap reduces the reactance of the armature winding and improves voltage regulation and stability. It is also necessary for ventilation. An obvious disadvantage of a long air gap is that it necessitates a greater field mmf to produce a specified air-gap flux.

The cooling problem in electrical apparatus in general increases in difficulty with increasing size, because the surface area from which the heat must be carried away increases roughly as the square of the dimensions, while the heat developed by the losses is roughly proportional to the volume and therefore increases approximately as the cube of the dimensions. Because of their compactness, this problem is a serious one with large turbine generators.

The use of a totally enclosed ventilating system brings up the possibility of using hydrogen as the cooling medium. Hydrogen has many properties which make it well suited to the purpose.

New Words and Expressions

synchronous machine	同步发电机
armature	n. 电枢
armature winding	电枢绕组
field winding	励磁绕组，磁极绕组
quantitative	a. 量的，数量的，定量的

salient	a. 凸出的，凸的，突出的
salient pole	凸极
saturation	n. 饱和，饱和度
cylindrical-rotor	隐极式转子，鼓极转子
steam-turbine-driven generator	汽轮发电机
Y-connected windings	星形连接绕组
turbine generator	涡轮发电机，汽轮发电机，水轮发电机
cps = cycles per second	周/秒，赫
rpm = revolutions per minute	转/分
steam turbine	汽轮机
rating	n. 额定值，额定参数；标称值，定额
efficiency	n. 效率
wedge	n. 楔[形]，楔形物，槽楔；v. 楔进，斜楔
concentric coil	同心线圈
slip ring	滑环
lead	n. ①导线，导管，引线　②铅；v. 超前，导前，引导
carbon brush	碳刷
mmf = magnetomotive force	磁动势
step wave	阶跃波
diameter	n. 直径
vibration	n. 振荡
field current	励磁电流
exciter	n. 励磁机
shaft	n. 轴
regulation	n. 调节
stability	n. 稳定性，稳定
ventilation	n. 通风，换气，通风装置
flux	n. 通量，磁力线

Notes

1. Because of the economies of high-speed high-temperature high-pressure steam turbines, much study and some real pioneering work have been devoted to improvements in materials and design of both generators and turbines, and the maximum ratings for which 3600-rpm machines have been built have approximately doubled before the decade.

   由于高速高温高压汽轮机的经济性，许多研究和一些富有开拓性的工作已改进了发电机和汽轮机的材料与设计，3600 转/分电机的最大容量较十年前已接近翻一番。

2. They usually consist of concentric coils of insulated copper strap laid flat in the slots. The rotor coil ends and ends connections are firmly held in place by retaining rings shrunk on over the ends of the coils. The leads are connected to slip rings which make contact with carbon brushes

through which the field current is introduced.

励磁绕组通常由平放在槽内并加以绝缘的铜排而形成的同心线圈所组成。转子线圈端接部分被热套在其上面的护环所固定。引线连至滑环，滑环与碳刷相接触，通过碳刷引入励磁电流。

用 词 的 增 省（三）

5. 增加原文中省略的词

原文中的某些成分已在前面出现，在后面往往省略，如并列句或并列成分中有相同的部分时。复合句中主句和从句的主语相同或其他成分相同时，从句中的主语或其他成分也都能省略。为了使译文能将原文意义表达清楚，需将这些省略部分补上。例如：

High voltage is necessary for long transmission line while low voltage for safe use. 远距离输电需要高压，安全用电需要低压。

When you turn a switch, you can easily operate lighting, heating or power-driven electrical devices. 旋转开关，就能轻而易举地控制照明装置、供热装置或电动装置。

The letter I represents the current in amperes, E the electromotive force in volts, and R the resistance in ohms. 字母 I 代表电流的安培数，E 代表电动势的伏特数，R 代表电阻的欧姆数。

6. 增加表示句子主语的词

当被动句中的谓语是表示"知道"、"了解"、"看见"、"认为"、"发现"、"考虑"等意思的动词时，通常可在其前增加"人们"、"我们"、"有人"等词语，译成汉语的主动句。例如：

With the development of modern electrical engineering, power can be transmitted to wherever it is needed. 随着现代化电气工程的发展，人们可以把电力输送到任何所需要的地方。

Weak magnetic fields are known to come from the human body. 我们知道，人体能产生微弱的磁场。

It is said that numerical control is the operation of machine tools by numbers. 人们说，数控就是机床用数字加以操纵。

7. 增加表示被动意义的词

英语中的被动句，当要强调动作或突出被动者时，译文常须增加"由"、"为"、"受"、"让"、"给"、"遭"、"加以"、"予以"、"为……所"等词。不定式作定语，如果是被动形式，都含有将来的意思，在译文时需增加"将要"、"应该"、"有待"、"设法"等词语。例如：

The method to be used is … 要采用的方法是……。

The lighthouse to be installed is eight meters high and 2.2 meters in diameter. 即将安装的灯塔高 8 米，直径 2.2 米。

8. 增加具体化、明确化的词语

有些英语句子如果直译成汉语，意思表达不够具体和明确，需要增译相关词语。

Floppy disks have always been *cheap* to make and relatively easy to copy. 软盘制作成本比较低，而且也比较容易拷贝。

At the moment, developed areas in Europe, the United States and Asia have already started studying *the possibility* of an electronic currency. 目前，欧洲、美国以及亚洲一些发达地区已经开

始研究推行电力货币的可能性。

Note again that considerable simplication in solving *the above* can be achieved if the data is made symmetrical. 还要注意，在解决上述问题时，如果使数据对称，就能得到很大程度的简化。

Exercises

I. Choose the best answer into the blank

1. The speed of a synchronous machine is directly proportional to _____ in its armature under steady-state conditions.

   A. the amplitude of the current   B. the frequency of the current

   C. the amplitude of the voltage   D. the flux

2. The field winding in a synchronous generator is supplied by _____ power source.

   A. a DC   B. an AC   C. no   D. any type

3. The cylindrical rotor machine is used in _____.

   A. low-speed motors

   B. high-speed motors

   C. high-speed steam-turbine-driven generators

   D. low-speed hydro-turbine-driven generators

4. The turbine generators with two poles for 60-cps are _____ machines.

   A. 3600-rpm   B. 1800-rpm   C. 5400-rpm   D.2400-rpm

5. The field current of a turbine generator is usually obtained from _____.

   A. a motor   B. an AC generator   C. an exciter   D. a battery

II. Answer the following questions according to the text

1. What types can synchronous machines be classified as?

2. What are the advantages of large synchronous generators?

3. Where are the field windings placed in a synchronous machine?

4. What functions do slip rings and carbon brushes have?

5. Why is the field winding of a synchronous generator designed as a low-voltage winding?

6. What advantages and disadvantages do turbine generators with air gaps have?

III. Translate the following into Chinese

A squirrel-cage rotor consists of a number of identical bars of copper or aluminum sunk into slots in a laminated steel core. It is cheap to produce, but has the disadvantage of a low starting torque and a lack of control of speed. In the case of large motors, it is desirable that there should be an adequate starting torque and some control over speed. For large motors therefore, a phase-wound rotor is used, with the windings connected at one end to each other and the other end to slip-rings, thus enabling the resistance of the rotor to be varied at will, providing a greater starting torque, and some speed control.

Section 4 Transformer

Types and construction of transformer

A transformer is a device that changes AC electric energy at one voltage level into AC electric energy at another voltage level through the action of a magnetic field. It consists of two or more coils of wire wrapped around a common ferromagnetic core. These coils are (usually) not directly connected. The only connection between the coils is the common magnetic flux present within the core.

One of the transformer windings is connected to a source of AC electric power, and the second (and perhaps third) transformer winding supplies electric power to loads. The transformer winding connected to the power source is called the primary winding or input winding, and the winding connected to the loads is called the secondary winding or output winding. If there is a third winding on the transformer, it is called the tertiary winding.

Power transformer are constructed on one of two types of cores. One type of construction consists of a simple rectangular laminated piece of steel with the transformer windings wrapped around two sides of the rectangle. This type of construction is known as core form. The other type consists of a three-legged laminated core with the windings wrapped around the center leg. This type of construction is known as shell form. In either case, the core is constructed of thin laminations electrically isolated from each other in order to reduce eddy currents to a minimum.

The primary and secondary windings in a physical transformer are wrapped one on top of the other with the low-voltage winding innermost. Such an arrangement serves two purposes: (i) It simplifies the problem of insulating the high-voltage winding from the core. (ii) It results in much less leakage flux than would be the two windings were separated by a distance on the core.

Power transformers are given a variety of different names, depending on their use in power systems. A transformer connected to the output of a generator and used to step its voltage up to the transmission levels is sometimes called a unit transformer. The transformer at the other end of the transmission line, which steps the voltage down from transmission levels to distribution levels, is called a substation transformer. Finally, the transformer that takes the distribution voltage and steps it down to the final voltage at which the power is actually used is called a distribution transformer. All these devices are essentially the same in their construction, the only difference among them is their intended use.

In addition to the various power transformers, two special-purpose transformers are used with electric machinery and power systems. The first of these special transformers is a device specially designed to sample a high voltage and produce a low secondary voltage directly proportional to it. Such a transformer is called a potential transformer. A power transformer also produces a secondary voltage directly proportional to its primary voltage; the difference between a potential transformer and a power transformer is that the potential transformer is designed to handle only a very small current. The second type of special transformer is a device designed to provide a secondary current much smaller than but directly proportional to its primary current[⑨]. This device is called a current transformer.

Equivalent circuit of transformer

The losses that occur in real transformers have to be accounted for in any accurate model of transformer behavior. The major items to be considered in the construction of such a model are:

(1) Copper (R_r) losses. Copper losses are the resistive heating losses in the primary and secondary windings of the transformer. They are proportional to the square of the current in the windings.

(2) Eddy current losses. Eddy current losses are resistive heating losses in the core of the transformer.

(3) Hysteresis losses. These losses are associated with the rearrangement of the magnetic domains in the core during each half-cycle.

(4) Leakage flux. The fluxes which escape the core and pass through only one of the transformer windings are leakage fluxes. These escaped fluxes produce a self-inductance in the primary and secondary coils, and the effects of this inductance must be accounted for.

It is possible to construct an equivalent circuit that takes into account all the major imperfections in real transformers. Each major imperfection will be considered in turn, and its effect will be included in the transformer model.

The easiest effect to model is the copper losses. Copper losses are resistive losses in the primary and secondary windings of the transformer core. They are modeled by placing a resistor R_P in the primary circuit of the transformer and a resistor R_S in the secondary circuit.

The leakage flux in the primary windings $\phi_{_{\it P}}$ produces a voltage e_{i_P} and the leakage flux in the secondary windings $\phi_{_{\it S}}$ produces a voltage e_{i_S}. Since much of the leakage flux path is through air, and since air has a constant reluctance much higher than the core reluctance, the flux $\phi_{_{\it P}}$ is directly proportional to the primary circuit current i_P and the flux $\phi_{_{\it S}}$ is directly proportional to the secondary current i_S

$$e_{i_P} = L_P \frac{\mathrm{d}i_P}{\mathrm{d}t}$$

$$e_{i_S} = L_S \frac{\mathrm{d}i_S}{\mathrm{d}t}$$

where L_P is the self-inductance of the primary coil, and L_S, is the self-inductance of the secondary coil. Therefore, the leakage flux will be modeled by primary and secondary inductors.

How can the core excitation effects be modeled? The magnetization current i_m is a current proportional (in the unsaturated region) to the voltage applied to the core, and lagging the applied voltage by 90°, so it can be modeled by a reactance X_m connected across the primary voltage source. The core-loss current i_{n+e} is a current proportional to the voltage applied to the core that is in phase with the applied voltage, so it can be modeled by a resistance R_m connected across the primary voltage source. (Remember that both these currents are really nonlinear, so the reactance X_m and the resistance R_m are at beast approximations of the real excitation effects.)

The resulting equivalent circuit is shown in Fig.4-4. Notice that the elements forming the excitation branch are placed inside the primary resistance R_P and the primary inductance L_P. This is because the voltage actually applied to the core is really equal to the input voltage less the internal voltage drops of the winding.

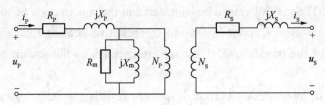

Fig.4-4　The model of a real transformer

New Words and Expressions

transformer	n. 变压器
wrap	v.; n. 包裹，包扎，缠绕，卷
ferromagnetic core	铁磁芯
primary winding	一次绕组，原绕组，初级绕组
secondary winding	二次绕组，副绕组，次级绕组
tertiary winding	三次绕组，第三绕组
power transformer	电力变压器
core form	铁芯式
shell form	壳式
innermost	a. 最内部的，最里面的，最深处的
leakage flux	漏磁通
unit transformer	单元（机组）变压器
substation transformer	配电变压器
distribution transformer	配电变压器
potential transformer	电压互感器
current transformer	电流互感器
copper loss	铜耗
hysteresis loss	磁滞损耗，磁滞损失
reluctance	n. 磁阻
self-inductance	自感应
core-loss	铁芯损耗

Notes

1. Power transformer are constructed on one of two types of cores. One type of construction consists of a simple rectangular laminated piece of steel with the transformer windings wrapped

around two sides of the rectangle.

电力变压器的铁芯分为两类。一类是由变压器绕组缠绕在一个简单的矩形钢片叠成的铁芯两边而构成。

2. The second type of special transformer is a device designed to provide a secondary current much smaller than but directly proportional to its primary current.

第二类特种变压器是专门用以提供比一次侧电流小得多却正比于一次电流的二次电流。

3. The magnetization current i_m is a current proportional (in the unsaturated region) to the voltage applied to the core, and lagging the applied voltage by 90°, so it can be modeled by a reactance X_m connected across the primary voltage source.

磁化电流 i_m 正比于作用于铁芯的电压，并滞后该电压 90°，因此可以采用并联于初级电压源的电抗 X_m 来建模。

用 词 的 增 省 （四）

在翻译过程中，根据"省词不省意"的原则，将原文中多余的词在译文中省略，使译文更加严谨、精练、明确。注意它不是删繁就简，也不是略去自己不懂的内容。用词的省略一是由于两种语言的语法不同而引起，二是可能由于技术上和修辞上的原因引起。

1. 冠词的省略

一般来说，英语的不定冠词 a 和 an、定冠词 the 在句中用作泛指，在译文中常可省略。对于定冠词 the 只有在特指前文中所提的人、物或事件时，才是例外，这时一般译成"这"、"那"、"该"等。而不定冠词 a 和 an 在表示数量，强调类别时不可省略，要译成"一个"、"一种"、"一类"等，表示单位时要译成"一"、"每"等。例如：

With *the* development of electrical engineering, power can be transmitted over long distance. 随着电气工程学的发展，电力能被输送到非常遥远的地方去。

With *an* equation we can work with *an* unknown quantity. 利用方程，我们可以求解未知量。

The greater *the* resistance of a wire, the less electric current will pass through it under *the* same pressure. 在电压相同的情况下，导线的电阻越大，流过的电流就越小。

2. 代词的省略

英语中表示泛指的人称代词、用作定语的物主代词、反身代词以及用于比较句中的指示代词，在翻译时，可根据汉语的表达习惯省略。例如：

When the signal *we* pick up has increased by 10 times as the gain may have been reduced by 8 times. 信号增大到 10 倍，增益降低到 1/8 。

There is not any established theory about how people store and retrieve information when *they* need *it*. 关于人们如何储存信息以及需要时如何检索信息，目前还没有已经确定的理论。

Turn the knob until *you* get a clear picture on the screen. 请转动旋钮直到屏幕上图像清晰为止。

Like silicon, gallium arsenide is a semiconductor—a material whose conductivity is between *that* of a conductor and an insulator. 像硅一样，砷化镓也是一种半导体材料，其导电率介于导体和绝缘体之间。

If *one* halves a bar magnet, each of the two halves will be a complete magnet. 如果把一根磁铁棒分成两段，那么其中每一段都仍是完整的磁铁。

Exercises

I. Choose the best answer into the blank

1. A transformer is a device that can converter one ac voltage to another ac voltage through the action of _____.

    A. an electric circuit   B. a magnetic field

    C. an electric field   D. a coupling circuit

2. The primary winding is connected to _____.

    A. the power source   B. the load

    C. the measurement instrument   D. the motor

3. The core construction consisting of a three-legged laminated core with the windings wrapped around the centre leg is called _____.

    A. core form   B. shell form   C. cylindrical form   D. global form

4. The transformer that takes the distribution voltage and steps it down to the final voltage at which the power is actually used is called a _____.

    A. distribution transformer   B. unit transformer

    C. substation transformer   D. potential transformer

5. Copper losses are _____ losses in the primary and secondary windings of the transformer core.

    A. inductive   B. capacitive

    C. resistive   D. reactive

II. Answer the following questions according to the text

1. How many types of core construction do power transformers have?

2. Why are thin laminations electrically isolated from each other used to construct the core ?

3. What function does a potential transformer have?

4. Are a power transformer and a potential transformer essentially the same in their con- struction?

5. What are the major losses items to be considered in the construction of such a equivalent circuit model?

III. Translate the following into Chinese

    There are sometimes occasion when it is desirable to change voltage levels by only a small amount. For example, it may be necessary to increase a voltage from 110V to 120V or from 13. 2kV to 13. 8kV. These small rises may be made necessary by voltage drops that occur in power systems a long way from the generators. In such circumstances, it is wasteful and excessively expensive to wind a transformer with two full windings, each rated at about the same voltage. A special-purpose transformer, called an autotransformer, is used instead.

Chapter 5　Computer

Section 1　Computer Basics

Most people can formulate a mental picture of a computer, but computers do so many things and come in such a variety of shapes and sizes that it might seem difficult to distill their common characteristics into an all-purpose definition. At its core, a computer is a device that accepts input, processes data, stores data, and produces output, all according to a series of stored instructions.

Computer **input** is whatever is put into a computer system. Input can be supplied by a person, by the environment, or by another computer. Examples of the kinds of input that a computer can accept include the words and symbols in a document, numbers for a calculation, pictures, temperatures from a thermostat, audio signals from a microphone, and instructions from a computer program. An input device, such as a keyboard or mouse, gathers input and transforms it into a series of electronic signals for the computer.

In the context of computing, **data** refers to the symbols that represent facts, objects, and ideas. Computers manipulate data in many ways, and we call this manipulation **processing**. The series of instructions that tell a computer how to carry out processing tasks is referred to as a **computer program**, or simply a "program." These programs form the software that sets up a computer to do a specific task. In a computer, most processing takes place in a component called the **central processing unit (CPU)**, which is sometimes described as the "brain" of the computer.

A computer stores data so that it will be available for processing. Most computers have more than one location for storing data, depending on how the data is being used. Memory is an area of a computer that temporarily holds data that is waiting to be processed, stored, or output. Storage is the area where data can be left on a permanent basis when it is not immediately needed for processing.

Output is the results produced by a computer. Some examples of computer output include reports, documents, music, graphs, and pictures. An output device displays, prints, or transmits the results of processing.

Computers are versatile machines, which are able to perform a truly amazing assortment of tasks, but some types of computer are better suited to certain tasks than other types of computers. Computers can be categorized as personal computer, handheld computers, workstations, mainframes, supercomputers, and servers.

A personal computer is a type of microcomputer, designed to meet the computing needs of an individual. It typically provides access to a wide variety of computing applications, such as word processing, photo editing, E-mail, and Internet access. Personal computers are available as desktop computers or notebook computers.

A handheld computer is designed to fit into a pocket, run on batteries, and be used while you are holding it. Also called a PDA (Personal Digital Assistant) and a palmtop computer, a computer in this category is typically used as an electronic appointment book, address book, calculator, and notepad. With its slow processing speed and small screen, a handheld computer is not powerful enough to handle many of the tasks that can be accomplished by desktop or notebook personal computers. A handheld computer is designed to be a computing accessory, rather than your primary computer.

Computers advertised as **workstation** are usually powerful desktop computers designed for specialized tasks. A workstation can tackle tasks that require a lot of processing speed, such as medical imaging and computer-aided design. Some workstations contain more than one microprocessor, and most have circuitry specially designed for creating and displaying three-dimensional and animated graphics. Because of its cost, a workstation is often dedicated to design tasks, and is not used for typical microcomputer applications, such as word processing, photo editing, and accessing the Web.

Ordinary personal computers that are connected to a local area network can also be called as workstations. A computer network is two or more computers and other devices that are connected for the purpose of sharing data and programs. A LAN (**local area network**) is simply a computer network that is located within a limited geographical area, such as a school computer lab or a small business.

A **mainframe computer** (or simply a "**mainframe**") is a large and expensive computer that is capable of simultaneously processing data for hundreds or thousands of users. Mainframes are generally used by businesses or governments to provide centralized storage, processing, and management for large amounts of data. Mainframes remain the computer of choice in situations where reliability, data security, and centralized control are necessary.

A computer falls into the **supercomputer** category if it is, at the time of construction, one of the fastest computers in the world. Because of their speed, supercomputers can tackle complex tasks that just would not be practical for other computers. Typical uses for supercomputers include breaking codes, modeling worldwide weather systems, and simulating nuclear explosions. One impressive simulation designed to run on a supercomputer tracked the movement of thousands of dust particles as they were tossed about by a tornado.

In the computer industry, the term "**server**" has several meanings. It can refer to computer hardware, to a specific type of software, or to a combination of hardware and software. In any case, the purpose of a server is to " serve " the computers on a network (such as the Internet or a LAN) by supplying them with data. A personal computer, workstation, or software that requests data from a server is referred to as a **client**. For example, on a network, a server might respond to a client's request for a Web page. Another server might handle the steady stream of e-mail that travels among clients from all over the Internet. A server might also allow clients within a LAN to share files or access a centralized printer.

PERSONAL COMPUTER SYSTEMS

A computer system usually refers to a computer and all of the input, output, and storage devices that are connected to it. At the core of a personal computer system is a desktop or notebook computer. Despite cosmetic differences among personal computers, a personal computer system usually includes the following equipment:

（1）**Computer system unit**. The system unit is the case that holds the main circuit boards, microprocessor, power supply, and storage devices. The system unit for most notebook computers holds a built-in keyboard and speakers too.

（2）**Display device**. Most desktop computers use a separate monitor as a display device, whereas notebook computers use a flat panel LCD screen (liquid crystal display screen) that is attached to the system unit.

（3）**Keyboard**. Most computers are equipped with a keyboard as the primary input device.

（4）**Mouse**. A mouse is an alternative input device designed to manipulate on-screen graphical objects and controls.

（5）**Floppy disk drive.** A floppy disk drive is a storage device that reads data from and writes data to floppy disks. A floppy disk is a round piece of flexible mylar plastic covered with a thin layer of magnetic oxide and sealed inside a protective casing. The floppies most commonly used on today's personal computers are 3 $^1/2''$ disks with a capacity of 1.44MB.

（6）**Hard disk drive.** A hard disk contains one or more metallic disks encased within a disk drive, which can store billions of characters of data in the form of magnetized spots. The storage capacity of a hard-disk unit is many times that of a floppy disk and much faster. It is usually mounted inside the computer's system unit.

（7）**CD-ROM or DVD drive.** A CD-ROM (compact disc read-only memory) drive is a storage device that uses laser technology to read data that is permanently stored on computer or audio CDs. A DVD (digital video disc) drive can read data from computer CDs, audio CDs, computer DVDs, or DVD movie disks. CD-ROM and DVD drives typically cannot be used to write data onto disks. The "RO" in "ROM" stands for "read-only" and means that the drive can read data from disks, but cannot be used to store new data on them.

（8）**CD-writer.** Many computers-especially desktop models——include a CD-writer that can be used to create and copy CDs.

（9）**Sound card and speakers.** Desktop computers have a rudimentary built-in speaker that's mostly limited to playing beeps. A small circuit board, called a sound card, is required for high-quality music, narration, and sound effects. A desktop computer's sound card sends signals to external speakers. A notebook's sound card sends signals to speakers that are built into the notebook system unit.

（10）**Modem.** Virtually every personal computer system includes a built-in modem that can be used to establish an Internet connection using a standard telephone line.

（11）**Printer.** A computer printer is an output device that produces computer-generated text or graphical images on paper.

In addition to these equipment mentioned above, some other **peripheral devices** might be added to a computer system to enhance its functionality, such as a digital camera, scanner, joystick, or graphics tablet.

New Words and Expressions

distill	v. 提取……的精华，蒸馏
instruction	n. 指令
document	n.文件
thermostat	n. 恒温器，定温器，温度自动调节器
audio signal	n. 声频信号，音频信号
program	n. 程序
keyboard	n. 键盘
software	n. 软件
central processing unit	中央处理单元
workstation	n. 工作站
videogame console	视频游戏操作板
mainframe	n. 主机，主机架
supercomputer	超级计算机
server	服务器
client	客户
microcomputer	微型计算机
desktop computer	台式计算机
notebook computer	笔记本电脑
handheld computer	掌上电脑
computer-aided	计算机辅助的
three-dimensional	三维的
animated graphics	动画图像
local area network (LAN)	局域网
LCD screen (liquid crystal display screen)	液晶显示屏
display device	显示设备
mouse	n. 鼠标
floppy disk drive	软盘驱动器
hard disk drive	硬盘驱动器
CD-ROM drive	CD-ROM 驱动器
DVD drive	DVD 驱动器
CD-writer	CD 写入器，刻录机
sound card	声卡
rudimentary	a. 基本的，基础的，初步的，根本的
built-in	a. 嵌入的，安装在内部的，内装的，机内的
modem	n. 调制解调器
peripheral device	外围设备

scanner	n. 扫描仪
digital camera	数码相机
joystick	n. 控制杆
graphics tablet	图形板
operating system	操作系统

Notes

1. Most people can formulate a mental picture of a computer, but computers do so many things and come in such a variety of shapes and sizes that it might seem difficult to distill their common characteristics into an all-purpose definition.

大多数人都能描绘一台计算机，但由于计算机能做许多事情，有许多形状和规格，以致人们难以提取其共同特征形成通用的定义。

2. The series of instructions that tell a computer how to carry out processing tasks is referred to as a computer program, or simply a "program".

告诉计算机如何执行处理任务的一系列指令被称为计算机程序，简称为程序。

用 词 的 增 省（五）

3. 连词的省略

英语中连词用得比较多，也比较严格，凡两个以上并列成分或并列句子都需要用连词连接。汉语则没有这种要求，时常可以省略。例如：

Like charges repel each other while opposite charges attract. 同性电荷相斥，异性电荷相吸。

Commercial business is very profitable, *and* most radio and TV stations depend on the income. 广告是很挣钱的生意，大部分电台和电视台都是靠广告费收入而生存的。

As the definition is quite clear, there is nothing more to be explained. 定义很清楚，因此不必再加以解释了。

4. 介词的省略

英语中介词的使用较多，句中词与词之间的关系多用介词表示，而汉语则不同，主要是通过语序与逻辑关系来表示。因此，在翻译时可以省略介词。例如：

In the transmission of electric power a high voltage is necessary. 远距离输电必须用高压。

The critical temperature is different *for* different kinds of steel. 不同种类的钢，临界温度各不相同。

In the absence *of* force, a body will either remain *at* rest, or continue to move *with* constant speed *in* a straight line. 尚无外力作用，物体则保持其静止状态，或做匀速直线运动。

Exercises

I. Choose the best answer into the blank

1. A computer works automatically according to _____.

A. a series of stored instructions   B. a series of instructions given by operators

C. a CPU   D. another computer

2. A keyboard or a mouse is _____ device.

  A. an output   B. an input   C. a storage   D. a data processing

3. The computer network for a university is usually described as _____.

  A. a city area   B. a wide area network

  C. a local area network   D. an Internet network

4. A computer that requests data from a server is called as _____.

  A. server   B. client   C. workstation   D. termination

5. A hard disk is referred to as _____ device.

  A. an output   B. an input   C. a storage   D. a data processing

II. Answer the following questions according to the text

1. Why is the central processing unit (CPU) sometimes described as the brain of the computer?

2. Which kinds can computers be categorized as?

3. Why do handled computers not take the place of desktop computers?

4. How many meanings does the term "server" have?

5. Which equipment is usually included in a personal computer system?

III. Translate the following into Chinese

A computer can be applied to many tasks, such as writing, number crunching, video editing, online shopping, etc. Computer software is also a core part of a computer system, because a computer cannot work without any computer software, or cannot work efficiently without appropriate software. A computer program is a sequence of detailed instructions designed to direct a computer to perform certain functions. These pre-written stored programs enable a computer to receive input, store information (data), make decisions arithmetically, manipulate and output data in the correct sequence and format. These programs are referred to as software. Software is generally categorized as either system software or application software. The primary purpose of application software is to help people carry outspecific tasks using a computer, and that of system software—your computer's operating system, device drivers, and utilities—is to help the computer carry out its basic operating functions.

Section2　Microprocessor and Memory

Microprocessor

A microprocessor (sometimes simply referred to as a "processor") is an integrated circuit designed to process instructions. It is the most important component of a computer, and usually the most expensive single component, containing as 50 million miniaturized electronic components. The miniaturized circuitry in a microprocessor is grouped into important functional areas, such as the ALU and the control unit.

The ALU (arithmetic logic unit) performs arithmetic operations, such as addition and subtraction. It also performs logical operations, such as comparing two numbers to see if they are the same. The ALU uses registers to hold data that is being processed. The microprocessor's control unit fetches each instruction. The computer loads data into the ALU's registers. Finally, the control unit gives the ALU the green light to begin processing.

The performance of a microprocessor is affected by several factors, including clock speed, word size, cache size, instruction set, and processing techniques.

The speed specifications that you see in a computer ad indicate the speed of the microprocessor clock—a timing device that sets the pace for executing instructions. Most computer ads specify the speed of a microprocessor in megahertz (MHz) or gigahertz (GHz). Megahertz means a million cycles per second. Gigahertz means a billion cycles per second.

A cycle is the smallest unit of time in a microprocessor's universe. Every action that a processor performs is measured by these cycles. It is important, however, to understand that the clock speed is not equal to the number of instructions that a processor can execute in one second. In many computers, some instructions occur within one cycle, but other instructions might require multiple cycles. Some processors can even execute several instructions in a single clock cycle.

Word size refers to the number of bits that a microprocessor can manipulate at one time. Word size is based on the size of the registers in the ALU, and the capacity of circuits that lead to those registers. A microprocessor with an 8-bit word size, for example, has 8-bit registers, processes eight bits at a time, and is referred to as an "8-bit processor." Processors with a larger word size can process more data during each processor cycle, a factor that leads to increased computer performance. Today's personal computers typically contain 32-bit or 64-bit processors.

Cache is sometimes called "RAM cache" or "cache memory." It is special high-speed memory that allows a microprocessor to access data more rapidly than from memory located elsewhere on the motherboard. Some computer ads specify cache type and capacity. A Level 1 cache (L1) is built into the processor chip, whereas a Level 2 cache (L2) is located on a separate chip and takes a little more time to get data to the processor. Cache capacity is usually measured in kilobytes.

As chip designers developed various instruction sets for microprocessors, they tended to add increasingly more complex instructions that each required several clock cycles for execution. A microprocessor with such an instruction set uses CISC (complex instruction set computer) technology. A microprocessor with a limited set of simple instructions uses RISC (reduced instruction set computer) technology. A RISC processor performs most instructions faster than a CISC processor. It might, however, require more of these simple instructions to complete a task than a CISC processor requires for the same task.

Some processors execute instructions "serially"—that is, one instruction at a time. With serial processing, the processor must complete all of the steps in the instruction cycle before it begins to execute the next instruction. However, using a technology called pipelining, a processor can begin executing an instruction before it completes the previous instruction. Many of today's microprocessors also perform parallel processing, in which multiple instructions are executed at the same time. Pipelining and parallel processing enhance processor performance.

RAM (Random Access Memory)

RAM is a temporary holding area for data, application program instructions, and the operating system. In a personal computer, RAM is usually several chips or small circuit boards that plug into the motherboard within the computer's system unit.

RAM is the "waiting room" for the computer's processor. It holds raw data that is waiting to be processed, as well as the program instructions for processing that data. In addition, RAM holds the results of processing until they can be stored more permanently on disk or tape, and operating system instructions that control the basic functions of a computer system. These instructions are loaded into RAM every time you start your computer, and they remain there until you turn off your computer.

In RAM, microscopic electronic parts called capacitors hold the bits that represent data. You can visualize the capacitors as microscopic lights that can be turned on or off. A charged capacitor is "turned on" and represents a "1" bit. A discharged capacitor is "turned off" and represents a "0" bit. Each bank of capacitors holds eight bits—one byte—of data. A RAM address on each bank helps the computer locate data, as needed, for processing.

The contents of RAM can be changed just by changing the charge of the capacitors. Unlike disk storage, most RAM is volatile, which means that it requires electrical power to hold data. If the computer is turned off, or if the power goes out, all data stored in RAM instantly and permanently disappears.

The capacity of RAM is usually expressed in megabytes (MB). Today's personal computers typically feature between 64 and 512 MB of RAM. The amount of RAM needed by your computer depends on the software that you use. RAM requirements are routinely specified on the outside of a software package. If it turns out that you need more RAM, you can purchase and install additional memory up to the limit set by the computer manufacturer. Today's personal computer operating systems are quite adept at allocating RAM space to multiple programs. If a program exceeds the allocated space, the operating system uses an area of the hard disk, called virtual memory, to store parts of a program or data file until they are needed. By selectively exchanging the data in RAM with the data in virtual memory, your computer effectively gains almost unlimited memory capacity. Too much dependence on virtual memory can have a negative affect on your computer's performance, however, because getting data from a mechanical device, such as a hard disk, is much slower than getting data from an electronic device, such as RAM.

RAM components vary in speed, technology, and configuration. RAM speed is often expressed in nanoseconds (ns). One nanosecond is 1 billionth of a second. With nanoseconds, lower numbers are better because it means that the RAM circuitry can react faster to update the data that it holds. RAM speed can also be expressed in MHz (million of cycles per second) just the opposite of nanoseconds, higher MHz ratings mean faster speeds.

ROM (Read-Only Memory)

ROM is a type of memory circuitry that holds the computer's startup routine. ROM is housed in a single integrated circuit—usually a fairly large, caterpillar-like DIP package—which is plugged into the motherboard.

Whereas RAM is temporary and volatile, ROM is permanent and non-volatile. ROM circuitry holds "hard-wired" instructions that remain in place even when the computer power is turned off. The instructions in ROM are permanent, and the only way to change them is to replace the ROM chip. In a personal computer, ROM contains a small set of instructions called the ROM BIOS (basic input/output system). These instructions tell the computer how to access the hard disk, find the operating system, and load it into RAM. Once the operating system is loaded, the computer can understand your input, display output, run software, and access your data.

CMOS MEMORY

In order to operate correctly, a computer must have some basic information about storage, memory, and display configurations. RAM goes blank when the computer power is turned off, so configuration information cannot be stored there. ROM would not be a good place for this information either because it holds data on a permanent basis. If, for example, your computer stored the memory size in ROM, you could never add more memory—well, you might be able to add it, but you couldn't change the size specification in ROM. To store some basic system information, your computer needs a type of memory that's more permanent than RAM, but less permanent than ROM. CMOS is just the ticket.

CMOS (complementary metal oxide semiconductor memory) is a type of chip that requires very little power to hold data. It can be powered by a small, rechargeable battery that's integrated into the motherboard. The battery trickles power to the CMOS chip so that it can retain vital data about your computer system configuration even when your computer is turned off. When you change the configuration of your computer system—by adding RAM, for example—the data in CMOS must be updated. Some operating systems recognize such changes and automatically perform the update. You can manually change CMOS settings by running the CMOS setup program.

New Words and Expressions

miniaturized	a. 小型的，小型化的
ALU (arithmetic logic unit)	算术逻辑单元
control unit	控制单元
register	n. 寄存器
cycle	n. 周期
clock cycle	时钟周期
word size	字长
cache	n. 高速缓冲存储器
instruction set	指令集
megahertz	n. 兆赫，兆赫兹
gigahertz	n. 吉赫，吉赫兹

motherboard	n. 母板，主板
chip	n. 芯片，晶片，组件
CISC (complex instruction set computer)	复杂指令集计算机
RISC (reduced instruction set computer)	简化指令集合计算机
serially	ad. 串行地
serial processing	串行处理
parallel processing	并行处理
pipelining	a. 流水线的
RAM (Random Access Memory)	随机存储器
operating system	操作系统
plug	v. 插入，插上；n. 插头，插入物
microscopic	a. 微观的，细微的，显微（镜）的，显微的
charge	v. 充电，带电，起电；n. 电荷，充电
discharge	v. 放电
bit	n. 位
byte	n. 字节
volatile	a. 易失的，挥发的，易挥发的，易变的，短暂的
megabytes (MB)	兆字节
software package	软件包
install	v. 安装
virtual memory	虚拟存储器
nanosecond	纳秒
SDRAM (synchronous dynamic RAM)	同步动态 RAM
ROM (Read-Only Memory)	只读存储器
startup	n. 起动
caterpillar-like	a. 履带式的
DIP ①= double in-line package 双列直插式组件　②=dual in-line package 双列式封装	
BIOS (basic input/output system)	基本输入输出系统
CMOS (complementary metal oxide semiconductor memory)	
rechargeable battery	充电电池
setup	安装
update	v. 更新，修改，校正

Notes

1. Finally, the control unit gives the ALU the green light to begin processing.
   最后，控制单元启动 ALU 开始处理。*green light* 有 "绿灯"、"放行"、"准许" 的意思，在此处作 "准许" 讲。

2. The speed specifications that you see in a computer ad indicate the speed of the micropro-cessor clock—a timing device that sets the pace for executing instructions.

计算机广告上的速度规范是指微处理器时钟的速度，它是设置指令执行步速的定时器件。

3. A Level 1 cache (L1) is built into the processor chip, whereas a Level 2 cache (L2) is located on a separate chip and takes a little more time to get data to the processor.

一级缓存位于处理器芯片内，而二级缓存在另外的芯片上，其获得数据给处理器所需时间较一级缓存多一点。

用 词 的 增 省（六）

5. 动词的省略

英语谓语必须用动词，而汉语不仅可以用动词作谓语，还可以用其他词类作为谓语。因此，翻译时往往可以省略原文中的谓语动词。例如：

The wire gets hot, for the current *becomes* too great. 电线发热，因为电流太大。

This chapter *provides* a brief review of applicable theory for computer. 本章简单回顾一下计算机的应用理论。

This diode *produces* about nine times more radiant power than that one. 这只二极管的辐射功率比那只大九倍左右。

6. 引导词的省略

英语中的两个引导词 "it" 和 "there"，翻译时可以省略。例如：

The invention of radio has made *it* possible for mankind to communication with each other over a long distance. 无线电的发明使人类有可能进行远距离通讯。

There exist neither perfect insulators nor perfect conductors. 既没有理想的绝缘体，也没有理想的导体。

It is demonstrated that it takes a year for the earth to go around the sun. 已经证实，地球绕太阳转一周需要一年的时间。

7. 同义词或近义词的省略

在英文专业文献中，为了表达确切，常对同一事物、同一概念使用不同词汇来描述。但在汉语中，这种不同词汇的翻译往往相同。因此在翻译时可将这类同义词省略。例如：

Semiconductor devices have no *filament or heaters*, hence they require no heating power or warmed up time. 半导体器件没有灯丝，因而不需加热功率或加热时间。

The mechanical energy can be changed back into electrical energy by means of a *generator* or *dynamo*. 利用发电机可以把机械能转变成电能。

Technology is the application of scientific method and knowledge to industry to satisfy our material *needs* and *wants*. 技术就是在工业上应用科学方法和科学知识以满足我们物质上的需求。

Exercises

I. Choose the best answer into the blank

1. Logical operations are performed in _____ of a microprocessor.

A. the control unit   B. the ALU   C. the registers   D. the stored area

2. The 16-bit processor can process _____ at a time.

   A. eight bits   B. sixteen bits   C. thirty-two bits   D. sixty-four bits

3. A microprocessor accesses data from cache memory _____ from memory located elsewhere on the motherboard.

   A. more rapidly than   B. more slowly than

   C. as rapidly as   D. as slowly as

4. Data stored in RAM _____ when the power of the computer is turned off.

   A. is held permanently   B. permanently disappears

   C. is held temporarily   D. temporarily disappears

5. The basic information about storage, memory, and display configurations in a computer is stored in _____.

   A. RAM   B. ROM   C. CMOS   D. EPROM

II. Answer the following questions according to the text

1. What parts is a microprocessor mainly composed of?

2. What factors can affect the performance of a microprocessor?

3. What is the smallest unit of time in a microprocessor?

4. What are the differences between serial processing and parallel processing?

5. What are the differences between RAM and ROM?

III. Translate the following into Chinese

Multimedia is one of the fastest-growing computer applications. The majority of microcomputer systems sold today are equipped for multimedia. The trend is expected to continue.

Multimedia, also called hypermedia, is the integration of all sorts of media into one form of presentation. These media may include video, music, voice, graphics, and text. An essential and unique feature of multimedia is user participation or interactivity. When experiencing a multimedia presentation, users typically can control the flow and content. This is done by selecting options that customize the presentation to the users' needs.

Once used almost exclusive for computer games, multimedia is now widely used in business, education, and the home. Business uses include high-quality interactive presentations, product demonstrations, and Web page design. In education, multimedia is primarily used for entertainment. In the very near future, however, higher-end multimedia applications such as interactive home shopping and video-on-demand services are expected.

Section 3   Input and Output Devices

Expansion Slots, Card, And Ports

Within a computer, data travels from one component to another over circuits called a data bus. One part of the data bus runs between RAM and the microprocessor. Another part of the data bus runs between RAM and various storage devices. The segment of the data bus that extends between

RAM and peripheral devices is called the expansion bus. As data moves along the expansion bus, it may travel through expansion slots, cards, ports, and cables.

An expansion slot is a long, narrow socket on the motherboard into which you can plug an expansion card. An expansion card is a small circuit board that provides a computer with the ability to control a storage device, an input device, or an output device. Expansion cards are also called "expansion boards", "controller cards", or "adapters".

Most desktop computers have four to eight expansion slots, but some of the slots usually contain expansion cards. A graphics card (sometimes called a "video card") provides a path for data traveling to the monitor. A modem provides a way to transmit data over phone lines or cable television lines. A sound card carries data out to speakers and headphones, or back from a microphone. A network card allows you to connect your computer to a local area network. You might add other expansion cards if you want to connect a scanner or download videos from a camera or VCR.

A desktop computer may have up to three types of expansion slots:

（1）ISA (industry standard architecture) slots are an old technology, used today only for some modems and other relatively slow devices. Many new computers have few or no ISA slots.

（2）PCI (peripheral component interconnect) slots offer fast transfer speeds and 32-bit or 64-bit data bus. These slots typically house a graphics card, sound card, video capture card, modem, or network interface card.

（3）AGP (accelerated graphics port) slots provide a high-speed data pathway that is primarily used for graphics cards.

Most notebook computers are equipped with a special type of external slot called a PCMCIA slot (personal computer memory card international association). Typically, a notebook computer has only one of these slots, but the slot can hold more than one PC card.

An expansion port is any connector that passes data in and out of a computer or peripheral device. Ports are sometimes called "jacks" or "connectors". An expansion port is often housed on an expansion card so that it is accessible through an opening in the back of the computer's system unit. A port might also be built into the system unit case of a desktop or notebook computer. The built-in ports that are supplied with a computer usually include a mouse port, keyboard port, serial port, and USB port. Ports that have been added with expansion cards usually protrude through rectangular cutouts in the back of the case.

DISPLAY DEVICES

The two key components of a computer display system include a graphics card and a display device, such as a monitor or LCD screen. A graphics card contains circuitry that generates the signals for displaying an image on the screen. It also contains special video memory, which stores screen images as they are processed, before they are displayed. Many graphics cards contain special graphics accelerator technology to boost performance for 3-D graphics applications, including computer games.

For many years, CRT monitors were the only game in town for desktop computer displays.

CRT (cathode ray tube) technology uses gun-like mechanisms to direct beams of electrons toward the screen and activate individual dots of color that form an image. As an alternative to CRT monitors, an LCD (liquid crystal display) produces an image by manipulating light within a layer of liquid crystal cells. LCDs are standard equipment on notebook computers. Recently, stand-alone LCDs, referred to as "LCD monitors" or "flat panel displays", have also become available for desktop computers.

Image quality is a factor of screen size, dot pitch, resolution, and color depth. Screen size is the measurement in inches from one corner of the screen diagonally across to the opposite corner. Typical monitor screen sizes range from 13" to 21". Dot pitch (dp) is a measure of image clarity. A smaller dot pitch means a crisper image. Technically, dot pitch is the distance in millimeters between like-colored pixels—the small dots of light that form an image. A dot pitch between .26 and .23 is typical for today's monitors.

Your computer's graphics card sends an image to the monitor at a specific resolution, defined as the maximum number of horizontal and vertical pixels that are displayed on the screen. Standard resolutions include 640×480, 800×600, and 1024×768. at higher resolutions, text and other objects appear smaller, but the computer can display a larger work area, such as an entire page of a document.

The number of colors that a monitor and graphics card can display is referred to as color depth or "bit depth". Most PCs have the capability to display millions of colors. When set at 24-bit color depth (sometimes called "True Color") your PC can display more than 16 million colors—and produce what are considered to be photographic-quality image. Windows allows you to select resolution and color depth. Most desktop owners choose 24-bit color at 1024×768 resolution.

PRINTERS

Printer technologies popularly include ink jet, laser, and dot matrix recently. These printers differ in resolution and speed, which affect the print quality and price.

Resolution. The quality or sharpness of printed images and text depends on the printer's resolution—the density of the gridwork of dots that create an image. Printer resolution is measured by the number of dots it can print per linear inch, abbreviated as dpi. At normal reading distance, a resolution of about 900 dots per inch appears solid to the human eye, but a close examination of color sections will reveal a dot pattern. Although 900 dpi might be considered sufficient for some magazines, expensive coffee-table books are typically produced on printers with 2,400 dpi or higher.

Print speed. Printer speeds are measured either by pages per minute (ppm) or characters per second (cps). Color printers typically take longer than black-and-white printouts. Pages that contain mostly text tend to print more rapidly than pages that contain graphics. Ten pages per minute is a typical speed for a personal computer printer.

An ink jet printer has a nozzle-like print head that sprays ink onto paper to form characters and graphics. Today's most popular printer technology, ink jet printers produce low-cost color or black-and-white printouts. The print head in a color ink jet printer consists of a series of nozzles, each with its own ink cartridge. Most ink jet printers use CMYK color, which requires only cyan (blue), magenta (pink), yellow, and black inks to create a printout that appears to have thousands of colors. Alternatively, some printers use six colors to print midtone shades that create slightly more realistic photographic images.

A laser printer uses the same technology as a photocopier to paint dots of light on a light-sensitive drum. Electrostatically charged ink is applied to the drum, then transferred to paper.

Laser printers accept print commands from a personal computer, but use their own printer language to construct a page before printing it. Printer Control Language is the most widely used printer language, but some printers use the PostScript language, which is preferred by many publishing professionals. Printer languages require memory, and most laser printers have between 2 MB and 8 MB. A large memory capacity is required to print color images and graphics-intensive documents.

A dot matrix printer produces characters and graphics by using a grid of fine wires. As the print head noisily clatters across the paper, the wires strike the ribbon and paper in a pattern prescribed by your PC. Dot matrix printers can print text and graphics—some even print in color using a multicolored ribbon.

Most printers include a cable that connects to one of your computer's ports. A parallel port is most commonly used, but some printers are designed to connect to a USB port or a serial port.

Many printers come packaged with device driver software. You must install that software following the manufacturer's directions. If your computer uses Windows, you'll probably have to use the Start button to access the Printers window, where you can select the newly installed printer as the "default printer"—the one you will use regularly.

New Words and Expressions

slot	n. 槽	
expansion slot	扩展槽	
port	n. 端口	
data bus	数据总线	
expansion bus	扩展总线	
socket	n. 插座，插口	
expansion card	扩展卡	
adapter	n. 适配器	
USB universal series bus	通用串行总线	
storage device	存储设备	
download	v.; n. 下载	
ISA (industry standard architecture)	工业标准结构	
PCI (peripheral component interconnect)	外部设备互连	
video capture card	视频捕获卡	
interface	n.; v. 接口	
AGP (accelerated graphics port)	加速图形端口	

serial port	串行端口
jack	n. 插座，插孔，插口，弹簧开关
protrude	v.（使）伸出，突出，推出
cutout	n. 中断装置，断流器，断路器
CRT (cathode ray tube)	阴极射线管
LCD (liquid crystal display)	液晶显示
dots of color	色点
stand-alone	独立的
diagonally	ad. 对角地
dot pitch	点距
clarity	n. 清晰度
pixel	n. 像素，图素，像元
resolution	n. 分辨率，分辨度
ink jet	喷墨
printout	n. 打印输出
nozzle	n. 喷管，喷头，喷嘴
cartridge	n. 夹头，卡盘
cyan	a.; n. 蓝绿色的，蓝绿色
magenta	a.; n. 深红色的，深红色
photocopier	n. 照相复印机，影印机
light-sensitive	a. 光敏的
drum	n. 磁鼓
electrostatically	ad. 静电地
multicolored	a. 多色的
default	n. 缺省，默认
ribbon	n. 色带

Notes

1. An expansion slot is a long, narrow socket on the motherboard into which you can plug an expansion card.

   扩展槽是主板上用于插入扩展卡的一种细长的插座。

2. VCR 是 video cassette recorder 的缩写，意思是"录像机"。

3. CRT (cathode ray tube) technology uses gun-like mechanisms to direct beams of electrons toward the screen and activate individual dots of color that form an image.

   CRT（阴极射线管）技术采用枪式机理将电子束射向屏幕，激活各色点以形成图像。

句 型 的 转 换

在翻译过程中，可以根据原文的具体情况，按照汉语的表达习惯，对原文句子结构进行调整和转换。有些转换方法已经在前面章节作过介绍，如长句分译法等。下面介绍其他几种较常用的转换方式：

1. 否定变肯定译法

该方法是将原文中否定的表达形式译成肯定形式。例如：

Until recently geneticists were not interested in particular genes. 基因学家们最近才开始对特定基因感兴趣。

Don't start working before having checked the instrument thoroughly. 要对仪器彻底检查才能开始工作。

The flowing of electricity through a wire is not unlike that of water through a pipe. 电流过导线就像水流过管子一样。

2. 肯定变否定译法

是将原文中肯定的表达形式译成否定形式。例如：

The influence of temperature on the conductivity of metals is slight. 温度对金属的导电性影响不大。

As rubber prevents electricity from passing through it, it is used as insulating material. 由于橡胶不导电，所以用作绝缘材料。

There are many other energy sources in store. 还有多种其他能源尚未开发。

3. 主动变被动译法

在具体文章中，如果原文主动句正面译出比较困难，或者译成汉语被动句更能准确表达原意、汉语行文更为方便时，可对原文主动句译成汉语的被动句。

The properties of materials have *dictated* nearly every design and every useful application that the engineer could devise. 工程师所能设想的每一种设计和每一种用途几乎都受到材料性能的限制。

Since prehistoric times the sketch *has served* as one of man's most effective communication techniques. 自从史前时期以来，草图一直被人类用作最有效的交际手段之一。

However, the development of the natural science began to gain speed only in the latter part of the 18th and the early part of the 19th centuries. 然而，只是到了十八世纪末和十九世纪初叶，自然科学才得到了迅速地发展。

还有被动语态译成汉语的主动句，见后面章节内容。

Exercises

I. Choose the best answer into the blank

1. _____ is used to connect your computer to a local area network.

   A. A graphics card   B. A modem   C. A network card   D. A sound card

2. _____ are primarily used for graphics cards.

   A. ISA slots   B. PCI slots   C. AGP slots   D. PCMCIA slots

3. The notebook computers use _____ as standard display equipment.

   A. CRT display   B. LCDs   C. LED   D. TV screen

4. Image clarity on a computer screen is measured with _____.

  A. screen size   B. dot pitch   C. resolution   D. color depth

5. _____ printer uses a grid of fine wires to produce characters and graphics.

  A. An ink jet printer   B. A thermal transfer printer

  C. A laser printer   D. A dot matrix printer

II. Answer the following questions according to the text

1. What names do expansion cards have also?

2. How many types of expansion slots may a desktop computer usually have?

3. What are the two key components of a computer display system?

4. How do the objects appearing on the screen of a computer change when a computer uses a higher resolution?

5. How to measure the printer resolution?

III. Translate the following into Chinese

A database is a collection of logically related data elements, and data elements may be structured in various ways to meet the multiple processing and retrieval needs of organizations and individuals.

Schemas and sets of subschemas organize a database logically. They comprise the database's logical design, which is the user's view of how the data appear to be arranged on the secondary storage media. Schemas are often complex. Three basic structures are used to organize the data elements: hierarchical, network, and relational.

The hierarchical database structure resembles an organizational chart of a corporation. Data can be structured in the same hierarchical way. One might view the structure as an upside-down tree.

The network database structure is similar to the hierarchical structure, it is more complex in nature, but is more flexible in accessing data items.

The relational database structure groups all the data into tables from which the actual data relationships can be built. A table consists of rows and columns: each row specifies a record, each column represents individual data items and the entire table represents a file.

A data base management system (DBMS) is a system software package that handles the tasks associated with creating, accessing, and maintaining data base records. To handle a database, the DBMS package must perform the following tasks:

Database Creation——defining and organizing the content, relationships and structure of the data needed to build a database.

Database interrogation——accessing the data in a database to support various information processing assignments that require information retrieval and report generations.

Database Maintenance——adding, deleting, updating, correcting and protecting the data in a database.

Section 4　Software Basics

software consists of computer programs, support modules, and data modules that work together to provide a computer with the instructions and data necessary for carrying out a specific type of task, such as document production, video editing, or web browsing.

Software typically includes files that contain computer programs. A computer program, or "program", is a set of self-contained instructions that tells a computer how to solve a problem or carry out a task.

A support module provides an auxiliary set of instructions that can be used in conjunction with the main software program. Each module is stored in its own file. Unlike a program file, a support module is not designed to be run by the computer user. Instead, these modules are "called" by the computer program, as needed.

A data module, as you might expect, contains any data that is necessary for a task, but not supplied by the user. For example, word processing software checks spelling by comparing the words in a document with the words in a dictionary file of correctly spelled words.

When a computer programmer develops or writes software, he has to select a suitable computer language that provides the tools that he uses to create software. These languages help the programmer produce a lengthy list of instruction, called source code, that defines the software environment in every detail—how it looks, how the user enters commands, and how it manipulates data. Most programmers today prefer to use high-level languages, such as C++, Java, COBOL, and Visual Basic, which have some similarities to human languages, and produce programs that are fairly easy to test and modify.

A computer's microprocessor only understands machine language in binary form—the instruct set that is "hard wired" within the microprocessor's circuits. Therefore, instructions written in a high-level language must be translated into machine language in binary form before a computer can use them. The process of translating instructions from a high-level language into machine language can be accomplished by two special types of programs: compilers and interpreters. A compiler translates all of the instructions in a program as a single batch, and the resulting machine language instructions, called object code, are placed in a new file. As an alternative to a compiler, an interpreter converts one instruction at a time while the program is running. This method of converting high-level instructions into machine language is more common with Web-based programs called scripts, written in languages such as JavaScript and VBScript. These scripts contain high-level instructions, which arrive as part of a Web page. An interpreter reads the first instruction in a script, converts it into machine language, and then sends it to the microprocessor. After the instruction is executed, the interpreter converts the next instruction, and so on.

Programs written for a computer may be in one of the following categories:

（1）Binary code. This is a sequence of instructions and operands in binary that list the exact representation of instructions as they appear in computer memory.

（2）Octal or hexadecimal code. This is an equivalent translation of the binary code to octal or hexadecimal representation.

（3）Symbolic code. The user employs symbols (letters, numbers, or special characters) for the operation part, the address part, and other part of the instruction code. Each symbolic instruction can be translated into one binary coded instruction. This translation is done by a special program called an assembler. Because an assembler translates the symbols, this type of symbolic program is referred to as an assembly language program.

（4）High-level programming languages. These are special languages developed to reflect the procedures used in the solution of a problem rather than be concerned with the computer hardware behavior. Examples of high-level programming languages are Fortran, C, C++, VC++, COBOL, VB, Delphi, etc. They employ problem-oriented symbols and formats. The programs are written in a sequence of statements in a form that people prefer to think in when solving a problem. However each statement must be translated into a sequence of binary instructions before the program can be executed in a computer.

Software is categorized as either system software or application software. System software helps you to manage your files, to load and execute programs, and to accept your commands from the mouse and keyboard. The system software programs that manage the computer are collectively known as an operating system, and differ from the application programs, such as Microsoft Word, or Netscape, or the programs that you write, which you normally run to get your work done. Windows and UNIX are the best known examples of an operating system.

The operating system is an essential part of the computer system. Like the hardware, it is made up of many components. A simplified representation of an operating system is shown in Fig.5-1. the most obvious element is the user interface that can be defined as the combination of hardware and software that helps people and computers communicate with each other. Your computer user interface includes the mouse and keyboard that accept your input and carry out your commands, as well as the display device that provides cues to help you use software, and displays error messages that alert you to problems. An operating system typically provides user interface tools, such as menus and toolbar buttons, which define the "look and feel" for all of its compatible software. Most computers today feature a graphical user interface. Sometimes abbreviated "GUI", a graphical user interface provides a way to point and click a mouse to select menu options and manipulate graphical objects that are displayed on the screen.

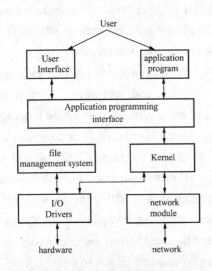

Fig.5-1　simplified operating system block diagram

The application program interface, or API, acts as

an interface for application programs and utilities to access the internal services provided by the operating system. These include file services, I/O services, data communication services, user interface services, program execution services, and more.

Many of the internal services are provided by the kernel module. The remaining services are provided by other modules that are controlled by the kernel. The kernel manages memory by locating and allocating space to programs that need it, schedules time for each application to execute, provides communication between programs that are being executed, manages and arranges services and resources that are provided by other modules, and provides security.

The file management system allocates and manages secondary storage space and translates file requests from their name-based form into specific I/O requests. The actual storage and retrieval of the files is performed by the I/O drivers that comprise the I/O component. Each I/O driver control one or more hardware devices of similar type.

Network module controls interaction between the computer system and the network(s) to which it is attached.

The operating system software is nearly always stored on a hard disk, but on a few systems the operating system is actually provided as a network service when the system is turned on. In either case, the bootstrap program in the operating system is stored within the computer using a type of memory known as ROM. The bootstrap program provides the tools to test the system and to load the remainder of the operating system from the disk or network.

One operating system might be better suited to some computing tasks than others. To provide clues to their strengths and weaknesses, operating systems are informally categorized and characterized using one or more of the following terms:

（1）A single-user operating system expects to deal with one set of input devices—those that can be controlled by one user at a time. Operating systems for handheld computers and many personal computers fit into the single-user category.

（2）A multiuser operating system is designed to deal with input, output, and processing requests from many users—all at the same time. One of its most difficult responsibilities is to schedule all of the processing requests that must be performed by a centralized computer—often a mainframe.

（3）A network operating system (also referred to as a "server operating system") provides communications and routing services that allow computers to share data, programs, and peripheral devices. Novell Netware, for example, is almost always referred to as a network operating system.

The difference between network services and multiuser services can seem a little hazy. The main difference , however, is that multiuser operating systems schedule requests for processing on a centralized computer, whereas a network operating system simply routes data and programs to each user's local computer, where the actual processing takes place.

（4）A multitasking operating system provides process and memory management services that allow two or more programs to run simultaneously. Most of today's personal computer operating systems offer multitasking services.

（5）A desktop operating system is one that's designed for a personal computer—either a desktop or notebook computer. The computer that you typically use at home, at school, or at work is most likely configured with a desktop operating system, such as Windows ME or MAC OS. Typically, these operating systems are designed to accommodate a single user, but may also provide networking capability. Today's desktop operating systems invariably provide multitasking capabilities.

New Words and Expressions

module	n. 模件，组件，模块
document	n. 文件，文献，公文
Web browsing	网页浏览
programmer	n. 程序员
computer language	计算机语言
binary	a.；n. 二进制的，二进位
source code	源代码
high-level language	高级语言
machine language	机器语言
batch	n. 批，一批
object code	目标代码
compiler	n. 编译程序
interpreter	n. 解释程序
script	n. 脚本
operand	n. 操作数
octal	a. 八进制的
hexadecimal	a. 十六进制的
assembler	n. 汇编程序
system software	系统软件
application software	应用软件
operation system	操作系统
user interface	用户界面，用户接口
menu	n. 菜单
toolbar	n. 工具条
button	n. 按钮
compatible	a. 兼容的，可共存的，兼容制的
graphical user interface	图形用户界面
click	v. 按
file management system	文件管理系统
bootstrap	n. 引导

bootstrap program	引导程序
single-user operating system	单用户操作系统
multiuser operating system	多用户操作系统
multitasking operating system	多任务操作系统

Notes

1. These languages help the programmer produce a lengthy list of instruction, called source code, that defines the software environment in every detail—how it looks, how the user enters commands, and how it manipulates data.

   这些语言有助于程序员编写很长的指令清单，这些指令称为源代码。

2. These are special languages developed to reflect the procedures used in the solution of a problem rather than be concerned with the computer hardware behavior.

   高级编程语言是用于反映解决问题的过程，而不涉及计算机硬件行为的特殊语言。

被动语态的翻译（一）

在英语专业文献中，大量使用被动语态，以突出所论证或说明的对象，使表述更客观，句子结构更简练。但在汉语中，并没有普遍使用被动语态的习惯。因此，在翻译英语被动语态时，大量的译成主动句，少数的仍可译成被动句，视具体情况而定。

译成汉语的主动句有以下几种不同情况：

1. 原主语在译文中仍作主语

If a machine part *is* not well *protected*, it will become rusty after a period of time. 如果机器部件不好好防护，过了一段时间后就会生锈。

Every moment of every day, energy *is being transformed* from one form into another. 每时每刻，能量都在由一种形式变成另一种形式。

At the receiving end, the composite signals *are applied* to band-pass filters. 在接收端，合成信号加到带通滤波器上。

This formula has already been mentioned above. 这个公式上面已经提到过。

2. 原主语在译文中作宾语，并增译主语使译文通顺流畅

The issue has not yet been thoroughly explored. 人们对这一问题迄今尚未进行过彻底探索。

New computer viruses and logic bombs are discovered every week. 每个星期，我们都能发现新型计算机病毒和逻辑炸弹。

If one of more electrons be removed, the atom is said to be positively charged. 如果原子失去一个或多个电子，我们就说，该原子带正电荷。

3. 原主语在译文中作宾语，而把行为主体或相当于行为主体的介词宾语译成主语

A new way of displaying time has been given by *electronics*. 电子技术提供了一种新的显示时间的方法。

Modern scientific discoveries lead to the conclusion that energy may be created from matter and that *matter*, in turn, may be created from *energy*. 近代科学的发现得出这样的结论：物质可以

产生能，能又可以产生物质。

Many jobs as to assemble parts in dangerous environment are done by robots in *some developed countries*. 一些发达国家用机器人去做危险环境下的零件组装工作。

4. 原文中的主语在译文中作宾语，译成无主句

一般来说，描述什么地方发生、存在或消失了什么事物的英语被动句，以及表示观点、态度、告诫、要求、号召等的被动句，汉译时往往采用无主句，有时还可在动词前加上"把"、"使"、"将"、"对"等词。

The mechanical energy can be changed back into electrical energy by means of a generator. 利用发电机，可以将机械能再转变成电能。

The resistance can be determined provided that the voltage and current are known. 只要知道电压和电流，就能测定电阻。

The quartz crystal in the watch is made to vibrate at a frequency of 56,000 times a second. 使钟表里的石英晶体以每秒 56,000 次的频率振荡。

5. 把主语并入谓语合译

英语中有些含有名词的动词短语用于被动语态在句子中作主语，翻译时应把主语和谓语合并，并按原动词短语的意思译出。

Attention must be paid to environmental protection in developing economy. 发展经济必须注意环境保护。

The unpleasant noise must *be* immediately *put an end to*. 必须立即终止这种讨厌的噪声。

Allowance must, no doubt, *be made for* the astonishing rapidity of communication in these days. 无疑要考虑到现代通信的惊人速度。

6. 由 "it" 引导的习惯性句型中的被动语态，可译作无人称主动句或不定人称主动句

It has been proved that energy cannot be destroyed; it can only be charged into other forms. 已经证明，能量是不可能消灭的，只能转换成其他形式。

It is generally recognized that light has a vast capacity for transmitting information. 一般认为，光传播信息的容量极大。

It can be seen that magnetic materials are used in a wide range of modern electronic equipment. 可见，磁性材料广泛用于现代电子设备中。

Exercises

I. Choose the best answer into the blank

1. _____ can be used in conjunction with the main software program to provide an auxiliary set instructions.

    A. Software   B. A support module

    C. A data module   D. A data module

2. A computer's microprocessor only understands _____.

    A. high-level languages   B. machine language

    C. human languages   D. assembly language

3. Delphi belongs to _____.

    A. low-level programming language

    B. high-level programming language

    C. a programming language concerned with the computer hardware behavior

    D. an assembly language

4. An operating system is considered as _____.

    A. system software   B. application software

    C. drive program   D. setup program

5. _____ allocates and manages secondary storage space and translates file requests from their name-based form into specific I/O requests.

    A. A bootstrap program   B. The file management system

    C. A network module   D. An application program

II. Answer the following questions according to the text

1. What types of programs can be used to translate a high-level language into machine language?

2. What are the characteristics of an assembly language program?

3. What are functional differences between system software and application software?

4. What is function of a bootstrap program?

5. What are the differences between a single-user system and a multiuser operating system?

III. Translate the following paragraph into Chinese

    A computer **virus** is one kind of threat to the security and integrity of computer systems. Like other threats, a computer virus can cause the loss or **alteration** of programs or data. A computer virus can spread from program to program and from system to system, without direct human intervention. In some cases, a virus may contain no intentionally harmful or disruptive instructions at all. Instead, it may cause damage by replicating itself and taking-up scarce resource, such as disk space, CPU times, or network connections. There are four main types of viruses: **shell**, **intrusive**, **operating system**, and **source code**.

    Shell viruses wrap themselves around a host program and do not modify the original program; intrusive viruses invade an existing program and actually insert a portion of themselves into the host program; operating system viruses work by replacing parts of the operating system with their own logic; source code viruses are intrusive programs that are inserted into a source program such as those written in PASCAL prior to the program being compiled, which are the least common viruses.

    There exists today three broad-based categories of **anti-virus** techniques: **Virus scanners**, **memory-resident monitors**, and **integrity checkers**.

Section 5   Computer Network Basics

    There are reasons why people wish to connect computers together. Some of the most important reasons are:

（1）Users working at their own computers, often in different locations, have access to programs, files, data from a data base, documents, and the like that are stored elsewhere. The users can also communicate using e-mail or "talk" services, or they can use groupware to work together on documents.

（2）It is often desirable to share valuable resources such as printers, a large disk facility, programs, or a data base among two or more computers.

（3）Users may connect their computers to powerful computer resources to obtain support services, conduct business, purchase goods, discuss common interests, play games, or simply socialize.

（4）Computers can be used together to increase system reliability by providing redundant processing. Two or more CPUs can be executing the same program, and the results can be compared by the computers continuously. Connecting computers together also makes it possible to switch processing to a backup computer in the event of failure of a CPU. Such systems are called fault-tolerant systems. Fault-tolerant systems often provide redundancy on other devices, such as disks, as well. Disk arrays are well suited for fault tolerant computing.

（5）Computer power can be increased by combining multiple CPUs or computers work together. Grouping multiple CPUs means that multiple processes can be executed simultaneously. As another approach, a program may be executed more rapidly by distributing its execution so that each connected CPU or computer may be executing different parts of the program.

Actually, it is rare today to see a computer that operates totally independently of other computers. Even home computers have modems that can be used to dial up a connection to an online service, a bulletin board, or another computer. Computers in businesses are generally interconnected into networks, so that the users may work together and share information with each other. Networks provide access to central data repositories, the Internet, e-mail, and resources such as printers and can be used to offer more overall processing power by dividing the workload among multiple systems. Networks of computers may be as small as a few computers in a single room or as large as millions of computers scattered all over the world, tied together into a giant network of networks called the Internet. It is also common for modern large systems to provide multiple CPUs within a single system for additional processing power or to handle specialized functions within the computer system, such as I/O.

Network Links

When computers are connected together they can share and exchange program code and data. In fact, the purpose of interconnection is to provide a means of communication between the computers. Data can travel from one network device to another over a cable or through the air. A communications channel, or "link", is a physical path or a frequency for a single transmission. Computer networks use a variety of links to carry data, the most common being twisted-pair cable, coaxial cable, fiber-optic cable, radio waves, microwaves, satellites, infrared light, and laser beams.

Twisted-pair cables typically contain four pairs of copper wires. Each pair of wires is independently insulated and then twisted around each other, which gives this cable its name. Twisted-pair cables can be shielded or unshielded. STP (shielded twisted pair) encases its twisted pairs with a foil shield, which reduces signal noise that might interfere with data transmission. UTP (unshielded twisted pair) contains no shielding. It is less expensive than shielded cable, but more susceptible to noise. Either type can be used for data com- munications.

Coaxial cable, often called "coax cable", consists of a copper wire encased in a non-conducting insulator, a foil shield, a woven metal outer shield, and a plastic outer coating.

Fiber-optic cable is a bundle of extremely thin tubes of glass. Each tube, called an optical fiber, is much thinner than a human hair. A fiber-optic cable usually consists of a strong inner support wire, multiple strands of optical fiber, and a tough outer covering. Unlike twisted pair and coaxial cables, fiber-optic cables do not conduct or transmit electrical signals. Instead, miniature lasers convert data into pulses of light, which flash through the cables. cables are an essential part of the Internet backbone, and are increasingly found on business and campus networks.

Bandwidth is the transmission capacity of a communications channel. A high-bandwidth communications channel can carry more data than a low-bandwidth channel. High-bandwidth communications systems, such as cable TV, are sometimes referred to as broadband, whereas systems with less capacity, such as the telephone system, are referred to as narrowband. The bandwidth of a digital channel is usually measured in bits per second (bps).

Network Devices

Each device that is connected to a network is referred to as a node. Many network nodes are computers—some of them busily serve out information, and others simply request information. Behind the scenes, several network devices handle specialized network tasks.

A modem is a device that converts the signals from a computer into signals that can travel over a wide area network, such as the telephone system or the Internet.

A network interface card is a small circuit board that converts the signals from a computer into signals that can travel over a local area network.

The term server often refers to any computer on a local area network or the Internet that contains the software to manage and process files for other network nodes. The term "server" can also refer to the software that provides a network service. E-mail servers, communications servers, file servers, and Web servers are some of the most common servers on today's networks.

A hub is a device that connects several nodes of a local area network. All of the devices that attach to a hub are part of the same local area network. Multiple hubs can be linked together to expand a local area network. To connect more than one local area network, or to connect a local area network to the Internet, requires an additional device, such as a router or a gateway.

A router is a device that is connected to at least two networks—sort of like a spider sitting in the middle of a Web. Routers make decision about the best route for data, based on the data's destination and the state of the available network links. A gateway is a device that performs functions similar to a router. Both routers and gateways can be incorporated on local area networks or the Internet.

A repeater is a device——found on LANs and the Internet—that amplifies and regenerates signals so that they can retain the necessary strength to reach their destinations.

New Words and Expressions

data base	数据库
redundant	a. 冗余的，多余的，
fault-tolerant	a. 容错的
redundancy	n. 冗余
disk array	磁盘阵列
home computer	家用电脑
dial up	拨号
repository	n. 仓库
twisted-pair	双绞的，双绞线的
coaxial cable	同轴电缆
fiber-optic cable	光缆，光纤电缆
microwave	n. 微波
infrared	a. 红外线的；n. 红外线
shielded	a. 屏蔽的
unshielded	a. 非屏蔽的
strand	n. 股，股线
bandwidth	n. 带宽
high-bandwidth	高带宽
low-bandwidth	低带宽
broadband	n. 宽带
narrowband	n. 窄带
hub	n. 集线器
router	n. 路由器
gateway	n. 网关
repeater	n. 中继器，转播器

Notes

1. Connecting computers together also makes it possible to switch processing to a backup computer in the event of failure of a CPU.

   计算机联网可实现在某一个 CPU 故障时能将处理工作切换到备用计算机上。

2. As another approach, a program may be executed more rapidly by distributing its execution so that each connected CPU or computer may be executing different parts of the program.

   另一种方法是将程序分布到每一个连接的 CPU 或计算机上执行，它们各执行程序的不同部分，会使程序的执行更快。

被动语态的翻译（二）

7. 译成汉语的被动句

当英语中某些被动句着重被动动作或被动者时，汉译时，可译成被动句，以突出其被动意义。由于汉语的动词无词形变化，只能用添加词的办法来表达被动，通常在谓语前加上"被"、"受"、"得到"、"以"、"加以"等。

The metric system is now *used* by almost all the countries in the world. 米制现在<u>被</u>全世界几乎所有的国家<u>采用</u>。

A machine *is assembled* of its separate components. 机器是<u>由</u>一些单独的部件<u>装配</u>而成的。

The discovery *is* highly *appreciated* in the circle of science. 这一发现在科学界<u>得到</u>很高的<u>评价</u>。

被动变主动译法

8. 译成汉语的判断句

凡是着重描述事物的过程、性质和状态的英语被动句，可译成"是……的"结构，起强调被动动作的作用。

The voltage *is* not *controlled* in that way. 电压不<u>是</u>用那样的方法<u>控制</u>的。

The volume *is* not *measured* in square millimeters. It *is measured* in cubic millimeters. 体积不<u>是</u>以平方毫米<u>计量的</u>。它<u>是</u>以立方毫米<u>计量的</u>。

Exercises

I. Choose the best answer into the blank

1. Twisted-pair cables typically contain _____ pairs of copper wires.

    A. one   B. two   C. three   D. four

2. _____ do not conduct or transmit electrical signals.

    A. Twisted pairs   B. Coaxial cables   C. Fiber-optic cables   D. Telephone wires

3. The transmission capacity of a communications channel is greater, then its bandwidth is _____.

    A. broader   B. more narrow   C. constant   D. unknown

4. _____ converts the signals from a computer into signals that can travel over a local area network.

    A. A modem   B. A network card   C. A hub   D. A router

5. _____ that connects at least two networks makes decision about the best route for data.

    A. A modem   B. A network card   C. A hub   D. A router

II. Answer the following questions according to the text

1. Why do people wish to connect their computers together to form a computer network?

2. What is a fault-tolerant system?

3. What links can be used to carry data in computer networks?

4. Why can computers that are used together increase system reliability?

5. Which is more susceptible to noise, shielded twisted pair or unshielded twisted pair?

III. Translate the following into Chinese

Network Topology

Various ways can be used to interconnect the nodes in a network. The layout used for a network is called the network topology or the network configuration.

Network designers use three basic alternative configurations, either singly or in combination, to connect together the nodes in a network. They are called bus, ring, and star topologies. Each configuration has its own advantages and disadvantages.

（1）With a bus configuration, each node is tapped in somewhere along the bus using a simple network interface between the bus and the computer or other device. The bus configuration is the easiest to wire. It is necessary only to run a single cable from a module at one end of the network to a module at the other. Each end of the bus is equipped with a terminator to prevent signals on the bus form echoing. The bus is a multipoint topology. A node transmits a message by placing it on the node, where it is broadcast to every other node on the bus. Access to the bus is passive. A nonsender simply listens for messages.

（2）A ring topology consists of a point-to-point connection from each node on the network to the next. The last node is connected back to the first to form a closed ring. The ring topology requires an active network interface unit for each node. Each node must retransmit the signal that it receives from the previous node to the next node in the ring. The links between nodes are unidirectional, so that data travels in only one direction around the ring. To simplify the ring, it is possible to purchase a single multistation access unit (MAU), which contains an active interface for each node, preconnected into a ring topology. Each computer node is then wired to one of the interfaces in the MAU. Although this arrangement has the physical appearance of a star topology, electrically it is still a ring.

（3）With a star configuration the network is controlled by a central station that acts as a steering device, passing data from one module to another as requested by each module. Each computer in the network is connected point-to-point to the control station. Most star networks are designed to receive messages in packet form. The central station then rebroadcasts the packets to every node. The central station may be active or passive.

Chapter 6　Electric Power Systems

Section 1　Introduction

The modern society depends on the electricity supply more heavily than ever before. It can not be imagined what the world should be if the electricity supply were interrupted all over the world. Electric power systems (or electric energy systems), providing electricity to the modern society, have become indispensable components of the industrial world.

The first complete electric power system (comprising a generator, cable, fuse, meter, and loads) was built by Thomas Edison – the historic Pearl Street Station in New York City which began operation in September 1882. This was a DC system consisting of a steam-engine-driven DC generator supplying power to 59 customers within an area roughly 1.5 km in radius. The load, which consisted entirely of incandescent lamps, was supplied at 110 V through an underground cable system. Within a few years similar systems were in operation in most large cities throughout the world. With the development of motors by Frank Sprague in 1884, motor loads were added to such systems. This was the beginning of what would develop into one of the largest industries in the world. In spite of the initial widespread use of DC systems, they were almost completely superseded by AC systems. By 1886, the limitations of DC systems were becoming increasingly apparent. They could deliver power only a short distance from generators. To keep transmission power losses (I^2R) and voltage drops to acceptable levels, voltage levels had to be high for long-distance power transmission. Such high voltages were not acceptable for generation and consumption of power; therefore, a convenient means for voltage transformation became a necessity.

The development of the transformer and AC transmission by L. Gaulard and J.D. Gibbs of Paris, France, led to AC electric power systems. In 1889, the first AC transmission line in North America was put into operation in Oregon between Willamette Falls and Portland. It was a single-phase line transmitting power at 4,000 V over a distance of 21 km. With the development of polyphase systems by Nikola Tesla, the AC system became even more attractive. By 1888, Tesla held several patents on AC motors, generators, transformers, and transmission systems. Westinghouse bought the patents to these early inventions, and they formed the basis of the present-day AC systems.

In the 1890s, there was considerable controversy over whether the electric utility industry should be standardized on DC or AC. By the turn of the century, the AC system had won out over the DC system for the following reasons:

（1）Voltage levels can be easily transformed in AC systems, thus providing the flexibility for use of different voltages for generation, transmission, and consumption.

（2）AC generators are much simpler than DC generators.

（3）AC motors are much simpler and cheaper than DC motors.

The first three-phase line in North America went into operation in 1893——a 2,300 V, 12 km line in southern California. In the early period of AC power transmission, frequency was not standardized. Many different frequencies were in use: 25, 50, 60, 125, and 133 Hz. This poses a problem for interconnection. Eventually 60 Hz was adopted as standard in North America, although 50 Hz was used in many other countries.

The increasing need for transmitting large amounts of power over longer distance created an incentive to use progressively high voltage levels. To avoid the proliferation of an unlimited number of voltages, the industry has standardized voltage levels. In U.S.A., the standards are 115, 138, 161, and 230 kV for the high voltage (HV) class, and 345, 500 and 765 kV for the extra-high voltage (EHV) class. In China, the voltage levels in use are 10, 35, 110 for HV class, and 220, 330 (only in Northwest China) and 500 kV for EHV class. The first 750 kV transmission line will be built in the near future in Northwest China.

With the development of the AC/DC converting equipment, high voltage DC (HVDC) transmission systems have become more attractive and economical in special situations. The HVDC transmission can be used for transmission of large blocks of power over long distance, and providing an asynchronous link between systems where AC interconnection would be impractical because of system stability consideration or because nominal frequencies of the systems are different.

The basic requirement to a power system is to provide an uninterrupted energy supply to customers with acceptable voltages and frequency. Because electricity can not be massively stored under a simple and economic way, the production and consumption of electricity must be done simultaneously. A fault or misoperation in any stages of a power system may possibly result in interruption of electricity supply to the customers. Therefore, a normal continuous operation of the power system to provide a reliable power supply to the customers is of paramount importance.

New Words and Expressions

electric power system	电力系统
cable	n. 电缆，缆，钢丝绳；v. 架设电缆，敷设电缆
fuse	n. 保险丝，熔断器；引信；v. 熔化，熔断
meter	n. 米；测量仪表，计量器
customer	n. 客户，用户
radius	n. 半径
incandescent lamp	白炽灯
transmission line	输电线路
power loss	功率损耗
voltage drop	电压降落
AC transmission	交流输电
transmission system	输电系统

utility	n. 公用事业，效用，中心电站
flexibility	n. 灵活性，机动性，适应性；柔性，柔度
interconnection	n. 相互连接，互联
asynchronous	a. 异步的
nominal frequency	额定频率
misoperation	n. 误操作，误动作
paramount	a. 最高的，头等的；高过，优于

Notes

1. The increasing need for transmitting large amounts of power over longer distance created an incentive to use progressively high voltage levels.

日益增长的对远距离大容量功率输送的需求导致所使用的电压水平不断提高。

2. The HVDC transmission can be used for transmission of large blocks of power over long distance, and providing an asynchronous link between systems where AC interconnection would be impractical because of system stability consideration or because nominal frequencies of the systems are different.

HVDC 可用来进行远距离大容量的功率输送，并且可以在由于系统稳定限制或系统额定频率不同使交流联网不能实现的情况下提供一个异步联网的手段。

否定句的翻译（一）

英语里表示否定意义的方法与汉语有很大不同。英语中，表示否定的形式多种多样，如全部否定、部分否定、双重否定、意义否定等，使用灵活、微妙。有的英语句子形式上是肯定的而实质上是否定的；有的形式上是否定的而实质上是肯定的。英语否定词的否定范围和重点有时难于判断，因此在翻译英语时，必须仔细分析，彻底理解其意义及否定的重点，再根据汉语的习惯进行翻译，正确表达。

一、全部否定

全部否定是对被否定的词、句的意义作全面的否定。表示全部否定时，常用 neither, neither…nor…, no, not, never, nothing, nobody, nowhere 等否定词。一般可照译为否定句。但有时需要改变否定词的词序。

Nothing in the world moves faster than light. 世界上<u>没有任何</u>东西比光传得更快了。

There is *no* sound evidence to prove this. <u>没有</u>可靠的证据可以证明这一点。

Whether any of this causes immediate harm is *not* known. 这是否会造成直接危害目前还<u>不</u>知道。

A gas has *neither* definite shape *nor* definite volume. 气体<u>既没有</u>一定的形状，<u>也没有</u>一定的体积。

二、部分否定

部分否定是对叙述的内容做部分的，而不是全部的否定。部分否定主要是由 all, both, every, each, often, always 等词与否定词构成，相当于汉语"不全是"、"不总是"、"并非都"、"未必都"、

"不是两个都"之意。这类否定句中的否定词 not 有时和谓语在一起，构成谓语否定。形式上很像全部否定，但实际上是部分否定，在翻译时要特别注意。

In a thermal power plant, *all* the chemical energy of the fuel is *not* converted into heat. 在热电厂，燃料的化学能<u>并未全部</u>转变成热能。

Friction is *not always* a disadvantage. In many instances it is highly important. 摩擦<u>并非总是不利的</u>，在许多情况下，它是非常重要的。

We are *not* familiar with *both* of the instruments. 我们对这两台仪器<u>不是都</u>熟悉。

All these metals are *not* good conductors. 这些金属并<u>不都是</u>良导体。

三、双重否定

在英文的同一句子中，出现两个否定词并用，或一个否定词与某些表示否定意义的词连用，构成双重否定，表达婉转或强调的语气。双重否定句可采用两种翻译手段，一种是采用反译法译成肯定句，另一种是采用双重否定方式。

1. 译成肯定句

The flowing of electricity through a wire is *not unlike* that of water through a pipe. 电流过导线<u>就像水流过管子一样</u>。

Despite the current oil glut, *no* serious observer believes that this is *anything but* a rapidly diminishing resource. 虽然目前石油供过于求，但任何一位认真的观察家<u>都</u>认为，石油是一种很快就要枯竭的资源。

Gases *cannot* be quickly compressed *without* generating heat. 气体迅速压缩就<u>一定会</u>产生热量。

2. 译成双重否定

It is not impossible to control industrial waste waters to preserve the usefulness of the receiving water. <u>不是不可能</u>控制工业废水以保护进水的可用性。

In fact, it is *impossible* for *no* force to be exerted on a body, since in this world everything is subject to the force of gravity. 事实上，物体<u>不受</u>外力作用是<u>不可能的</u>，因为在这个世界上任何物体都要受到重力的作用。

There can *never* be a force acting in nature *unless* two bodies are involved. 在自然界中<u>不牵</u>涉两个物体，就<u>不会</u>有作用力。

Exercises

I. Choose the best answer into the blank

1. The first complete power system was built in _____, it was _____ power system.

　　A. 1889, an AC　　　B. 1882, a DC　　　C. 1882, an AC　　　　D. 1889, a DC

2. The first three-phase AC transmission line in North America was put into operation in _____.

　　A. 1889　　　　　　B. 1882　　　　　　C. 1893　　　　　　　D. 1890

3. Power system interconnections are usually formed at the _____ level.

　　A. transmission system　　　　　　B. subtransmission system

　　C. distribution system　　　　　　D. generating station

4. In North American _____ is adopted as standard frequency in electric power system.

    A. 25Hz   B. 50Hz   C. 60Hz   D. 125Hz

5. _____ can provide an asynchronous link between two ac electric power systems with different nominal frequencies.

    A. The HVDC transmission   B. The EHV AC transmission

    C. The AC distribution   D. Generators

II. Answer the following questions according to the text

1. When was the first AC transmission line put into operation in North America?

2. Why did the AC system win out over the DC system at the turn of the century?

3. What voltage levels are in use for EHV class in China?

4. Why have HVDC transmission systems become more attractive?

5. What is the basic requirement to a power system?

III. Translate the following into Chinese

Power system stability may be broadly defined as the property of a power system that enables it to remain in a state of operating equilibrium under normal operating conditions and to regain an acceptable state of equilibrium after being subjected to a disturbance.

Instability in a power system may be manifested in many different ways depending on the system configuration and operating mode. Traditionally, the stability problem has been one of maintaining synchronous operation. Since power systems rely on synchronous machines for generation of electrical power, a necessary condition for satisfactory system operation is that all synchronous machines remain in synchronism or, colloquially "in step". This aspect of stability is influenced by the dynamics of generator rotor angles and power-angle relationships, and then referred to "*rotor angle stability*".

Section 2   Components of Power Systems

Modern power systems are usually large-scale, geographically distributed, and with hundreds to thousands of generators operating in parallel and synchronously. They may vary in size and structure from one to another, but they all have the same basic characteristics:

（1）Are comprised of three-phase AC systems operating essentially at constant voltage. Generation and transmission facilities use three-phase equipment. Industrial loads are invariably three-phase; single-phase residential and commercial loads are distributed equally among the phases so as to effectively form a balanced three-phase system.

（2）Use synchronous machines for generation of electricity. Prime movers convert the primary energy (fossil, nuclear, and hydraulic) to mechanical energy that is, in turn, converted to electrical energy by synchronous generators.

（3）Transmit power over significant distances to consumers spread over a wide area. This requires a transmission system comprising subsystems operating at different voltage levels.

The basic elements of a modern power system in USA. are shown in Fig.6-1. Electric power is produced at generating stations (GS) and transmitted to consumers through a complex network of individual components, including transmission lines, transformers, and switching devices. It is common practice to classify the transmission network into the following subsystems: Transmission system; Subtransmission system; Distribution system.

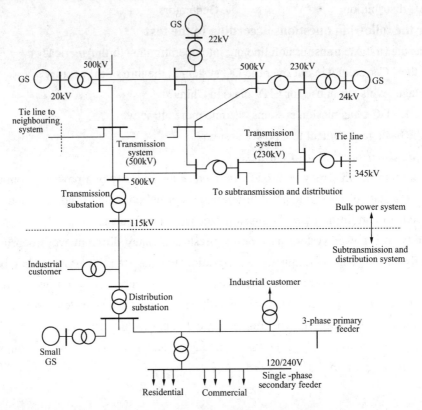

Fig.6-1　Basic elements of a power system

The transmission system interconnects all major generating stations and main load centers in the system. It forms the backbone of the integrated power system and operates at the highest voltage levels (typically, 230 kV and above in U.S.A.). The generator voltages are usually in the range of 11 to 35 kV. These are stepped up to the transmission voltage level, and power is transmitted to transmission substations where the voltages are stepped down to the subtransmission level (typically, 69 to 138 kV). The generation and transmission subsystems are often referred to as the bulk power system.

The subtransmisson system transmits power in small quantities from the transmission substations to the distribution substations. Large industrial customers are commonly supplied directly from the subtransmission system. In some systems, there is no clear demarcation between subtransmission and transmission circuits. As the system expands and higher voltage levels become necessary for transmission, the older transmission lines are often relegated to subtransmission function.

The distribution system represents the final stage in the transfer of power to the individual customers. The primary distribution voltage is typically between 4.0 kV and 34.5 kV. Small industrial customers are supplied by primary feeders at this voltage level. The secondary distribution feeders supply residential and commercial customers at 120/240 V.

Small generating plants located near the load are also connected to the subtransmission or distribution system directly. Interconnections to neighboring power systems are usually formed at the transmission system level. The overall system thus consists of multiple generating sources and several layers of transmission networks. This provides a high degree of structural redundancy that enables the system to withstand unusual contingencies without service disruption to the customers.

New Words and Expressions

in parallel	并联地
synchronously	ad. 同步地
facility	n. ①容易，方便　②灵活，熟练　③（便利）条件
	④（常用复数）设备，装置，工具，器材
primary energy	一次能源
fossil	n. 化石，石块
hydraulic	a. 水力[学]的，水压的，液压的，液力的
mechanical energy	机械能
subsystem	n. 子系统，分系统，辅助系统
switching device	开关装置，开关设备
subtransmission	n. 二次输电
subtransmission system	分支输电系统，二次输电系统
distribution system	配电系统
substation	n. 变电所，变电站，分站，分所
feeder	n. 馈线，馈电电路
redundancy	n. 多余，冗余
contingency	n. 意外事故，偶然事故

Notes

Modern power systems are usually large-scale, geographically distributed, and with hundreds to thousands of generators operating in parallel and synchronously.

现代电力系统通常是规模大，地域分布广，具有成百上千并列同步运行的发电机组。

否定句的翻译（二）

四、意义上的肯定

英语中有的否定词与其他词连用形成一个固定结构，这种结构在形式上是否定的，但意义上是肯定的，常见的有 nothing like（没有什么比得上……），cannot... too（越……越好），no/not/nothing + more + than（不过），no/not/nothing + less + than（多达）等。

The importance of the project *can hardly* be exaggerated. 这项工程的重要性怎么说<u>也不过分</u>。

It is *impossible to overestimate* the value of the invention. 这项发明的价值无论怎样估计<u>也不会太高</u>。

Pesticides can cause a lot of harm, so you can *never be too* careful when using pesticides. 杀虫剂会造成很大危害，所以当使用杀虫剂时<u>应</u>特别小心。

五、含蓄否定

英语里有些词或词组形式上是肯定的，但意义往往是否定的。由这类词或词组表达的否定称为含蓄否定。翻译时，一般要把否定的意义明确译出，可译成"不"、"没"、"没有"、"非"等。

1. 动词或动词短语引起的否定

常见的有 deny 拒绝，否认，fail 失败，lack 缺乏，refuse 拒绝，stop 停止，protect … from，保护……免受，keep … from 避免，overlook 忽视，忽略，miss 失败，错过等。

The experiment *failed* of success. 实验<u>没有</u>成功。

The value of loss in this equation is so small that we can *overlook* it . 在此方程中，损耗值太小，可以<u>忽略不计</u>。

The specification *lacks* detail. 这份说明书<u>不够</u>详尽。

2. 名词引起的否定

常见的有 neglect 忽视，absence 缺乏，loss 失去，exclusion 排除，ignorance 无知等。

A few instruments are in a state of *neglect*. 一些仪器处于<u>无人管理</u>状态。

3. 形容词或形容词短语引起的否定

常见的有 free from 不受……影响，ignorant of 不知道，short of 缺乏，last 最不，little 少，few 少等。

The precision instrument must be kept *free from* dust. 精密仪器必须保持<u>无尘</u>。

This equation is *far from* being complicated. 这个方程式一点也<u>不</u>复杂。

4. 介词或介词短语引起的否定

常见的有 beyond 超出，above 超出……之外，beneath 不值得，beside 同……无关，instead of 而不是等。

The problem is *beyond* the reach of my understanding. 这个问题我<u>无法</u>理解。

The Theory of Relativity worked out by Einstein is now *above* many people's comprehension. 爱因斯坦提出的"相对论"，现在还有不少人理解<u>不了</u>。

5. 连词及其某些短语引起的否定

常见的有 before 在……以前，尚未……，but 而不，would rather…than 宁可……而不愿，与其……不如，rather than 而不……，too…to 太……不等。

Never start to do the experiment *before* you have checked the meter. <u>没有</u>检查好仪表，切勿开始做试验。

Exercises

I. Choose the best answer into the blank

1. In power plants _____ convert the primary energy to mechanical energy, and _____ con- vert

mechanical energy to electric energy.

A. synchronous generators, prime movers

B. prime movers, synchronous generators

C. prime movers, asynchronous generators

D. prime movers, prime movers

2. The generator voltages are usually stepped up to the transmission voltage level by _____.

A. series capacitors B. parallel reactors

C. step-up transformers D. step-down transformers

3. Residential and commercial customers are supplied by the secondary distribution feeders at _____.

A. 120/240 V B. 220/380 V C. 110/220 V D. 48/110 V

4. In USA, the voltages of the transmission system are typically _____.

A. 345kV B. 500kV

C. 230kV and above D. 115kV and above

II. Answer the following questions according to the text

1. What components is a modern power system comprised of?

2. What is the function of the distribution system?

3. What is the function of the transmission system?

4. What is the function of the subtransmission system?

5. What is the characteristics of a modern power system in network structure?

III. Translate the following into Chinese

Instability may also be encountered without loss of synchronism. For example, a system consisting of a synchronous generator feeding an induction motor load through a transmission line can become unstable because of the collapse of load voltage. Maintenance of synchronism is not an issue in this instance; instead, the concern is stability and control of voltage. This form of instability can also occur in loads covering an extensive area supplied by a large system. This kind of stability is referred to "voltage stability".

Rotor angle stability is the ability of interconnected synchronous machines of a power system to remain in synchronism. It is most important to power system stability problems. The stability problem involves the study of the electromechanical oscillations inherent in power system. A fundamental factor in this problem is the manner in which the power outputs of synchronous machines vary as their rotors oscillate.

Section 3 Operation and Control of Power Systems

The purpose of a power system is to deliver the power the customers require in real time, on demand, within acceptable voltage and frequency limits, and in a reliable and economic manner. In normal operation of a power system, the total power generation is balanced by the total load and transmission losses. The system frequency and voltages on all the buses are within the required limits, while no overloads on lines or equipment are resulted. However, loads are constantly changed in small or large extents, so some control actions must be applied to maintain the power system in the normal and economic operation state.

Optimal economic operation

It is an important problem how to operate a power system to supply all the (complex) loads at minimum cost. The basic task is to consider the cost of generating the power and to assign the allocation of generation (P_{Gi}) to each generator to minimize the total "production cost" while satisfying the loads and the losses on the transmission lines. The total cost of operation includes fuel, labor, and maintenance costs, but for simplicity the only variable costs usually considered are fuel costs. The fuel-cost curves for each generating unit are specified, the cost of the fuel used per hour is defined as a function of the generator power output. When hydro-generation is not considered, it is reasonable to choose the P_{Gi} on an instantaneous basis (i.e. always to minimize the present production cost rate). With hydro-generation, however, in dry periods, the replenishment of the water supply may be a problem. The water used today may not be available in the future when its use might be more advantageous. Even without the element of the prediction involved, the problem of minimizing production cost over time becomes much more complicated.

It should be mentioned that economy of operation is not the only possible consideration. If the "optimal" economic dispatch requires all the power to be imported from a neighboring utility through a single transmission link, considerations of system security might preclude that solution. When water used for hydro-generation is also used for irrigation, nonoptimal releases of water may be required. Under adverse atmospheric conditions it may be necessary to limit generation at certain fossil-fuel plants to reduce emissions.

In general, costs, security and emissions are all areas of concern in power plant operation, and in practice the system is operated to effect a compromise between the frequently conflicting requirements.

Power system control

Power system control is very important issue to maintain the normal operation of a system. System voltage levels, frequency, tie-line flows, line currents, and equipment loading must be kept within limits determined to be safe in order to provide satisfactory service to the power system customers.

Voltage levels, line currents, and equipment loading may vary from location to location within a system, and control is on a relatively local basis. For example, generator voltage is determined by the field current of each particular generating unit; however, if the generator voltages are not coordinated, excess var flows will result. Similarly, loading on individual generating units is determined by the throttle control on thermal units or the gate controls on hydro-units. Each machine will respond individually to the energy input to its prime mover. Transmission line loadings are affected by power input from generating units and their loadings, the connected loads, parallel paths for power to flow on other lines, and their relative impedances.

Active power and frequency control

For satisfactory operation of a power system, the frequency should remain nearly constant. Relatively close control of frequency ensures constancy of speed of induction and synchronous motors. Constancy of speed of motor drives is particularly important for satisfactory performance of all the auxiliary drives associated with the fuel, the feed-water and the combustion air supply systems. In a network, considerable drop in frequency could result in high magnetizing currents in induction motors and transformers. The extensive use of electric clocks and the use of frequency for other timing purpose require accurate maintenance of synchronous time which is proportional to integral of frequency. As a consequence, it is necessary to regulate not only the frequency itself but also its integral. The frequency of a system is dependant on active power balance. As frequency is a common factor throughout the system, a change in active power demand at one point is reflected throughout the system by a change in frequency. Because there are many generators supplying power into the system, some means must be provided to allocate change in demand to the generators. A speed governor on each generating unit provides the primary speed control function, while supplementary control originating at a central control center allocates generation.

In an interconnected system with two or more independently controlled areas, in addition to control of frequency, the generation within each area has to be controlled so as to maintain scheduled power interchange. The control of generation and frequency is commonly referred to as load-frequency control (LFC).

The control measures of power and frequency include:

（1）Regulation of the generator's speed governor

（2）Underfrequency load shedding

（3）Automatic generation control (AGC)

AGC is an effective means for power and frequency control in large-scale power systems. In an interconnected power system, the primary objectives of AGC are to regulate frequency to the specified nominal value and to maintain the interchange power between control areas at the scheduled values by adjusting the output of the selected generators. This function is commonly referred to as *load-frequency control*. A secondary objective is to distribute the required change in generation among units to minimize operating costs.

In an isolated power system, maintenance of interchange power is not an issue. Therefore, the function of AGC is to restore frequency to the specified nominal value. This is accomplished by adding a reset or integral control which acts on the load reference setting of the governors of unit on AGC. The integral control action ensures zero frequency error in the steady state. The supplementary generation control action is much slower than the primary speed control action. As such it takes effect after the primary speed control (which acts on all units on regulation) has stabilized the system frequency. Thus, AGC adjusts load reference settings of selected units, and hence their output power, to override the effects of the composite frequency regulation characteristics of the power system. In so doing, it restores the generation of all other units not on AGC to scheduled values.

Reactive power and voltage control

For efficient and reliable operation of power systems, the control of voltage and reactive power should satisfy the following objectives:

（1）Voltages at the terminals of all equipment in the system are within acceptable limits. Both utility equipment and customer equipment are designed to operate at a certain voltage rating. Prolonged operation of the equipment at voltages outside the allowable range could adversely affect their performance and possibly cause them damage.

（2）System stability is enhanced to maximize utilization of the transmission system.

（3）The reactive power flow is minimized so as to reduce RI^2 and XI^2 losses to a practical minimum. This ensures that the transmission system operates efficiently, i.e. mainly for active power transfer.

The problem of maintaining voltages within the required limits is complicated by the fact that the power system supplies power to a vast number of loads and is fed from many generating units. As loads vary, the reactive power requirements of the transmission system vary. Since reactive power can not transmitted over long distances, voltage control has to be effected by using special devices dispersed throughout the system. This is in contrast to the control of frequency which depends on the overall system active power balance. The proper selection and coordination of equipment for controlling reactive power and voltage are among the major challenges of power system engineering.

The control of voltage levels is accomplished by controlling the production, absorption, and flow of reactive power at all levels in the system. The generating units provide the basic means of voltage control; the automatic voltage regulators control field excitation to maintain a scheduled voltage level at the terminals of the generators. Additional means are usually required to control voltage throughout the system. The devices used for this purpose may be classified as follows:

（1）Sources or sinks of reactive power, such as shunt capacitors, shunt reactors, synchro- nous condensers, and static var compensators (SVCs).

·（2）Line reactance compensators, such as series capacitors.

（3）Regulating transformers, such as tap-changing transformers and boosters.

Shunt capacitors and reactors, and series capacitors provide passive compensation. They are either permanently connected to the transmission and distribution system, or switched. They contribute to voltage control by modifying the network characteristics. Synchronous condensers and SVCs provide active compensation, the reactive power absorbed/supplied by them is automatically adjusted so as to maintain voltages of the buses to which they are connected. Together with the generating units, they establish voltages at specific points in the system. Voltages at other locations in the system are determined by active and reactive power flows through various circuit elements, including the passive compensating devices.

New Words and Expressions

reliable   a. 可靠的

bus	n. 母线
overload	n. 过载，超载，过负荷
optimal	a. 优化的，最优的，最佳的
production cost	生产成本，生产费用
hydro-generation	n. 水力发电
dry period	枯水期
replenishment	n. （再）补充，充实，充满
economic dispatch	经济调度
economic operation	经济运行
security	n. 安全性，可靠性
emission	n. 排放，放出，散放
tie-line	n. 联络线
var flow	无功潮流
throttle	n. 阀门，节流阀，调速汽门
thermal unit	热力机组，热力单位
magnetizing current	激磁电流，励磁电流
electric clock	电钟
active power balance	有功功率平衡
supplementary control	辅助控制
load-frequency control (LFC)	负荷频率控制
speed governor	调速器
underfrequency load shedding	低周减载，低频减负荷
automatic generation control (AGC)	自动发电控制
stabilize	v. 使……稳定
reactive power	无功功率
active power	有功功率
automatic voltage regulator	自动电压调节器
shunt capacitor	并联电容器，并联电容
shunt reactor	并联电抗器，并联电抗
synchronous condenser	同步调相机
static var compensators (SVCs)	静止无功补偿器
series capacitor	串联电容器
tap-changing transformer	可调分接头变压器
booster	n. 升压器，增压器，加压泵

Notes

1. The water used today may not be available in the future when its use might be more advantageous.

   今天用掉的水可能在未来更有用时不能再得到。

2. In general, costs, security, and emissions are all areas of concern in power plant operation, and in practice the system is operated to effect a compromise between the frequently conflicting requirements.

一般来讲，成本、安全和排放问题都是电厂运行需要考虑的方面，通常的做法是系统的运行需在各种矛盾的要求之间折中考虑。

3. Constancy of speed of motor drives is particularly important for satisfactory performance of all the auxiliary drives associated with the fuel, the feed-water and the combustion air supply systems.

电动机转速的恒定对与燃料、给水和送风等有关的辅机设备的良好运行是特别重要的。

4. The extensive use of electric clocks and the use of frequency for other timing purpose require accurate maintenance of synchronous time which is proportional to integral of frequency. As a consequence, it is necessary to regulate not only the frequency itself but also its integral.

电钟和其他使用频率定时的设备的广泛应用要求维持准确的同步时间，该时间正比于频率的积分。所以，不仅需要调整频率自身而且需要调整它的积分。

5. In an interconnected power system, the primary objectives of AGC are to regulate frequency to the specified nominal value and to maintain the interchange power between control areas at the scheduled values by adjusting the output of the selected generators.

在互联电力系统中，AGC 的主要目标是通过调节指定发电机的输出将系统频率调整到额定值，并且将区域间的功率交换维持在所要求的水平。

6. Synchronous condensers and SVCs provide active compensation, the reactive power absorbed/ supplied by them is automatically adjusted so as to maintain voltages of the buses to which they are connected.

同步调相机和 SVCs 提供有源补偿，它们吸收或发出的无功功率可以自动调整以维持它们所连母线的电压水平。该句中的"active"的含义是"有源的"，与"passive"（无源的）相对应。

数量词的翻译（一）

在科技英语和专业英语中大量出现数量词。由于英语与汉语在数量的表达方法和方式上差别较大，翻译时往往需要换算。因此，在翻译时，需要仔细分析，以免发生翻译错误，引起严重后果。

1. 句型：as + 形容词 + as 数词 + ……

as high as…　　　可译成"高达……"；

as heavy as…　　可译成"重达……"；

as large as…　　 可译成"大到（至）……"；

as low as…　　　可译成"低到（至）……"；

as many as…　　 可译成"多到……"。

The temperature at the sun's center is *as high as* 10000000°C. 太阳中心的温度高达摄氏 1000 万度。

The outer portion of the wheel may travel *as fast as* 600 miles per hour. 轮子外缘的运动速度

可能<u>高达</u>每小时六百英里。

2. 数量增加的翻译

（1）句型："be *n* times as +形容词（或副词）+as…"，"be *n* times +比较级+than"，"be + 比较级 + than + 名词 + by *n* times"，"be + 比较级 + by a factor of *n*"，可译成"是……的 *n* 倍"、"*n* 倍于"或"比……大（*n*-1）倍"。

The new machine turns *three times as fast as* the old one. 新机器的转速是旧机器的<u>3 倍</u>。（或译成：新机器的转速比旧机器快 2 倍。）

The oxygen atom is 16 *times heavier than* the hydrogen atom. 氧原子的重量是氢原子的<u>16 倍</u>。

Mercury weighs *more than* water *by about* 14 *times*. 水银比水重约 <u>13 倍</u>。

The error probability of binary AM is *greater* than for binary *FM by a factor of at least* 6. 二进制调幅误差概率比二进制调频至少<u>大 5 倍</u>。

（2）句型："as + 形容词或副词 + again as"，"again as + 形容词或副词 + as"，可译成"是……的 2 倍"，或"比……多（大，长……）一倍"。如果 again 前加 half，则表示"是……的 1.5 倍"或"比……多（大，长……）半倍"。

This wire is *as long again as* that one. 这根金属线的长度是那根的<u>2 倍</u>。

The amount left was estimated to be *again as much as* all the zinc that has been mined. 当时估计，剩余的锌储量是已开采量的<u>2 倍</u>。

The resistance of aluminum is approximately *half again as great as* that of copper for the same dimensions. 尺寸相同时，铝的电阻约为铜的<u>一倍半</u>。

（3）用带有"增大"意思的动词（increase, rise, grow 等）和含有数字的词语配合。句型有："动词 + *n* times"，"动词 + by + *n* times"，"动词 + to + *n* times"，"动词 + *n*-fold"，"动词 + by a factor of + *n*"，可译成"增加到 *n* 倍"，"增加了（*n*-1）倍"；"(by) *n* +单位（或 *n*%）"表示净增量，数词可照译。

The production has *increased three times*. 生产<u>增加了 2 倍</u>。

The strength of the attraction *increases by four times* if the distance between the original charges is behalved. 如果原电荷的距离缩短一半，则引力就<u>增大到</u>原来的<u>4 倍</u>。

This year, the production of this kind of machine in our plant is estimated to *increase to* 3 *times* compared with 1980. 今年我厂这种机器的产量预计比 1980 年<u>增长 2 倍</u>。

Since the first transatlantic telephone cable was laid the annual total of telephone calls between UK and Canada has *increased sevenfold*. 自从第一条横跨大西洋的电话电缆敷设以来，英国与加拿大之间的年通话量<u>增加了 6 倍</u>。

If *X* is doubled, *Y* is increased by *a factor of* 4. 若 *X* 增加到 2 倍，则 *Y* <u>增加到 4 倍</u>。

Automation will help us to raise the output of production *by thirty percent*. 自动化能帮助我们<u>提高产量 30%</u>。

（4）用表示倍数的动词表示的量的增加。例如，double 可译成"增加一倍"，"翻一番"，"是……2 倍"；treble 可译成"增加 2 倍"，"增加到 3 倍"；quadruple 可译成"增加 3 倍"，"翻两番"。

As the high voltage was abruptly *trebled* all the values burnt. 由于高压突然<u>增加了 2 倍</u>，管子都烧坏了。

The new airport will double the capacity of the existing one. 新机场是现有机场容量的 2 倍。

Exercises

I. Choose the best answer into the blank

1. The objective of the optimal economic operation of power systems is _____.

    A. to minimize the total production cost

    B. to maintain frequency constant

    C. to maintain voltages constant

    D. to ensure balance between generation and load

2. The frequency of a power system is determined mainly by _____.

    A. bus voltages   B. active power generation

    C. reactive power generation   D. active power generation and consumption

3. The voltage levels at the terminals of generators are controlled mainly by _____.

    A. static var compensators   B. series capacitors

    C. automatic voltage regulators   D. shunt reactors

4. When the system frequency is changed away from the rating, _____ must be regulated.

    A. system voltages   B. reactive power

    C. active power   D. generators' excitation

5. Regulation of the generator's speed governor can change its _____ output.

    A. reactive power   B. active power

    C. terminal voltage   D. reactive current

II. Answer the following questions according to the text

1. What parts are included in the total cost of operation?

2. In an interconnected power system, what is the main function of an AGC system?

3. What measures can be used for voltage control in a power system?

4. Why is the problem of maintaining voltages within the required limits complicated?

5. How does the active power loss of a power system vary as the reactive power flow decreases?

III. Translate the following into Chinese

    When two or more synchronous machines are interconnected, the stator voltages and currents of all the machines must have the same frequency and the rotor mechanical speed of each is synchronized to this frequency. Therefore, the rotors of all interconnected machines must be in synchronism. In a generator, the electromagnetic torque opposes rotation of the rotor, so that mechanical torque must be applied by the prime mover to sustain rotation. The electrical torque (or power) output of the generator is changed only by changing the mechanical torque input by the prime mover. The effect of increasing the mechanical torque input is to advance the rotor to a new position relative to the revolving magnetic field of the stator. Conversely, a reduction of mechanical torque or power input will retard the rotor position. In a synchronous motor, the roles of electrical and mechanical torques are reversed compared to those in a generator.

Section 4　Power System Stability

Power versus angle relationship

An important characteristic that has a bearing on power system stability is the relationship between interchange power and angular positions of the rotors of the synchronous machines. This relationship is highly nonlinear. To illustrate this let us consider the simple system shown in Fig.6-2(a). It consists of two synchronous machines connected by a transmission line having an inductive reactance X_L but negligible resistance and capacitance. Let us assume that machine 1 represents a generator feeding power to a synchronous motor represented by machine 2.

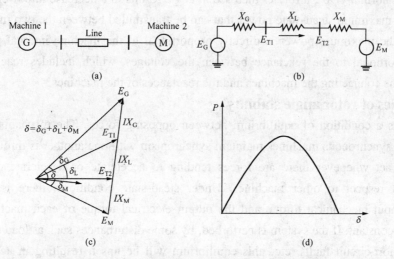

Fig.6-2　Power transfer characteristic of a two-machine system

(a) Single-line diagram;　　　　(b) Idealized model;

(c) Phasor diagram;　　　　(d) Power-angle curve

The power transferred from the generator to the motor is a function of angular separation (δ) between the rotors of the two machines. This angular separation is due to three components: generator internal angle δ_G (angle by which the generator rotor leads the revolving field of the stator); angular difference between the terminal voltages of the generator and motor (angle by which the stator field of the generator leads that of the motor); and the internal angle of the motor (angle by which the rotor lags the revolving stator field). Fig.6-2(b) shows a model of the system that can be used to determine the power versus angle relationship. A simple model comprising an internal voltage behind an effective reactance is used to represent each synchronous machine. The value of the machine reactance used depends on the purpose of the study. For analysis of stead-state performance; it is appropriate to use the synchronous reactance with the internal voltage equal to the excitation voltage.

A phasor diagram identifying the relationships between generator and motor voltages is shown in Fig.6-2(c). The power transferred from the generator to the motor is given by

$$P = \frac{E_G E_M}{X_T} \sin \delta$$

where

$$X_T = X_G + X_L + X_M$$

The corresponding power versus angle relationship is plotted in Fig.6-2(d). With the somewhat idealized models used for representing the synchronous machines, the power varies as a sine of the angle: a highly nonlinear relationship. With more accurate machine models including the effects of automatic voltage regulators, the variation in power with angle would deviate significantly from the sinusoidal relationship; however, the general form would be similar. When the angle is zero, no power is transferred. As the angle is increased, the power transfer increases up to a maximum. After a certain angle, normally 90°, a further increase in angle results in a decrease in power transferred. There is thus a maximum stead-state power that can be transmitted between the two machines. The magnitude of the maximum power is directly proportional to the machine internal voltages and inversely proportional to the reactance between the voltages, which includes reactance of the transmission line connecting the machines and the reactances of the machines.

Categories of rotor angle stability

Stability is a condition of equilibrium between opposing forces. The mechanism by which interconnected synchronous machines maintain synchronism with one another is through restoring forces, which act whenever there are forces tending to accelerate or decelerate one or more machines with respect to other machines. Under stead-state conditions, there is equilibrium between the input mechanical torque and the output electrical torque of each machine, and the speed remains constant. If the system is perturbed, by some disturbances such as load changes, line outages and short-circuit faults, etc., this equilibrium will be upset, resulting in acceleration or deceleration of the rotors of the machines according to the laws of motion of a rotating body. If one generator temporarily runs faster than another, the angular position of its rotor relative to that of the slower machine will advance. The resulting angular difference transfers part of the load from the slow machine to the fast machine, depending on the power-angle relationship. This tends to reduce the speed difference and hence the angular separation. The power-angle relationship, as discussed above, is highly nonlinear, beyond a certain limit, an increase in angular separation is accompanied by a decrease in power transfer; this increases the angular separation further and leads to instability. For any given situation, the stability of the system depends on whether or not the deviations in angular positions of the rotors result in sufficient restoring torques.

When a synchronous machine losses synchronism or "falls out of step" with the rest of the system, its rotor runs at a higher or lower speed than that required to generate voltages at system frequency. The "slip" between rotating stator field (corresponding to the system frequency) and the rotor field results in large fluctuations in the machine power output, current and voltage; this cause the protection system to isolate the unstable machine from the system. Loss of synchronism can occur between one machine to the rest of the system or between groups of machines. In the latter case synchronism may be maintained within each group after its separation from others.

Rotor angle stability can usually be classified as *small-signal stability* and *transient stability*, according to the severity of the disturbances applied.

Small-signal stability or *small disturbance stability* is the ability of power system to maintain synchronism under small disturbances. Such disturbances occur continually on the system because of small variations in loads and generation. The disturbances are considered sufficiently small for linearization of system equations to be permissible for purposes of analysis. Instability that may result can be of two forms: (i) steady increase in rotor angle due to lack of sufficient synchronizing torque, or (ii) rotor oscillations of increasing amplitude due to lack of sufficient damping torque. The nature of the system response to small disturbances depends on a number factors including the initial operating point, the transmission system strength, and the type of generator excitation controls used. For a generator connected radially to a large power system, in the absence of automatic voltage regulators (i.e., with constant field voltage) the instability is due to lack of sufficient synchronizing torque. This results in instability through a non-oscillatory mode. With continuously acting voltage regulators, the small-disturbance stability problem is one of ensuring sufficient damping of system oscillations. Instability is normally through oscillations of increasing amplitude. In today's practical power systems, small-signal stability is largely a problem of insufficient damping of oscillations.

Transient stability is the ability of the power system to maintain synchronism when subjected to a severe transient disturbance. The resulting system response involves large excursions of generator rotor angles and is influenced by the nonlinear power-angle relationship. Stability depends on both the initial operating state of the system and the severity of the disturbance. Usually, the system is altered so that the post-disturbance steady-state operation differs from that prior to the disturbance.

Fig.6-3 illustrates the behavior of a synchronous machine for stable and unstable situations. It shows the rotor angle responses for a stable case and for two unstable cases. In the stable case (Case 1), the rotor angle increases to a maximum, then decreases and oscillates with decreasing amplitude until it reaches a steady state. In Case 2, the rotor angle continues to increase steadily until synchronism is lost. This form of instability is referred to as first-swing instability and is caused by insufficient synchronizing torque. In Case 3, the system is stable in the first swing but becomes unstable as a result of growing oscillations as the end state is approached. This form of instability generally occurs when the post-disturbance steady-state condition itself is "small-signal" unstable, and not as a result of the transient disturbance.

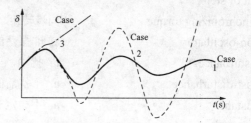

Fig.6-3   Rotor angle response to a transient disturbance

In large power systems, transient instability may not always occur as first-swing instability; it could be the result of the superposition of several modes of oscillation causing large excursions of rotor angle beyond the first-swing.

New Words and Expressions

angular	a. 角的，角度的
power versus angle relationship	功角关系
synchronous reactance	同步电抗，功率—角度关系
excitation voltage	励磁电压
angular displacement	角位移
rotor angle stability	转角稳定性，功角稳定性
voltage stability	电压稳定性
electromechanical	a. 机电的
electromagnetic	a. 电磁的
equilibrium	n. 平衡，均衡
mechanism	n. 机理，机制；机构，装置；结构
synchronism	n. 同步
accelerate	v. 加速，促进
decelerate	v. 减速
mechanical torque	机械转矩
electrical torque	电气转矩
outage	n. 停电，断电，中断，停运，停机，事故
short-circuit fault	短路故障
power-angle relationship	功角关系
fluctuation	n. 波动，起伏
small-signal stability	小信号稳定性
transient stability	暂态稳定性
small disturbance stability	小干扰稳定性
damp	v. 阻尼，（使）减弱，减幅；n. 阻尼，衰减
damping torque	阻尼转矩
instability	不稳定性
out of step	失步
synchronizing torque	同步转矩
non-oscillatory	a. 非振荡的，非周期的
disturbance	n. 扰动，干扰
post-disturbance	a. 干扰后的，扰动后的，事故后的
unstable	a. 不稳定的
first-swing	n.; a. 第一次摇摆

Notes

1. For example, a system consisting of a synchronous generator feeding an induction motor load

through a transmission line can become unstable because of the collapse of load voltage.

例如，一个发电机通过一条输电线向感应电动机负荷供电的系统可能由于负荷电压的崩溃而失去稳定。

2. The mechanism by which interconnected synchronous machines maintain synchronism with one another is through restoring forces, which act whenever there are forces tending to accelerate or decelerate one or more machines with respect to other machines.

互联同步发电机之间维持同步的机制是恢复力，无论何时有导致一台或多台发电机相对于其他发电机加速或减速的力量存在，恢复力将起作用。

数 量 词 的 翻 译 （二）

3. 数量减少的翻译

（1）用带有"减少"意思的动词和含有数词的词语配合。句型有："动词 + n times"，"动词 +by +n times"，"n times as + 形容词或副词 + as"，"动词 + by a factor of + n"，可译成"减少了 n 分之（n-1）倍"，"减少到 n 分之一"。汉语的分母不习惯用小数，若英语减少的倍数中有小数点时，应换算成分数。

The pre-heating time for the new type thermal meter *is shortened 5 times*. 这种新型热电式仪表的预热时间缩短 4/5。

The new equipment will *reduce* the error probability by *seven times*. 新设备的误差概率将降低 6/7。

The leads of the new condenser are *shortened three times as long as* those of the old. 新型电容器的导线比旧式电容器的导线缩短了 1/3。

Tests indicate this *might reduce* activity *by a factor between* 10 *and* 100. 测试结果表明，这可将放射性降低到原来的 1/10~1/100 。

（2）用表示"减少"的动词连接"by n（或 n%）"以及连系动词连接"n less (than)"，表示净减量，所减数字可照译。

The bandwidth *was reduced by two-thirds*. 频带宽度减少了 2/3。

The prime cost decreased by sixty percent . 主要成本降低了 60%。

（3）英语中用表示"减少"的动词连接"to + n（或 n%）"表示"减少到 n（或 n%）"。

The pressure will *be reduced to one-fourth* of its original value. 压力将减小到原来数值的 1/4。

The pollution was reduced to 25%. 污染减少到了 25%。

By the year 2003 the world's annual oil output is expected to fall to 33%. 到 2003 年，世界石油年产量预计将下降到 33%。

（4）句型："half as much as …"、"twice less than…"，可译成"比……少一半"或"比……少 1/2"。

The power output of the machine is *twice less than* its input. 该机器的输出功率比输入功率小 1/2。

The line AB is *half as long as* the line CD. AB 线比 CD 线短一半。

Exercises

I. Choose the best answer into the blank

1. In a single machine power system, the maximum power transfer from the generator to the system is directly proportional to _____.

    A. bus voltage   B. the system frequency

    C. the machine internal voltage   D. the line reactance

2. If the input mechanical torque is greater than the output electrical torque in a generator, the speed of its rotor will _____.

    A. decrease   B. increase

    C. maintain equilibrium   D. keep synchronous speed

3. If the synchronizing torque is insufficient in a disturbed system, _____ will occur.

    A. voltage instability   B. dynamic instability

    C. oscillatory instability   D. non-oscillatory instability

4. If an electric power system lacking of sufficient damping torque under a certain operation state suffers a disturbance, _____ will occur.

    A. voltage instability   B. dynamic instability

    C. oscillatory instability   D. non-oscillatory instability

5. After a large disturbance, the system is sometimes stable in the first swing but becomes unstable as a result of growing oscillations as the end state is approached, this is because _____.

    A. the disturbance is too severe

    B. the post-disturbance steady-state condition of the system is 'small signal' unstable

    C. the duration time of the disturbance is too long

    D. the initial rotor angle is too big

II. Answer the following questions according to the text.

1. What is the difference between the terms 'transient stability' and 'small-signal stability'?

2. May instability occur without loss of synchronism among the generators?

3. According to the power-angle curve of a single-machine system, when the maximum power transfer is obtained?

4. What is the first-swing instability of a power system?

5. What factors does transient stability depend on?

III. Translate the following into Chinese

Voltage Stability

Voltage stability is the ability of a power system to maintain steady acceptable voltages at all buses in the system under normal operating conditions and after being subjected to a disturbance. A system enters a state of voltage instability when a disturbance, increase in load demand, or change in system condition causes a progressive and uncontrollable drop in voltage. The main factor causing instability is the inability of the power system to meet the demand for reactive power. The heart of the problem is usually the voltage drop that occurs when active power and reactive power flow through inductive reactances associated with the transmission network.

Progressive drop in bus voltages can also be associated with rotor angles going out of step. For example, the gradual loss of synchronism of machines as rotor angles between two groups of machines approach or exceed 180° would result in very low voltages at intermediate points in the network. In contrast, the type of sustained fall of voltage that is related to voltage instability occurs where rotor angle stability is not an issue.

Voltage instability is essentially a local phenomenon; however, its consequences may have a widespread impact. Voltage collapse is more complex than simple voltage instability and is usually the result of a sequence of events accompanying voltage instability leading to a low-voltage profile in a significant part of the power system. Voltage instability may occur in different ways. For purpose of analysis, voltage stability is usually classified into the following two subclasses:

(1) *Large-disturbance voltage stability* is concerned with a system's ability to control voltages following large disturbances such as system faults, loss of generation, or circuit contingencies. This ability is determined by the system load characteristics and the interactions of both continuous and discrete controls and protections. A criterion for large-disturbance voltage stability is that, following a given disturbance and following system-control actions, voltages at all buses reach acceptable steady-state levels.

(2) *Small-disturbance voltage stability* is concerned with a system's ability to control voltages following small perturbations such as incremental changes in system load. This form of stability is determined by the characteristics of load, continuous controls, and discrete controls at a given instant of time. A criterion for small-disturbance voltage stability is that, at a given operating condition for every bus in the system, the bus voltage magnitude increases as the reactive power injection at the same bus is increased. A system is voltage-unstable if, for at least one bus in the system, the bus voltage magnitude decreases as the reactive power injection at the same bus is increased.

Voltage instability does not always occur in its pure form. Often the angle and voltage instabilities go hand in hand. One may lead to the other and the distinction may not be clear. However, a distinction between angle stability and voltage stability is important for understanding of the underlying causes of the problems in order to develop appropriate design and operating procedures.

Chapter 7   Power System Protections

Section 1   Introduction

The steady-state operation of a power system is frequently disturbed by various faults on electrical equipment. To maintain the proper operation of the power system, an effective, efficient and reliable protection scheme is required. Power system components are designed to operate under normal operating conditions. However, if due to any reason, say a fault, there is an abnormality, it is necessary that there should be a device which senses these abnormal conditions and if so, the element or component where such an abnormality has taken place is removed, i.e. deleted from the rest of the system as soon as possible. This is necessary because the power system component can never be designed to withstand the worst possible conditions due to the fact that this will make the whole system highly uneconomical. And therefore, if such an abnormality takes place in any element or component of the power system network, it is desirable that the affected element / component is removed from the rest of the system reliably and quickly in order to restore power in the remaining system under the normal condition as soon as possible.

The protection scheme includes both the protective relays and switching circuits, i.e. circuit breakers. The protective relay which functions as a brain is a very important component. The protective relay is a sensing device, which senses the fault, determines its location and then send command to the proper circuit breaker by closing its trip coil. The circuit breaker after getting command from the protective relay, disconnects only the faulted element. This is why the protective relay must be reliable, maintainable and fast in operation.

In early days, there used to be electromechanical relay of induction disk-type. However, very soon the disk was replaced by inverted cup, i.e. hollow cylinder and the new relay obtained was known as an induction cup or induction cylinder relay. This relay, which is still in use, possesses several important features such as higher speed, higher torque for a given power input and more uniform torque.

However, with the advent of electronic tubes, electronic relays having distinct features were developed during 1940s. With the discovery of solid state components during 1950s, static relays with numerous advantages were developed. The use of digital computers for protective relaying purposes has been engaging the attention of research and practicing engineers since late 1960s and 1980s. Now, the microprocessor/mini computer-based relaying scheme, because of its numerous advantages such as self-checking feature and flexibility, has been widely used in power systems all over the world.

The overall system protection is divided into following sections: (i) Generator protection, (ii) Transformer protection, (iii) Bus protection, (iv) Feeder protection, (v) Transmission line protection.

Basic Requirements to Protective Relays

Any protection scheme, which is required to safeguard the power system components against abnormal conditions such as faults, consists basically of two elements: (i) Protective relay and (ii) Circuit breaker. The protective relay which is primarily the brain behind the whole scheme plays a very important role. Therefore proper care should be taken in selecting an appropriate protective relay which is reliable, efficient and fast in operation. The protective relay must satisfy the following requirements:

（1）Since faults on a well designed and healthy system are normally rare, the relays are called upon to operate only occasionally. This means that the relaying scheme is normally idle and must operate whenever fault occurs. In other words, it must be reliable.

（2）Since the reliability partly depends upon the maintenance, the relay must be easily maintainable.

（3）The maloperation of the relay can be in two ways. One is the failure to operate in case a fault occurs and second is the relay operation when there is no fault. As a matter of fact, relay must operate if there is a fault and must not operate if there is no fault.

（4）Relaying scheme must be sensitive enough to distinguish between normal and the faulty system.

Protective Relays

The function of the protective relays is to sense the fault and energize the trip coil of the circuit breaker. The following types of protective relays are used for the apparatus such as synchronous machines, bus bar, transformer and the other apparatus and transmission line protection.

（1）Overcurrent relays.

（2）Undervoltage relays.

（3）Underfrequency relays.

（4）Directional relays.

（5）Thermal relays.

（6）Phase sequence relays such as (i) negative sequence relays and, (ii) zero sequence relays.

（7）Differential relays and percentage differential relays.

（8）Distance relays such as (i) plane impedance relays, (ii) angle impedance relays, i.e. Ohm or reactance relays, (iii) angle admittance relays, i.e. Mho relays and, (iv) offset and restricted relays.

（9）Pilot relays such as (i) wire pilot relays, (ii) carrier channel pilot relays, (iii) microwave pilot relays.

There are different types of the relaying scheme based on construction. They are: (i) electromechanical type, (ii) thermal relays, (iii) transductor relays, (iv) rectifier bridge relay, (v) electronic relays, (vi) static relays, (vii) digital relaying schemes.

New Words and Expressions

power system protection	电力系统保护，电力系统继电保护
abnormality	n. 异常，反常，不正常
sense	v. 检测，读出，断定；感觉，感受，感到
relay	n. 继电器，中继器；v. 中继，转播，用继电器控制
circuit breaker	断路器
trip coil	跳闸线圈，脱扣线圈
electromechanical relay	电磁继电器
protective relay	保护继电器
solid state	固态
static relay	静态继电器，无触点继电器
self-checking	自检，自校
maloperation	n. 误操作，误动作，维护不当
energize	v. 激励，激磁，驱动，通以电流
overcurrent relay	过电流继电器
undervoltage relay	低电压继电器，欠压继电器
underfrequency relay	低周继电器，低频继电器
directional relay	方向继电器
thermal relay	热继电器，温度继电器，热敏继电器
phase sequence relay	相序继电器
negative sequence relay	负序继电器
zero sequence relay	零序继电器
differential relay	差动继电器
percentage differential relay	比率差动继电器
distance relay	距离继电器
plane impedance relay	平面阻抗继电器
angle impedance relay	角度阻抗继电器
angle admittance relay	角度导纳继电器
Mho relay	姆欧继电器，电导继电器
offset relay	偏置继电器
restricted relay	制约式继电器
pilot relay	控制继电器，辅助继电器
wire pilot relay	有线控制继电器
carrier channel pilot relay	载波控制继电器
microwave pilot relay	微波控制继电器
transductor relay	饱和电抗型继电器
rectifier bridge relay	整流桥型继电器
electronic relay	电子继电器

Notes

1. However, if due to any reason, say a fault, there is an abnormality, it is necessary that there should be a device which senses these abnormal conditions and if so, the element or component where such an abnormality has taken place is removed, i.e. deleted from the rest of the system as soon as possible.

   然而，由于任何原因，比如说故障，出现非正常运行状态，有必要采用一个装置来感知这种非正常状态，然后这种出现非正常状态的元件可以被切除，也就是说，尽可能快地将该元件与系统其他部分相隔离。

2. The protective relay is a sensing device, which senses the fault, determines its location and then send command to the proper circuit breaker by closing its trip coil.

   保护继电器是一个感知装置，它感知故障、确定故障的位置，并且通过闭合相应断路器的跳闸线圈来发出跳闸命令。

简　　历 (Resume)

简历是个人经历的文字记载。撰写个人简历是为了一定的目的，向特定的读者或机构介绍个人的有关情况，如申请攻读学位或求职等均须递交申请信、推荐信和简历。

简历写作要求做到实事求是，简明扼要，语言正确，格式规范。简历的内容和篇幅因人、因事及个人资历而异，一个较为完整的简历大体包括：个人情况，教育状况，工作经历，著作和论文出版与发表情况，所参加的学术团体，推荐人等项目。作者可根据实际需要取舍或增添，有重点地突出有关的内容。

1. 个人情况（Personal）

个人情况通常包括姓名、性别、出身年月、出生日期、国籍、婚姻状态、配偶资料、健康状况、常驻地址、通信地址、电话及电子信箱等内容。有时还需写明个人身高、体重以及爱好等。

2. 教育状况（Education）

教育状况主要写明何地何校毕业、何时何处被授予何种学位。若为获得学位，最好注明所学主要科目。根据需要，还应当写明自己的外语程度。编写顺序一般最高学历或最近学历先写，时间安排成倒叙的顺序。

3. 工作经历（Experience）

工作经历可写成 Experience，还可视具体情况写成 working Experience，Research Experience，Teaching Experience，Professional Experience，Employment 等。工作经历一般应包括工作单位、工作时间、工作内容、工作成效以及担任的职务等。叙述的顺序也可按由近及远的倒序方法。

4. 出版物（Publication）

出版物可包括个人的著作、论文。若有著作，以 Books 为题列出书籍的名称、出版机构、出版年份、总页数等。论文另立一项 Papers，列出主要论文的作者（包括合作者）、标题、刊名、刊期、页码等。翻译的文献以 Translation 为题列出。出版物的书写体例一般按写作参考文献的规定。出版物一般按时间顺序由远及近。

下面举一个例子。

RESUME

PERSONAL

Name: Zhang Feng

Address: 182 North jianshe Road, Shanxi 030013, The People's Republic of China

Telephone: (0351) 2646301

Email: zhangfeng123@sina.com

Date of Birth: July 15, 1964

Place of Birth: Taiyuan, Shanxi Province, China

Nationality: Chinese

Sex: Male

Marital Status: Married with one child

Health: Excellent

Hobbies: Violin and Football

EDUCATION

1990~1993　　Zhejiang University; M.S.E. Research Direction for Electric Power System and Automation

1981~1985　　Tianjin University, B.E.E Major in Electrical Engineering and Automation

1979~1981　　Taiyuan No.10 Middle School, Senior High School

1976~1979　　Taiyuan No.10 Middle School, Junior High School

WORK EXPERIENCE

1993~present　　Shanxi Electric Power Research Institute, High-level Electrical Engineer

1985~1990　　Shanxi Electric Power Transmission and Transformation Engineering Company; Electrical Engineer.

REFERENCE

Available on request

Exercises

I. Choose the best answer into the blank

1. The protective relay disconnects faulted elements in a power system by _____.

　　A. determining its location　　　　　　B. acting as a brain

　　C. tripping the proper circuit breakers　　D. sensing the fault

2. When the trip coil of a circuit breaker is excited by a protective relay, the circuit breaker is _____.

　　A. switched on　　　　　　　　　　B. switched off

　　C. connected to a fault element　　　　D. turned on

3. Any protection scheme consists basically of _____.

　　A. two elements　　B. three elements　　C. four elements　　D. five elements

4. The _____ of a protective relay is that it must operate correctly if there is a fault and must not operate if there is no fault.

A. sensitivity   B. selectivity   C. rapidity   D. reliability

5. The protective scheme that senses zero sequence current and operates as necessary is called as _____.

A. overcurrent protection   B. zero sequence protection

C. negative sequence protection   D. directional protection

II. Answer the following questions according to the text

1. What is the main function of the protection system in a power system?

2. Why is the protective relay analogized to a brain in protective schemes?

3. What requirements must be satisfied for protective relay?

4. Why is the computer-based relaying scheme widely used in modern power systems?

III. Translate the following into Chinese

The relays used for power system protection are usually divided into two groups: (i) primary relays, (ii) backup relays, according to their roles in the overall system protection.

The primary relays are the first line of defense. They sense the fault and, if it exists, send the signal to the proper circuit breaker by closing its trip coil and hence clear the fault. The fault may not be cleared if the relay maloperation or the circuit breaker fails to operate. The causes of failure in the circuit breaker are either failure of supply to its trip coil or a struck mechanical lever. The failures in protective relay are because of wrong setting of the relay, bad contacts or open circuit in the relay coil. In such cases, the backup relays are used as the second line of defense. They have longer operating time even though they sense the fault along with the primary relays. Relay operating time is defined as the time interval between sensing of fault by the relay and sending the trip signal to the proper circuit breaker. Backup relays are arranged in two ways, viz. they may be located at the same place as the primary relay, i.e. local backup and operate the same breaker. In the other case, they are located different stations, i.e. remote backup, and operate different circuit breaker. The remote backup is preferred because it is more reliable even though it disconnects a longer section of the line. In order to attain the desired reliability, the power system network is divided into different protection zones.

Section 2   Faults and Their Damages on Power Systems

Faults on Transmission Lines

Because transmission lines are exposed to lightning and other atmospheric hazards, faults on them occur more frequently than those in apparatus. The types of faults taking place on a transmission line are listed, in the order of severity, as following:

（1） 3-ϕ fault (LLL fault) or 3-ϕ to ground fault (LLLG fault) with or without fault impedance. This fault which is most severe but least common is only one in number.

（2）Double line to ground (LLG) fault with or without fault impedance. This fault is less severe but more common than 3-φ fault. However, this type of faults are three in number.

（3）Line to line (LL) fault. This fault is more common but less severe than the above faults. These faults are also three in number.

（4）Single line to ground (LG) fault. This fault is the least severe but the most common one. These faults are also three in number.

From the above, we conclude that there are four types of faults which are ten in number. The first three faults such as LLL or LLLG, LLG and LL faults involving two or more phases are known as phase fault while the fourth fault, namely, LG fault, is called ground fault. All of the line faults will bring the system into abnormal operating conditions, and may damage electrical equipment. Therefore, the faulty lines must be isolated from the system by protection relays.

Faults in Synchronous Machines

Generators are subjected to varieties of possible hazards when they are in operation. The possible hazards or faults which may occur in a synchronous generator can broadly be classified into two categories: (i) internal faults within the generator, (ii) abnormal operating and/or abnormal system conditions caused by external faults. Internal faults of a generator mainly include stator faults and rotor faults.

Stator Faults—Within the stator winding, faults can occur due to failure of insulation (i.e. dielectric) and open circuit of conductor. Failure of insulation can lead to the short circuit between: (i) two or more phases, (ii) phase and core, (iii) two or more turns of the same phase (i.e. interturn fault).

Failure of insulation can occur due to overvoltage, overheating caused by unbalanced loading, by overloading, by ventilation troubles, and by improper cooling of lubrication oil. It may also be caused by conductor movement due to forces exerted by short circuit currents or out of step operation. The most common fault in the stator winding is ground fault; about 85% of the faults are phase to ground faults in any generator winding. Phase to ground fault if persists may lead to phase to phase fault and even to phase-phase-phase fault (three-phase short circuit), which is the most severe fault though least common. The cause of overvoltage which ultimately results into failure of insulation can be due to overspeed of the prime mover, or due to defective voltage regulator; however, these days governors and voltage regulators act very fast and prevent any damage to the winding insulation.

Rotor Faults—In the rotor winding also failure of insulation between field winding and core or two or more turns can occur. These faults may ultimately result in unbalanced currents and heating of the rotor. If the rotor is ungrounded, first earth fault does not show any effect but a second earth fault increases the current in the affected portion of winding which may cause distortion and permanent damage. It is advisable to open the field circuit breaker even with single earth fault to avoid second earth fault so as to prevent local heating.

Abnormal operating conditions / miscellaneous faults—There are a number of abnormal conditions which do not occur in the stator or rotor winding, but are undesirable since they can damage the generator. Each of these conditions is discussed in the following.

（1）Loss of synchronism. This condition can occur either due to loss of field excitation or governor becomes defective. During out of step condition, as the swing angle between the generated voltage of the machine and that of other units in the system changes, the current in any such unit varies in magnitude. The current surges that result are cyclical in nature, their frequency being a function of reactive rate of slip of the poles in the machine. The resulted high peak currents and off-frequency operation can cause winding stresses, and pulsating torques which can excite mechanical resonances that can be potentially damaging to the generator and to the shifts. Thus generator should be tripped without any delay within the first slip cycle to avoid any major damage.

（2）Overspeed. The cause of overspeed is sudden loss of a very large load; sometimes this happens due to tripping of circuit breaker near the generator end. In the case of steam turbine, the steam can be shut off immediately but in case of hydro turbine, the water flow cannot be stopped quickly, due to the mechanical and hydraulic inertia. The governor controls the over speeding so as to avoid any high voltage, high frequency and mechanical damage to the generators. The setting of an overspeed rating may be 115% for steam turbines and 140% for hydro-turbines.

（3）Motoring. In a multi-generator system, when prime mover fails to provide required speed, the generator may act as a motor, drawing power from the system, instead of supplying power. Generally motoring is prevented by sensitive reverse power relay which operates on about 0.5% reverse power.

（4）Underspeed. Due to failure of steam or water supply to the prime mover, the speed of the generator will reduce and if the reverse power relay fails, then underspeed and/or underfrequency relay comes into picture and trips the circuit breaker.

（5）Loss of excitation. Excitation failure may be caused by a faulty field circuit breaker or failure of the exciter. It can be detected by an undercurrent dc relay. Due to failure of excitation, the synchronous generator may act as an induction generator thereby absorbing reactive power (i.e. sink of reactive power). Turbine generator tends to overheat the rotor and the slot wedges under these conditions because of heavy currents induced in these parts and sometimes arcing occurs at metal wedges in the slots.

（6）Overvoltage. This may be caused due to overspeed or overexcitation when speed governor or voltage regulator fails to act as desired.

（7）Stator overheating. Overheating may occur due to bearing failure, overloading, inadequate lubrication, or improper cooling of lubricating oil, etc. Overheating affects the dielectric strength of insulation.

（8）External faults. Whenever abnormal conditions occur beyond the generator protection zone, the generator is also affected since the very source of power to the external fault is the generator itself. These conditions can be detected by the magnitude of negative sequence current, second harmonic current in field current and line overcurrent relay.

New Words and Expressions

3-ϕ fault   三相故障

3-φ to ground fault	三相接地短路故障
double line to ground fault	两相短路接地故障
line to line fault	相间短路故障
single line to ground fault	单相接地故障
ground fault	接地故障
internal fault	内部故障
external fault	外部故障
interturn fault	匝间故障
overvoltage	n. 过电压
overheat	v. 过热，使过热
overheating	n. 过热，超温
lubrication oil	润滑油
out of step	失步
overspeed	n.; v.; a. 超速，过速，超转速，过速的
miscellaneous	a. 杂的，杂项的，各种的；n. 其他
resonance	n. 谐振，共振
trip	v. （使）断开，（使）跳闸，切断，关闭
mechanical resonance	机械共振
hydro turbine	水轮机
inertia	n. 惯性，惯量
undercurrent	n. 欠电流，电流不足；a. 欠电流的，低电流的
arcing	n. 飞弧，发弧，弧击穿
overexcitation	n. 过励

Notes

The resulted high peak currents and off-frequency operation can cause winding stresses, and pulsating torques which can excite mechanical resonances that can be potentially damaging to the generator and to the shifts.

所产生的峰值很高的电流和异步运行可在绕组中引起过度的应力，并产生可能激发机械共振的脉动转矩，而这种共振可能破坏发电机和它的轴系。该句中"off-frequency"的含义为"异步的、非同步的"。

商 务 信 函

　　商务信函是商务贸易活动过程中信息交流、传递的重要媒介。随着对外交流和对外商务贸易活动的增多，掌握商务信函的写作是非常必要的。

　　在格式上和写作要求上与社交信函相差较大。常用的商业信函格式有两种：齐头式和混合式。其中齐头式较为方便，因而也最流行。使用齐头式一般省略除正文以外所有的标点符号。混合式的日期可放在右边，事由可居中，结束敬语居右或居中，其他与齐头式相同。下面所列为齐头式格式。

CENTRE ELECTRICAL APPLIANCES CO., LTD
FOREIGN TRADE MANSION
269 SICHUAN ROAD
（信头）

4 May 2002   （日期）
Our ref: C/125   （查考号码）
John S. Waters President
XYZ Inc
890 Broadway
Metropolis NY 112211   （信内地址）

Dear Mr. Waters   （称呼）
Re: Block left   （事由）

Business letters are increasingly entirely "flush left" or "block left". All the lines begin at the left-hand typing margin, with no indentation at all. There are no tabs for paragraph indents, for date indents, or for signature/title indents.

_____

_____ （正文）

Sincerely yours   （结束敬语）
（Signature）   （签名）

Encl.   （附件）
C.C.   （抄送副本）
P.S.   （附言）

在写商业信函时，需要注意以下几点。

（1）查考号码项。用于经常通信的双方，对来往信函进行编号，便于整理和查找。

（2）信内地址项。如果信是写给某一机构的某一部门，信内地址应按照机构全名、部门名称、详细地址这一顺序逐行书写。如：

Electric Power Research Institute of China

Distribution System Department

15 Xiaoying Road

Beijing 100085

如果是写给个人，书写的顺序是：Mr.（或 Mrs., Miss, Ms）加上对方全名，对方职称或职务、所在公司或机构名称，详细地址。如：

Mr. Zhang Wei

General Manager

Taiyuan Power Supply Company

113 Bingzhou Road

Taiyuan 030020

（3）事由项。是用几个词来简明扼要地概括信文内容。一般事由写在称呼下面两个行距处，与称呼排齐。一般要大写名词的第一个字母，由"Subject:"或"Re:"引出，并下划线以区别于其他文字。近来英美商人趋向于只写标题，并下划线，省略 "Subject:" 或 "Re:"。

（4）信的正文。商务信无论从内容还是语气上都应正规而严肃，但近年来国外的商务信函却发展的日趋口语化。有的商务信像电报一样简短，有的则较长，语气也较亲切。

（5）结束敬语。商务信函的结束敬语比较单一，变化不多。常用 Yours sincerely (Sincerely yours), Yours faithfully (Faithfully yours), Yours truly (Truly yours)。

Exercises

I. Choose the best answer into the blank

1. At the fault point in electrical equipment, there may be _____.

　　A. arcing　　　　　　　　　　　　B. high temperatures

　　C. destructive mechanical forces　　D. all of the above

2. Among the following faults on a transmission line, the most severe one is usually the _____.

　　A. 3-ϕ fault　　　　　　　　　　　B. double line to ground fault

　　C. line to line fault　　　　　　　　D. single line to ground fault

3. Among the following faults on a transmission line, the most common one is the _____.

　　A. 3-ϕ fault　　　　　　　　　　　B. double line to ground fault

　　C. line to line fault　　　　　　　　D. single line to ground fault

4. The most common fault in the generator's stator winding is _____.

　　A. three-phase short circuit fault　　B. phase to ground fault

　　C. phase to phase fault　　　　　　　D. interturn fault

5. If generator overspeed occurs in a thermal power plant, the action most possibly undertaken is _____.

　　A. to shut off the steam　　　　　　B. to stop the water flow

　　C. to trip the terminal circuit break　D. to shed the load

II. Answer the following questions according to the text

1. Why do faults more frequently occur on transmission lines?

2. What fault types belong to ground fault?

3. What hazards may overvoltage bring to a synchronous generator?

4. How many fault categories can broadly be classified into in a synchronous generator? What are they?

5. What problems may loss of excitation bring to a synchronous generator?

III. Translate the following into Chinese

　　All cases of abnormal operation such as faults in a transformer can be broadly divided into two categories: (i) external faults, (ii) internal faults. External faults include problems like short duration overloading, short circuits external to the transformer, etc. .Internal faults may be grouped into 3 categories: (i) incipient faults, (ii) terminal faults, (iii) winding faults.

　　Incipient faults are those faults, which are initially minor in nature and of no immediate hazard but which could grow slowly into major faults if left unattended, thus causing damage to the transformer. Examples of such faults are:

（1）Core faults due to breakdown of insulation of lamination, of bolts or of clamping rings, causing limited arcing inside oil.

（2）Poor electrical connection of conductors.

（3）Coolant failure i.e. failure of cooling arrangement.

（4）Improper oil flow, loss or blockage of oil causing development of local hot spots.

（5）Regulator failure and improper load sharing between transformers operating in parallel, causing circulating current.

Terminal faults include the following: (i) phase to phase fault on H.V. or L.V. terminals, (ii) phase to earth fault on H.V. or L.V. terminals, (iii) three phase faults on H.V. or L.V. terminals.

Winding faults are as follows: (i) phase to phase fault on H.V. or L.V. windings, (ii) phase to earth fault on H.V. or L.V. windings, (iii) short circuit between turns of H.V. windings or L.V. windings, (iv) short circuit between turns of tertiary windings, (v) earth fault on tertiary windings.

Section 3   Circuit Breakers

A circuit breaker is a mechanical switching device capable of making, and breaking currents under normal circuit conditions and also making, carrying for a specified time, and breaking currents under specified abnormal conditions such as those of short circuit. The medium in which circuit interruption is performed may be designated by a suitable prefix, for example, air-blast circuit breaker, oil circuit breaker. The circuit breakers currently in use can be classified into the following categories according to the arc-quenching principles: air switches, oil circuit breakers, minimum-oil circuit breakers, air-blast circuit breakers, the magnetic air circuit breakers, SF_6 circuit breakers and vacuum circuit breakers. They are rated by voltage, insulation level, current, interrupting capabilities, transient recovery voltage, interrupting time, and trip delay. The nameplate on a circuit breaker usually indicates: (i) the maximum steady-state current it can carry, (ii) the maximum interrupting current, (iii) the maximum line voltage, (iv) the interrupting time in cycles. The interrupting time may last from 3 to 8 cycles on a 60 Hz system. To interrupt large currents quickly, we have to ensure rapid cooling. High-speed interruption limits the damage to transmission lines and equipment and, equally important, it helps to maintain the stability of the system whenever a contingency occurs. The main parts of a circuit breaker are usually: arc-quenching chamber (or interrupter with moving and fixed contacts), operating mechanism and supporting structures.

Air Switches—With increasing currents and voltages, spring-action driving mechanisms were developed to reduce contact burning by faster-opening operation. Later, main contacts were fitted with arcing contacts of special material and shape, which opened after and closed before the main contacts. Further improvements of the air switch were the brush-type contact with a wiping and cleaning function, the insulating barrier leading to arc chutes, and blowout coils with excellent arc-extinguishing properties. These features, as well as the horn gap contact, are still in use in low voltage as and dc breakers.

Oil Circuit Breaker—Around 1900, in order to cope with the new requirement for "interrupting capacity", AC switches were immersed in a tank of oil. Oil is very effective in quenching the arc and establishing the open break after current zero. Deion grids, oil-blast features, pressure-tight joints and vents, new operating mechanisms, and multiple interrupter were introduced over several decades to make the oil circuit breaker a reliable apparatus for system voltages up to 362kV.

Minimum-Oil Circuit Breaker—These breakers were developed after 1930. They make use of special low-oil-volume interrupting champers of extra—light weight. By means of current-dependent oil streams in different directions and supported by oil injection, the arc is cooled and extinguished effectively. The interrupters are mounted on porcelain or molded-resin supports, thus avoiding oil as an insulating medium to ground. For both oil and minimum-oil circuit breakers, standard transformer oil can be used. Fig.7-1 shows the minimum-oil circuit breakers in a 220kV substation.

Fig.7-1　220kV outdoor minimum-oil circuit breakers

Air-Blast Circuit Breaker—Further increase of system voltages and generating capacities triggered the search for faster and stronger circuit breakers utilizing oilless arc interruption. After 1940, the air-blast circuit breaker was developed, making use of the good insulating and arc-quenching properties of dry and clean compressed air.

The Magnetic Air Circuit Breaker—It uses a combination of a strong magnetic field (coil or soft-iron plates) with a special arc chute to lengthen the arc until the system voltage cannot maintain the arc circuit any longer. This interrupting principle is applied mainly in the distribution voltage range in metal-clad switchgear.

SF_6 Circuit Breaker—The excellent arc quenching and insulating properties of SF_6 gas stimulated this breaker development in the early 1950s. Both live- and dead-tank design were introduced into the 1960s in outdoor circuit breakers from 15 to 800 kV. Dead-tank SF_6 breaker designs were incorporated into gas-insulated substations (GISs) up to 800kV in the 1960s and 1970s. GIS offers space savings and environmental advantages over conventional outdoor substations. The SF_6 breaker provides an alternative to oil and vacuum for metal-clad and metal-enclosed switching up to 38 kV.

Vacuum Circuit Breaker—This has been the most recent advancement in new arc-interrupting and breaker development. Vacuum-bottle interrupters are designed for higher system voltage, current and interrupting ratings. Increased application of vacuum circuit breakers spreads at distribution systems both in metal-clad and metal-enclosed switchgear.

New Words and Expressions

air-blast circuit breaker   压缩空气断路器

oil circuit breaker   油断路器，多油断路器

quench   v.; n. 熄灭，熄弧

arc-quenching   n. 灭弧

minimum-oil circuit breaker   少油断路器

magnetic air circuit breaker   磁吹断路器

SF_6 circuit breaker   六氟化硫（SF_6）断路器

vacuum circuit breaker   真空断路器

interrupting capability   开断容量，遮断容量

deion grid   去电离栅极，灭弧栅

interrupting time   开断时间，遮断时间

nameplate   n. 铭牌

operating mechanism   （断路器的）操动机构

horn gap   角隙，角放电器火花源

horn gap contact   带灭弧功能的触头

air switch   空气开关

spring-action   弹簧动作

spring-action driving mechanism   弹簧操作机构

insulating barrier   绝缘隔板

arc chute   灭弧罩，灭弧隔板，电弧隔板

blowout coil   灭弧线圈，消弧线圈

arc-extinguishing   a. 灭弧的，消弧的

molded-resin   模制树脂，浇铸树脂

trigger   n. 触发，起动；v. 触发，起动，激发，引起

outdoor   a. 户外的

live-tank   带电箱体

dead-tank   接地箱体

gas-insulated substations (GISs)   气体绝缘变电站

vacuum-bottle   n. 真空罐

switchgear   n. 开关设备，配电设备，配电装置

Notes

The circuit breakers currently in use can be classified into the following categories according to the arc-quenching principles: air switches, oil circuit breakers, minimum-oil circuit breakers, air-blast circuit breakers, the magnetic air circuit breakers, SF_6 circuit breakers and vacuum circuit breakers.

根据断路器的灭弧原理，当前使用的断路器可以归纳为如下几类：空气开关、多油断路器、少

油断路器、压缩空气断路器、磁吹断路器、六氟化硫断路器和真空断路器。

产 品 技 术 说 明 书

　　产品说明书是生产单位向用户介绍产品的特点、性能、用途、使用、保养维修等的文字说明。主要是让用户了解、熟悉产品，所以产品说明书要求语言平实、简洁、准确、条理分明，注重内容的科学性和实用性。

　　产品说明书从结构上讲一般由标题、前言、正文、落款等部分组成。

　　（1）标题一般采用产品名称，或产品名称加文种（"说明书"或"使用说明书"），例如：

　　　　Pressure Relief Device Service Manual

　　（2）前言也称概述。用简练的语言概括介绍产品的主要特点，适用范围等。

　　（3）正文，是产品说明书的主体部分，一般包括以下几方面的内容：

　　1）产品的研究、开发及制作工艺；

　　2）产品的性质、性能、特征、特点等；

　　3）产品的适用范围和用途等；

　　4）产品的安装及使用方法；

　　5）产品的保养、维修方法及注意事项等；

　　6）产品的工作原理、主要技术指标等。

　　根据不同的产品，产品说明书的内容也各有侧重。

　　产品说明书正文的写作形式多种多样，有条文式、表格式等，使用的说明方法也有很多，可以采用定义说明、图表说明、分类说明、数字说明等说明方法。

　　对于内容较为复杂的产品说明书，常印成小册子或手册，由封面、目录、前言、正文、封底及插图等组成。

Exercises

I. Choose the best answer into the blank

1. The use of transformer oil in a minimum-oil circuit breaker is ＿＿＿＿＿.

　　A. to quench the arc and establish an insulated break between the contacts

　　B. to quench the arc and build insulation between the arc-quenching chamber and ground

　　C. to establish an insulated break between the contacts and build insulation between the arc-quenching chamber and ground

　　D. to protect the circuit breaker from firing

2. A circuit breaker mainly consists of ＿＿＿＿＿ parts.

　　A. two　　　　　　B. three　　　　　　C. four　　　　　　D. five

3. The air-blast circuit breaker makes use the arc-quenching properties of ＿＿＿＿＿.

　　A. transformer oil　　　　　　　　B. a strong magnetic field

　　C. SF_6　　　　　　　　　　　　　D. dry and clean compressed air

4. The reason that the SF_6 circuit breaker is widely used is _____ properties of SF_6.

   A. the arc quenching　　　　　　　　B. the excellent insulating

   C. the space saving　　　　　　　　　D. the excellent arc quenching and insulating

5. Vacuum-bottle interrupters are designed for _____.

   A. the higher voltage system　　　　　B. the low voltage distribution system

   C. higher system voltage, current　　　D. 38kV systems

II. Answer the following questions according to the text

1. How many kinds can circuit breakers be classified into according to their arc-quenching medium?

2. What rated quantities are included on the nameplate of a circuit breaker?

3. What are the main parts of a circuit breaker?

4. Why are SF6 circuit breakers widely used in power systems recently?

5. What properties do the air-blast circuit breakers make use of?

III. Translate the following into Chinese

A fuse is a device that, by the fusion of one or more of its specially designed and proportioned components, opens the circuit in which it is inserted and breaks the current when this exceeds a given value for a sufficient time. A fuse consists of a fuse-holder (which comprises a fuse and a fuse carrier) and a fuselink. A fuselink is a device comprising a fuse element or several fuse elements connected in parallel enclosed in a cartridge, usually filled with an arc-extinguishing medium and connected to terminations, the fuselink is the part of a fuse which requires replacing after the fuse has operated.

The powder-filled fuse is the most advanced type of fuselink, with great advantages in limitation of short circuit currents and very high breaking capacity. 'Miniature fuses' are used in electronic and similar apparatus, and 'semi-closed fuses' are the rewirable type still extensively used in consumer units and other applications where only limited breaking capacity is required.

Other types of fuse, such as the liquid-quenched and the expulsion fuse, which employ some mechanical feature to assist the circuit-breaking process, are available. These are used mainly for high voltage overhead-line networks.

The fuse is a weak link in a circuit, and, as such, possesses one important advantage over mechanical interrupting devices such as circuit breakers. Because the element in the fuse is of much smaller cross-sectional area than the cable it protects (assuming, of course, that they are of the same material) the element will reach its melting point before the cable. The larger the current the quicker the element melts. If deterioration of the element should occur it operates even faster; a fuse is therefore a device that "fails safe". A comparison of the modern fuse with mechanical interrupters shows that the fuse has one outstanding property not possessed by the latter, namely the ability to interrupt very large currents in a much shorter time —so short in fact that the current will be "cut off" before it reaches its peak value. Serious overheating and electromagnetic forces in the system will thus be avoided. It is not unusual for a fuse to be used as "back-up" protection for a circuit-breaker that might, by itself, have inadequate breaking capacity. In addition the sealed cartridge fuse is silent in operation and does not emit flame. Being sealed, it is tamper-proof and with fuse elements of, say silver, it is non-deteriorating and gives a consistent and reliable performance.

Section 4   Distance Protection

When faults occur on a power transmission line, a protection system is required to isolate the faulted transmission line. To guarantee reliable and quick isolation of the faulted line, several protection systems with different principles are usually employed to protect one transmission line. Among them, distance protection system is one of the most important protections applied for transmission lines.

The operation of distance protection depends on the basic fact that on the occurrence of a fault, the distance between any point in the power system and the fault is proportional to the ratio of voltage to current at the point. In an interconnected network in which there may be a number of power stations, the voltage-to-current ratio is a maximum at the power station and decreases along the various feeders to the fault where it is almost zero. Relays responding to this voltage/current ratio can therefore be used at various points on the system to give a measure of the distance or length of the line to the fault. By arranging the relays such that those nearest to the fault operate quicker than those at a farther distance, discriminative tripping of the circuit breakers controlling the various feeders can be obtained. Usually, a 3-zone distance protection schemes is employed for transmission line protection.

Standard 3-zone Protection The conventional distance relaying uses three distance measuring units (physically separate units or one unit for first and second zones with a timing unit to increase the reach of the former and a second unit for the third zone). The first zone unit which is set to cover usually between 80% and 90% of the first section, is an instantaneous high speed relay while the second zone unit which is set to cover about 25% of the second section and the third zone unit which is set to cover up to the end of the second section are time-delayed relays. The time delays T_2 and T_3 for the second and third zones, respectively, are provided by a separate timer relay. Setting in the first zone for less than 100% of the length is made to avoid overreach of the relay into adjacent section. The overreach would occur because of the following: (i) Transient overreach of the relay, (ii) Errors in the relay, (iii) Errors in the current transformers (CTs) and voltage transformers (VTs), (iv) Errors in the data on which the impedance settings are made.

The main object of the second zone unit is to provide protection to the end zone of the first section and also to give remote back-up to the next section up to about 25% of its length. It should be adjusted such that it will be able to operate even for arcing faults at the end of the first section. Also the tendency to underreach by the relay due to the effect of intermediate current sources and the other errors as mentioned above, should be taken into account. The time delay (T_2) with the second zone unit is normally between 0.2 and 0.5s.

The third zone unit provides backup protection (remote) for faults in the adjoining line sections. As far as possible its reach should extend beyond the end of the largest adjoining line section under conditions that cause the maximum amount of underreach, namely arcs and intermediate current sources. The third zone time delay (T_3) is usually between 0.4 and 1.0s.

In many cases, where the consecutive line sections differ very much in length, alterations in the above scheme, in the number of steps or time delays, may be necessary to give optimum selectivity and protection.

A schematic diagram of a 3-zone protection scheme is given by Fig.7-2.

Distance Protection requirements
Three basic features are necessary from distance relays. They are: (i) response to direction, (ii) response to impedance,

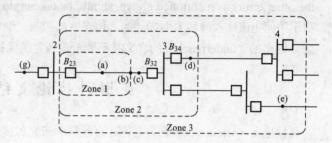

Fig.7-2   Schematic diagram of 3-zone protection

(iii) timing. These features need not necessarily be provided by the separate relay elements but they are fundamental to all distance schemes. As far as the directional and measuring relays are concerned, the actual number required in any scheme is governed by the consideration that in a three phase system, three phase, phase-to-phase, phase-to-earth and double phase-to-earth faults must be taken care of.

It is common practice therefore to provide two separate sets of distance relays, one set for phase faults and the other set for earth faults. These between them cater for three phase and double phase-to-earth faults. Each set of these relays contains three individual relays (one for each pair of phases for phase fault scheme and one for each phase for the earth fault scheme). Each relay again consists of 2 or 3 elements for the three-zone scheme as described earlier. Thus distance protective schemes are inevitably complicated by many relays necessary. These are sometimes reduced by using a single relay for a number of duties (switched distance schemes) but excessive combinations like this will involve intricate selector circuits and may result in delayed operation. Polyphase distance schemes have been developed without any switching, etc.

New Words and Expressions

voltage-to-current ratio	电压电流比
time-delayed relay	延时继电器
timer relay	时间继电器
overreach	v.; n. 越过，伸得过长
current transformer	电流互感器
voltage transformer	电压互感器
remote back-up	远后备
arcing fault	闪络故障
underreach	v.; n. 达不到

backup　　　　　　n. 后备，支持，备份；a. 后备的，备用的，备份的
response　　　　　n. 响应，反应

Notes

Also the tendency to underreach by the relay due to the effect of intermediate current sources and the other errors as mentioned above, should be taken into account.

由于中间电流注入源和上面提到的其他误差的影响，继电器保护区域缩短的可能性也应该被考虑。这里的"underreach"的含义是不能覆盖预定的保护区域。

英语科技论文结构

科技论文（science papers）是论述自然科学研究和技术开发成果的说理性文章。按写作目的可分为学术论文、学位论文、科技报告。按研究性质可分为基础理论研究、试验研究和应用研究等。

科技报告由于内容多，论述详尽，篇幅长，一般单独印刷成册。它基本上由三部分组成，即前部、正文、后部，具体编排顺序如下：

前部

  Front cover 封面

  Title page 扉页

  Letter of transmittal (forwarding letter)提交报告书

  Distribution list 分发范围

  Preface or Foreword 序或前言

  Acknowledgements 致谢

  Abstract 摘要

  Contents 目录

  List of tables 表格目录

  List of illustrations 插图目录

正文

  Introduction 引言

  Main body 论文主体

  Conclusion 结论

后部

  List of references 参考文献

  Appendices 附录

  Table 表

  Graphs 图

  List of abbreviations, signs and symbols 缩写、记号及符号表

  Index 索引

  Back cover 封底

在科技报告中，根据写作内容的不同，前部和后部中的一些项目可以省略，但各项之间的顺序必须遵守。

在科技报告的封面上一般包括以下内容：

Title 标题

Contract or job number 合同或任务编号

Author or Authors 作者

Date of issue 完成日期

Report number and serial number 报告编号及系列编号

Organization responsible for the report 研究单位

Classification notice (confidential, secret ,etc) 密级（机密、保密等）

对于期刊论文，也即我们说的专业学术论文，其结构形式编排如下：

Title 标题

Authors 作者

Organizations and address 作者所在单位与联系地址

Abstract 摘要

Key words 关键词

Introduction 引言

Main body of papers 论文主体

Conclusion or Summary 结论或总结

References 参考文献

Exercises

I. Choose the best answer into the blank

1. The conventional distance relaying uses _____ distance measuring units.

A. one   B. two   C. three   D. four

2. The main objective of the second zone unit is to protect _____ and also to give remote back-up to the next section up to about 25% of its length.

A. the first section wholly   B. the second section wholly

C. the first section partly   D. the third section partly

3. According to the paragraphs, three basic features of distance relays are responding to direction, responding to impedance, and _____.

A. delaying   B. operating   C. complicating   D. timing

4. The distance protection is applied to protect _____.

A. transformers   B. generators   C. transmission lines   D. buses

5. The objective of the third zone unit is to provide _____ for faults in the adjoining line sections.

A. back protection   B. instantaneous high speed protection

C. close back protection   D. current measure

II. Answer the following questions according to the text

1. What is the basic principle of distance protection?

2. What are distance measuring units used in the conventional distance relaying?

3. What is the range of the first zone protection for the first section of a transmission line?

4. How many is usually the third zone time delay?

5. What fault kinds of transmission lines are taken care of in a distance protection system?

III. Translate the following into Chinese

Distance relays responsive to voltage and current are required to operate when the complex impedance Z_L represented by the ratio U/I is less than some predetermined value known as the setting impedance Z_R. The magnitude of Z_R may in some cases depend on the phase angle of Z_R, i.e. the angle between the voltage and current. The operating point of a distance relay is most conveniently defined as some point in the complex impedance plane such that a line drawn from the origin to the point represent a complex impedance of magnitude Z_R and phase angle θ. The locus of this operating point is known as the polar characteristic of the relay.

A fault on a transmission line with a single source is shown in Fig.7-3 (a), the fault area with the effect of the fault resistance on the complex impedance plane is demonstrated by Fig.7-3 (b). The fault resistance (R_f) has two components, the resistance of the arc and the resistance of the earth return path. In the case of interphase faults only the arc is involved, while with earth faults, the resistance of the fault path through the tower, tower footing resistance and earth return should be added to the arc resistance. The arc resistance actually decreases slightly as the fault point approaches the relay location. When the line length is under 15 km or less at the higher voltages the effect of the arc resistance becomes pronounced. The Zone-2 and Zone-3 relays are usually influenced significantly by the arc resistance, and the Zone-1 is almost always unaffected by the arc resistance where the line is not very short.

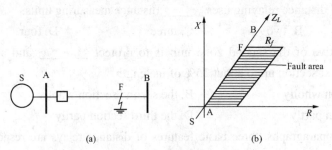

(a)   (b)

Fig.7-3   Arc phenomenon in a fault

Section 5　Lightning Arresters

When lightning strikes a transmission line or the overhead ground wire that shields the line, a very high voltage surge will usually occur on the transmission line. To protect transformers and other electrical apparatus in substation from damaging, a lightning arrester (also called surge arrester) is designed to limit the over-voltage that may occur across them due either to lightning or switching surges. The upper end of the arrester is connected to the line or the terminal of the apparatus that has to be protected, while the lower end is solidly connected to ground. Ideally, a lightning arrester clips any voltage in excess of a specified maximum, by permitting a large current, if need be, to be diverted to ground. In this way the arrester absorbs energy from the incoming surge. The *E-I* characteristic of an ideal lightning arrester is, therefore, a horizontal line whose level corresponds to the maximum permissible surge voltage. In practice the *E-I* characteristic slopes upwards, but is still considered to be reasonably flat.

Some arresters are composed of an external porcelain tube containing an ingenious arrangement of stacked discs, air gaps, ionizers, and coils. The discs (or valve blocks) are composed of a silicon carbide material. The resistance of this material decreases dramatically with increasing voltage.

Under normal voltage conditions, spark gaps prevent the current from flowing through the tubular column. Consequently, the resistance of the arrester is infinite. However, if a serious over-voltage occurs, the spark gaps break down and the surge discharges to ground. The 60Hz follow-through current is limited by the resistance of the valve blocks and the arc is simultaneously stretched and cooled in series of arc chambers. The arc is quickly snuffed out and the arrester is then ready to protect the line against the next voltage surge. The discharge period is very short, rarely lasting more than a fraction of a millisecond.

A more modern type of arrester has valve blocks made of stacked zinc-oxide discs without using any air gaps or other auxiliary devices. Its *E-I* characteristic is similar to that of a silicon carbide arrester, except that it is much flatter and therefore more effecting in diverting surge currents. These metal-oxide varistor (MOV) arresters are widely used today.

Lightning arresters with very flat characteristics also enable us to reduce the BIL (basic impulse insulation level) requirements of apparatus installed in substations. The BIL of a device is its ability to withstand an impulse voltage of extremely short duration. As the BIL rises, we must increase the amount of insulation which, in turn, increases the size and cost of equipment. Therefore, the reduction in BIL significantly reduces the cost of the installed apparatus in HV and EHV systems. Fig.7-4 shows a lightning arrester installed in an EHV substation.

Fig.7-4   MOV lighting arresters protect an EHV transformer

New Words and Expressions

lightning	n. 雷（电），闪电；a. 闪电（般）的
lightning arrester	避雷器
overhead ground wire	架空地线
surge	n.; v. 电[浪]涌，冲击，波动

surge arrester	避雷器
over-voltage	n. 过电压
switching surge	操作冲击，操作浪涌
clip	n. 线夹，接线柱，夹子；v. 夹住，箍，钳牢，固定
ionizer	n. 电离装置，游离装置
silicon carbide	碳化硅，金刚砂
spark gap	火[电]花隙，放电器，避雷器
valve block	阀片
break down	击穿，断裂，破裂
arc chamber	电弧室
zinc-oxide	n.氧化锌
metal-oxide varistor	金属氧化物压敏电阻器
basic impulse insulation level (BIL)	基本冲击绝缘水平

Notes

1. HV	high voltage	高电压，或高压
2. EHV	extra high voltage	超高压

学术论文写作（一）——论文标题

　　论文标题一般应对称地写在文章首行的正中央，不宜过长（一般不超过两行）。如果题目过长，一行之内排不开，则可排成倒金字塔状，但是，词或短语不要分开写。标题中，除介词、连词外，每个词的词首需大写，也有些学术会议论文集的论文标题的所有字母都大写。

　　标题是论文的总纲，以表明论文的中心内容及意义。要求论文标题要简单明了，力戒冗长累赘。一般采用各种名词性结构，即中心词（名词）+修饰语（介词短语、分词短语、不定式短语等），例如：

An Adaptive Fuzzy Logic Power System stabilizer

A Digital Processor of Neural Networks

A Constant-Power Battery Charger with Inherent Soft Switching and Power Factor Correction

Improved small-signal analysis for the phase-shifted PWM power converter

Application of the Principle of Phase Comparison of Fault Component to Transformer Protection.

To Apply (Applying) the Principle of Phase Comparison of Fault Component to Transformer Protection.

　　论文标题中，有些冠词可以省略，例如：

Summary on Development of Switched Reluctance Machine　开关磁阻电机发展综述（在Summary 前省略了定冠词 The）。

　　在论文标题中常出现的词汇归纳如下：

summary（综述），development（发展），application（应用），comparison（比较），study

（研究），research（研究），experimental research（实验研究），application research（应用研究），design（设计），analysis（分析），method（方法），principle（原则），investigation（调查），discussion（讨论）。

Exercises

I. Choose the best answer into the blank

1. Lightning arresters with very flat characteristics may reduce requirements to _____ of apparatus installed in substations.

   A. the supporting structure   B. the arc chamber

   C. the protection system   D. the basic impulse insulation level

2. The objective of a lightning arrester is to limit _____.

   A. the over-voltage   B. the over-current

   C. the overload   D. the low-voltage

3. The resistance of a silicon carbide material _____ with decreasing voltage.

   A. decreases   B. increases   C. keeps constant   D. does not change

4. Under normal voltage conditions, the resistance of the arrester is ideally _____.

   A. infinite   B. smaller   C. zero   D. changeable

5. The increasing in BIL _____ the cost of the installed apparatus in HV and EHV systems.

   A. reduces   B. increases   C. does not change   D. changes

II. Answer the following questions according to the text

1. How is the lightning arrester connected to a power system?

2. What is the principle of the lightning arrester?

3. What is the property of the valve blocks that are composed of a silicon carbide material?

4. Why are the metal-oxide varistor arresters used more widely than the silicon carbide arresters?

III. Translate the following into Chinese

Differential Protection

The general idea involved in the differential protection scheme is to compare the operating quantity (voltage or current) at the input and output ends, i.e. terminal of the equipment being protected. This is a vector comparison since the quantity being compared has the magnitude and the phase angle associated with it. Tripping is initiated if the magnitude of the difference exceeds a pre-determined constant value (i.e. base value).

For a transformer, the differential protection scheme is shown in Fig.7-5. The CTs have been connected at the two sites (i.e. primary and secondary sides) of the transformer and I_1 and I_2 represent the currents on the primary and secondary side. By properly choosing the turn ratios of CTs and reversing its connections to that of the main transformer being protected, CTs secondary currents are made nearly the same during normal load conditions or external faults. However, during internal fault in the transformer, the current I_1 on the primary side of the transformer will differ from the current I_2 on the secondary in magnitude and/or in phase. The trip signal is given if the vector difference of these currents flowing in the operating coil exceeded in the base value. Hence for tripping

$$|I_1 - I_2| \geqslant k$$

where k is a constant (i.e. base value).

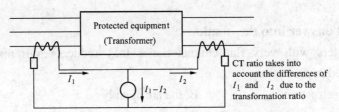

Fig.7-5   The basic unbiased differential connection (only one phase is shown)

Chapter 8　Electric Power Generation

Section 1　Coal-Fired Power Plants

In fossil-fuel power plants, coal, oil, or natural gas is burned in a furnace, the combustion products heat water, converting it to steam, and the steam drives a turbine which is mechanically coupled to an electric power generator. A schematic diagram showing a typical coal-fired power plant is given in Fig.8-1. In very brief outline, the operation of the plant is as follows. Coal is taken from storage and fed to a pulverizer (or a mill), mixed with preheated air, and blown into the furnace, where it is burned. The furnace contains a complex of tubes and drums called a *boiler* through which water is pumped, its temperature rising in the process until it evaporates into stream. The steam passes on to the turbine, while the combustion gases (flue gases) are passed through mechanical and electrostatic precipitators which removed upward of 99% of the solid particles (ash) before being released to the chimney or stack.

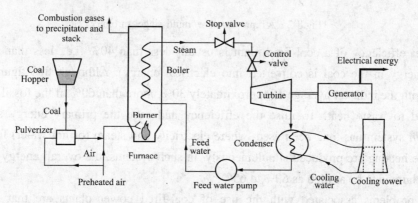

Fig.8-1　Basic principles of a coal-fired power plant

The unit just described, with pulverized coal, air, and water as an input and steam as a useful output, is variously called a steam generating unit, or furnace, or boiler. When the combustion process is under consideration the term *furnace* is usually used, while the term *boiler* is more frequently used when the water-steam cycle is consideration. The steam, at a typical pressure of 3500 psi and a temperature of 1050°F, is supplied through control and stop (shutoff) valves to the steam turbine. The thermal energy of the steam is converted into mechanical energy by the turbine. The exhaust steam from the turbine is cooled in a heat exchanger called condenser, and as feed-water, is pumped back to the boiler again. The control valve permits the output of the turbine-generator unit (turbogenerator) to be varied by adjusting steam flow. The stop valve has a protective function; it is normally fully open but can be "tripped" shut to prevent overspeed of the turbine-generator unit if the electrical output drops suddenly (due to circuit-breaker action) and the control valve does not close.

Fig.8-1 suggests a "single-stage" turbine, but in practice a more complex "multi-stage" arrangement is used to achieve relatively higher thermal efficiencies. The schematic diagram of a representative "multi-stage" arrangement is given in Fig.8-2. Here four turbines with different steam pressures are mechanically coupled in tandem. In routine outline, high-pressure steam from the boiler (superheater) enters the high-pressure (HP) turbine. Upon leaving the HP turbine it is returned to a section of the boiler (reheater) and then directed to the intermediate-pressure (IP) turbine. Leaving the IP turbine, steam (at lower pressure and much expended) is directed to the low-pressure (LP) turbines. The exhaust steam from the LP turbines is cooled in a condenser, and as feed-water, is reheated (with steam extracted from the turbines) and pumped back to the boiler.

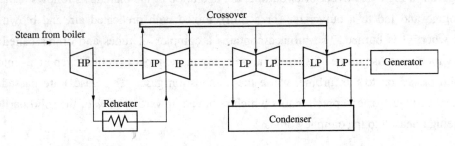

Fig.8-2　A representative "multi-stage" turbine

The net efficiency of a coal-fired plant is usually less than 40% (i.e., less than 40% of the chemical energy in the coal is converted into electrical energy). Although this figure compares favorably with the industry average of approximately 30%, more than 60% of the fossil-fuel energy is converted to waste heat! To raise the efficiency and save the primary energy sources, the *cogeneration* system has long been used, where electricity and steam (or hot water) for industrial use or space heating are produced simultaneously. In such systems, the overall energy efficiencies have been claimed to be as high as 60% to 65%.

Some problems associated with the use of coal-fired power plants are that mining and transportation of coal present safety hazards and other social costs. Coal-fired plants share environmental problems with some other types of fossil-fuel plants: these include "acid rain" and the "greenhouse" effect.

New Words and Expressions

coal-fired	a.	燃煤的
furnace	n.	炉，炉膛，燃烧室
pulverizer	n.	磨煤机，粉煤机
preheated	a.	预热的
boiler	n.	锅炉，蒸发器，蒸汽发生器
flue gas		烟气，废气，排烟
electrostatic	a.	静电的
precipitator	n.	除尘器

electrostatic precipitator	电除尘
chimney	n.（高）烟囱，烟筒
coal hopper	煤斗
burner	n. 燃烧器，喷燃器
cooling tower	冷却塔
feed water pump	给水泵
psi	磅/平方英寸（压强单位）
shutoff	n. 关闭，切断，断路
exhaust steam	乏汽
heater exchanger	热交换器
condenser	n. 凝结器，冷凝器
feed-water	给水
turbogenerator	n. 涡轮发电机
single-stage turbine	单级汽轮机
thermal efficiency	热效率
multi-stage turbine	多级汽轮机
tandem	a.; ad. 级联（的），串联的，前后排列的；n. 前后排列使用的一组事物
in tandem	前后地，协力地，相互合作地
superheater	n. 过热器
high-pressure turbine	高压汽轮机
reheater	n. 再热器
intermediate-pressure turbine	中压汽轮机
low-pressure turbine	低压汽轮机
cogeneration	n. 热电联产，热电联供
acid rain	酸雨
greenhouse effect	温室效应

学术论文写作（二）——论文作者姓名、单位与联系地址

论文作者姓名写在论文标题的正下方中央处。根据在研究中或论文主要工作中的作用大小，对作者进行排名，第一作者的姓名排在最前面。外国作者的姓写在名字的后面，对于中国作者的姓可写在名字的前面，也可写在名字的后面，视具体要求而定；姓和名的首写字母都要大写；名字中的两个字之间可以用破折号隔开，或直接连写。作者的姓与名之间需空一格，作者之间也需空一格。

单位与联系地址写在作者下方，按作者顺序尽可能与作者位置对齐。先写作者所在单位，后写联系地址，也可二者合一。对于具有多层次关系的单位，按先小单位后大单位的次序书写，例如：

Dept. of Electr. Power Eng., Xian Jiaotong Univ., Shanxi, China

Department of Electric Power Engineering, Project College of Shanxi University, Shanxi, China

Electr. Power & Power Electron. Center, Illinois Inst. of Technol., Chicago, IL, USA

Dept. of Autom., Tsinghua Univ., Beijing, China

由上面的例子可以看出，为了缩短书写的长度，尽可能采用缩略形式。

下面几个例子包括了标题、作者姓名、单位与地址：

例1（选自 IEEE TRANSACTIONS ON POWER DELIVERY, VOL. 17, NO. 4, OCTOBER 2002）

Three-Phase-to-Four-Phase Transformer for Four-Phase Power-Transmission Systems

Liu Guangye[1]   Yang Yihan[2]

1 Hunan University, Changsha, Hunan, China.
2 North China Electric Power University, Beijing, China.

例2（摘自 IEEE TRANSACTIONS ON POWER SYSTEMS, VOL. 18, NO. 1, FEBRUARY 2003）

Purchase Allocation and Demand Bidding in Electric Power Markets

Ya'an Liu[1]   Xiaohong Guan[2]

1 Systems Engineering Institute, SKLMS Lab., Xian Jiaotong University, Shanxi 710049, China.
2 Center for Intelligent and Networked Systems, Tsinghua University, Beijing 10084, China.

例3〔引自 Electric Power Systems Research 65 (2003)〕

Enhancing small signal power system stability by coordinating unified power flow controller with power system stabilizer

Wanliang Fang [a], H.W. Ngan [b],*

a   Department of Electric Power Engineering, Xi'an Jiaotong University, Xi'an, PR China
b   Department of Electrical Engineering, The Hong Kong Polytechnic University, Hong Kong, China

Exercises

I. Choose the best answer into the blank

1. In a coal-fired power plant, an electrostatic precipitator is used to remove _____ from the

combustion gases.

   A. solid particles   B. SO$_2$ C. CO   D. water vapour

2. The thermal energy of the steam is converted into _____ energy by the turbine.

   A. electrical   B. mechanical   C. chemical   D. potential

3. The net efficiency of a coal-fired plant is usually less than _____.

   A. 30%   B. 40%   C. 50%   D. 60%

4. In cogeneration systems, the overall energy efficiencies are raised by _____.

   A. improving the combustion process

   B. providing thermal energy to the customers

   C. raising the steam temperature

   D. reducing SO$_2$ emissions

5. Upon leaving the HP turbine, the steam is returned to the _____ and then directed to the intermed.ate-pressure turbine.

   A. boiler   B. superheater   C. reheater   D. cooling tower

II. Answer the following questions according to the text

1. What is the production process of power generation in a coal-fired power plant?

2. How to process the exhaust steam from the turbine?

3. Why are multi-stage turbines used in some thermal power plants?

4. What is more than 60% of the fossil fuel energy consumed to?

5. What are the advantages of the cogeneration system?

III. Translate the following into Chinese

Basic Process of Power Generation

The basic principle of power generation is to convert mechanical energy from the prime mover into electrical energy by a synchronous generator, as shown in Fig.8-3. The prime mover turns the rotor of the generator in whose stator three (phase) windings are embedded. In the process mechanical power from the prime mover drive is converted to three-phase alternating current at voltages in the range 11 to 30kV line to line at frequency of 50Hz in China or 60 Hz in U.S.A. and some other countries. The electrical energy is then transferred to a transmission system with very high voltages by step-up transformers. The highest voltage level for power transmission on the earth is currently about 1000kV in Russia. The primary sources of electrical energy supplied by generators are the kinetic energy of water and the thermal energy derived from fossil fuels and nuclear fission. The prime movers convert these sources of energy into mechanical energy that is, in turn, converted to electrical energy by synchronous generators. The prime mover governing systems provide a means of controlling power and frequency to maintain stable operation of the generating unit, a function commonly referred to as load –frequency control or automatic generation control.

Power plants are commonly classified, according to the types of the prime energy sources, into the following categories: fossil-fuel power plant, hydropower plant and nuclear power plant, etc.

The main electrical systems from generators to transmission systems in different kinds of power plants are very similar. The only differences are in the structures of the prime movers and the process converting the primary energy to mechanical energy.

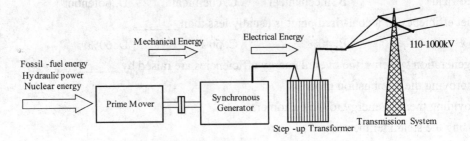

Fig.8-3   General Process of Electric Power Generation

Section 2   Hydropower Plants

Hydropower is an important source of power for electricity generation. In contrast to the thermal power plants, the energy in the hydropower plant is derived from falling water. The power output of such plants is directly related to the product of the flow rate of water, measured in cubic meters per second, the distance through which this water falls, measured by the head in meters, and a suitable constant. The essential elements of the hydroelectric plant thus involve water storage (the dam), a means for delivering the falling water (the penstock), the electric generator, and related auxiliary equipment.

Hydroplants are classified as *high head* (over 100 ft) and *low head*. The head refers to the difference of elevation between the upper reservoir above the turbine and the tail race or discharge point just below the turbine. For very high heads (600 to 6000ft) Pelton wheels or impulse turbines are used; these consist of a bucket wheel rotor with one or more nozzles directed at the periphery. At medium-high heads (120 to 1600ft) Francis turbines are used. These turn on a vertical axis with the water entering through a spiral casing and then inward through adjustable "gates" (i.e., valves) to a "runner" (i.e., turbine wheel) with fixed blades. The low-head Kaplan type turbine is similar but with adjustable blades in the runner. The efficiency of these turbines is fairly high, in the neighborhood of 88% to 93% when operating at their most efficient points.

Fig.8-4 shows a cross section through a hydroelectric plant with a Kaplan turbine. Some of the generator features should be noted. The rotation axis is vertical. With a speed of 144 rpm we should have 50 poles to generate 60 Hz. These poles are mounted on the periphery of a spoked wheel called a *spider*. There is space between the poles to accommodate the pole windings. The rotor called by the descriptive title *salient pole*.

We note a highly desirable feature of hydropower plants: the speed with which they may be started up, brought up to speed, connected to the power network, and "loaded" up. This can be done in under 5 minutes, in contrast to many hours in the case of thermal plants; the job is also much simpler and adaptable to remote control. The hydropower is well suited for turning on and off at a dispatcher's command to meet changing power needs. We note that when water is in short supply, it is desirable to use the limited available potential energy sparingly, for periods of short duration, to meet the peak-load demands. When water is plentiful with the excess flowing over the spillway of the dam, base-loading use is indicated.

The desirable feature of hydropower in effectively meeting peak demand may be obtained in locations without suitable water flows by using *pumped storage*. In this scheme water is pumped from a lower reservoir to a higher one during off-peak times (generally at night) and the water is allowed to flow downhill in the conventional hydroelectric mode during times of

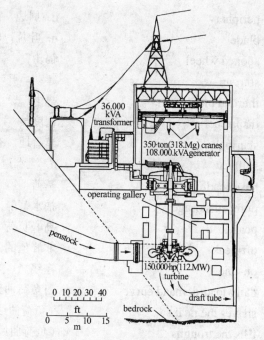

Fig.8-4   Cross section through a hydroelectric plant with a Kaplan turbine

peak demand. Off peak, the generators, operating as synchronous motors, drive the turbines in reverse in a pumping mode. The overall efficiency is only about 65% to 70%, but the economics are frequently favorable when one considers the economics of the overall system, including the thermal units. Consider the followings. It is not practical to shut down the largest and most efficient thermal units at night, so they are kept "on-line" supplying relatively small (light) loads. When operating in this mode the pumping power may be supplied at low incremental costs. On the other hand, at the time of peak demand the pumped storage scheme provides power that would otherwise have to be supplied by less efficient (older) plants. In a sense, from the point of view of the thermal part of the system, the pumped storage scheme "shaves the peaks" and "fills the troughs" of the daily load-demand curve.

New Words and Expressions

hydropower	n. 水力，水力发电
cubic	a. 立体的，三次的，体积的，正六面体的
dam	n. 坝，堰
penstock	n. 水道，压力水管
hydroplant	n. 水电厂，水电站
high head	高水头
low head	低水头
tail race	尾水渠，退水渠
nozzle	n. 喷嘴

periphery	n. 周边，周围，外围，范围
blade	n. 叶片，轮叶
spoked wheel	辐轮
start up	起动，开动，触发
thermal plant	热电厂
dispatcher	调度员
sparingly	节省地，有节制地，少量地
spillway	n. 泄水道，溢水孔
base-loading	基荷
pumped storage	抽水蓄能
peak load	高峰负荷
off-peak	非峰值的
on-line	在线
daily load-demand curve	日负荷曲线
shaves the peaks	（负荷曲线的）削峰
fills the troughs	（负荷曲线的）填谷
tail race	（水电厂的）尾水渠
bucket wheel rotor	勺轮转子

Notes

1. These turn on a vertical axis with the water entering through a spiral casing and then inward through adjustable "gates" (i.e., valves) to a "runner" (i.e., turbine wheel) with fixed blades.

   这些水轮机靠立式轴旋转，水流通过螺旋状通道和一个可调的阀门向内流向带有固定叶片的涡轮。

2. In this scheme water is pumped from a lower reservoir to a higher one during off-peak times (generally at night) and the water is allowed to flow downhill in the conventional hydroelectric mode during times of peak demand.

   在这种系统中，非高峰负荷期间（通常是夜间）水被从低处的水库抽到高处的水库，而在高峰负荷期间水流按通常的水力发电模式从高处流下来。

3. In a sense, from the point of view of the thermal part of the system, the pumped storage scheme "shaves the peaks" and "fills the troughs" of the daily load-demand curve.

   从系统热力发电部分的角度来看，在某种意义上抽水蓄能电站的运行是对日负荷曲线进行"削峰"和"填谷"。

学术论文写作（三）——摘要

摘要是以提供论文梗概为目的，不加评论和补充解释，以精练的语言简单扼要、重点突出、确切地讲明本文所介绍或阐述的重要内容的短文。摘要中通常包括 4 个要素，即研究目的、研究方法、研究结果和结论。

（1）研究目的是指研究、研制、调查等的前提、目的任务，以及所涉及的主题范围；

（2）研究方法是指所采用的新原理、理论、条件、材料、工艺、结构、手段、装备和程序等；

（3）研究结果是指实验或研究的结果、数据、得到的关系、观察的现象、性能等；

（4）结论是对结果的分析、研究、比较、评价和应用，提出的问题，今后的课题，假设，启发，建议预测等。

在有些情况下，摘要中也可包括研究工作的主要对象和范围，以及具有情报价值的其他重要的信息。但不应有引言中出现的内容，也不要对论文内容作诠释和评论，不得简单重复题名中已有的信息。摘要的句型力求简单，语句顺畅，使作者或审稿人能够一目了然，把握住论文的主题和必要信息。篇幅不宜过长，一般不超过 200 个单词。

摘要多采用过去时态叙述作者工作，以现在时态叙述作者结论。一般使用第三人称，而不使用第一、第二人称。

例〔引自 Electric Power Systems Research 35 (1995)〕

A procedure for optimal allocation of sectionalizing switches in radial distribution systems is proposed. This procedure is aimed at minimizing unsupplied energy caused by network failures. Opportunities for alternative source supply made possible by network reconfiguration are considered. Two applications of this procedure are explored: when the allocation of alternative supply tie-lines is given and when the optimal allocation of a specified number of tie-lines, as well as the allocation of sectionalizers, must be determined. The procedure is based upon the genetic algorithm, a search technique motivated by natural evolution. The basic operators of the genetic algorithm are adapted to solve the problems considered. Performance enchancing modifications of the algorithm are suggested when applicable. A medium-scale, practical example is presented to illustrate the validity and effectiveness of the proposed method.

摘要中常用到的词汇归纳如下：

be described（描述），be introduced（介绍），be expounded（详细解释），be proposed（提出），be discussed（讨论），be analyzed（分析），be offered（提供），be pointed out（指出），be inferred（推导），be developed（开发），be tested（验证），be testified（验证），be diagnosed（诊断），be used（使用），be built（建立），be adopted（采用），be applied（应用），be investigated（调查），be proved（证明），be compared（比较），be concluded（得出结论），be considered（考虑），be improved（改进），be presented（提出），be studied（研究），be shown（表明），be given（给出），be examined（检查），be reviewed（回顾），be outlined（概括），be revealed（揭示），be put forward（提出）。

Exercises

I. Choose the best answer into the blank

1. In hydropower plants, _____ are frequently used for medium heads.

    A. Pelton wheel turbines　　　　　　B. Kaplan type turbines

    C. impulse turbines　　　　　　　　D. Francis turbines

2. During times of the off-peak load, a pumped-storage plant should _____.

 A. provide energy to the power network

 B. stop its operation

 C. absorb energy from the power network

 D. feed energy to some synchronous motors

3. The overall efficiency of a pumped storage plant is usually about _____.

 A. 30%~40%　　　B. 50%~55%　　　　C. 60%~65%　　D. 65%~70%

4. The start-up speed of a hydropower plant is _____ that of a thermal plant.

 A. faster than　　　B. slower than　　　C. equal to　　　D. as fast as

5. The hydropower is well suited for switching according to _____ command to meet changing power needs.

 A. a consumer's　　B. a user's　　　　C. a dispatcher's　　D. an operator's

II. Answer the following questions according to the text

1. What part of the load do hydropower plants supply when water is plentiful with the excess flowing over the spillway of the dam?

2. What is the main advantages of a hydropower plant compared to a coal-fired power plant?

3. What essential elements are include in a hydroelectric plant?

4. How does a pumped storage set operate?

III. Translate the following into Chinese

Cooling Towers

If a thermal power plant is located in a dry region, or far away from a river or lake, we still have to cool the condenser, one way or another. We often use *evaporation* to produce the cooling effect. To understand the principle, consider a lake that exposes a large surface to the surrounding air. A lake evaporates continually, even at low temperatures, and it is known that for every kilogram of water that evaporates, the lake loses 2.4MJ of heat. Consequently, evaporation causes the lake to cool down.

Consider now a tub containing 100kg of water at a certain temperature. If we can somehow cause 1kg of water to evaporate, the temperature of the remaining 99kg will inevitably drop by 5.8°C. We conclude that whenever 1 percent of a body of water evaporates, the temperature of the remaining water drops by 5.8°C. Evaporation is therefore a very effective cooling process.

But how can we produce evaporation? Surprisingly, all that is needed is to expose a large surface of water to the surrounding air. The simplest way to do this is to break up the water into small droplets, and blow air through this artificial rain.

In the case of a thermal station, the warm cooling water flowing out of the condenser is piped to the top of a cooling tower (Fig.8-5) where it is broken up into small droplets. As

Fig.8-5　Cooling tower installed in a nuclear power station

the droplets fall toward the open reservoir below, evaporation takes place and the droplets are chilled. The cool water is pumped from the reservoir and recirculated through the condenser, where it again removes heat from the condensing steam. The cycle then repeats. Approximately, 2 percent of the cooling water that flows through the condenser is lost by evaporation. This loss can be made up by a stream, or a small lake.

Section 3   Nuclear Power Plants

Controlled nuclear fission is the source of energy in a nuclear power plant. In the process of fission, heat is generated which is transferred to a coolant flowing through the reactor. Water is the most common coolant, but gases, organic compounds, liquid metals, and molten salts have also been used.

In USA, the two common types, collectively called *light-water reactors* (to distinguish them from a type using "heavy water"), are the *boiling-water reactor* (*BWR*) and the *pressured-water reactor* (*PWR*), and both use water as coolant.

In the BWR the water is allowed to boil in the reactor core; the steam is then directed to the turbine. In the PWR there may be two or more cycles or loops linked by heat exchangers but otherwise isolated from each other. In all but the last stage (the secondary of which carries steam to the turbine) the water is pressurized to prevent the generation of steam. A schematic diagram of a two-loop system with a single heat exchanger (called steam generator) is shown in Fig.8-6.

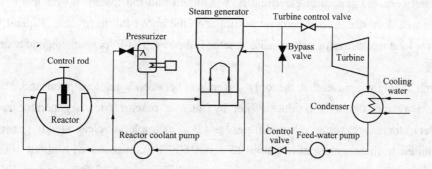

Fig.8-6   Power generation in a nuclear power plant with a pressured-water reactor

The coolant circuit in a PWR acts as a heat transport medium as well as a nuclear reaction moderating medium. As a moderator, the coolant is used to slow down high energy neutrons to thermal energy levels, thus facilitating the nuclear fission reaction. This function provides a mechanism for self-regulation of the reactor process. An increase of reactor power results in an increase of the coolant temperature and a corresponding decrease of the fluid density. This lowers the nuclear fission reaction rate, thereby acting as a negative feedback in the reactor process dynamics. The coolant pressure control is facilitated by the use of a *pressurizer*, which comprises a liquid-filled tank feeding the coolant circuit. A steam space at the top of the tank is used to maintain the pressure at setpoint by means of electric water heaters and water sprays. The liquid level in the tank is controlled by using a make-up and let-down system of valves. The fluid flow in the reactor is sustained by means of large electrically driven *reactor coolant pumps*. The control of the reactor power is achieved by means of neutron-absorbing *control rods* which are inserted to a variable depth in the reactor core. The controller directs the movement of preselected groups of control rod clusters to increase or decrease reactor power as required to maintain the average coolant temperature at a programmed setpoint. A neutron flux signal and a turbine power signal are used to enhance the controller's response to load variations. Long-term regulation of core reactivity is accomplished by adjusting the concentration of neutron-absorbing boric acid in the reactor coolant.

The operation of the PWR is best visualized by considering its response to an increase in load demand. The control valves open to let more steam into the turbine to meet the increased demand. This in turn causes the water level in the steam generator to drop. The feed-water flow then increases to restore the water level. The mismatch between the reactor power level and the steam generator load results in a decrease of the reactor's coolant temperature and pressure, and a corresponding decrease in the moderating fluid's density. This change in density results in an increase of the neutron multiplication rate which provides the initial rise in the reactor power level. In response to the decreased coolant temperature, the reactor control system initiates a control absorber rod withdrawal to raise reactor power. The coolant pressure control system responds to the pressure change by operating the pressurized heaters. Finally, the pressurized water level is restored by the make-up and let-down system. A new steady-state condition is established when the equilibrium between the generator electrical power output and the reactor power level is reached. The response to a decrease in load demand is similar to the above but in reverse. Typically, a PWR is capable of a load manoeuvring rate of $\pm5\%$ reactor full power (RFP) per minute, and a step change of $\pm10\%$ RFP.

Although it might appear that the only difference between a nuclear plant and a fossil-fuel plant is the way the steam is produced (i.e. by nuclear reactor /steam generator rather than furnace/boiler), there are some other differences. For example, nuclear steam generators are presently limited in their temperature output to about 600°F (compared with about 1000°F for a fossil-fuel plant). This has a negative impact on thermal efficiency (30% instead of 40%) and in steam conditions in the turbines. There are of course major differences in fuel cycle (supply and disposal) and in requirements for plant safety.

New Words and Expressions

fission	n.; v. 裂变，分裂，剥离
nuclear power plant	核电站，核电厂
reactor	n. 反应堆，反应器；电抗器，电抗线圈
coolant	n. 冷却剂，冷却液
light-water reactor	轻水反应堆

boiling-water reactor （BWR）	沸水反应堆
pressured-water reactor (PWR)	压水反应堆
reactor core	反应堆堆芯，反应堆活性区
bypass valve	旁路阀门
reactor coolant pump	反应堆冷却泵
moderator	n. 减速剂，慢化剂
self-regulation	自调整
negative feedback	负反馈
pressurize	v. 增压，对……加压，产生压力
pressurizer	n. 保持压力装置，增压装置
moderator	n. 减速器，减速剂
setpoint	设定值，给定值
make-up	补给[水]，补充
let-down	下泄
control rod	（反应堆的）控制棒，控制杆
visualize	v. 使……可视化，具体化，形象化
manoeuvre	n. 调动，策略；v. 调动，操纵

Notes

In USA, the two common types, collectively called light-water reactors (to distinguish them from a type using "heavy water"), are the boiling-water reactor (BWR) and the pressured-water reactor (PWR), and both use water as coolant.

在美国，使用着两种反应堆：沸水反应堆（BWR），压水反应堆（PWR），两者统称为轻水反应堆（区别于"重水"反应堆），并且都是使用水作为冷却剂。

学术论文写作（四）——关键词和引言

1. 关键词

关键词是为了便于二次文献检索，提取出最能集中反映本文的理论、技术特点的关键性单词或词组。关键词应从标题和正文中被反复论及的词语或领域中提取。紧跟在摘要之后，另起一行。关键词规定是 3～10 个，实际中以 3～5 个为多见。关键词之间应有 2～3 个空格或者分号隔开。

例 1 ［引自 Computers and Electrical Engineering 30 (2004)：Markov-chain based reliability analysis for distributed systems］

Keywords: distributed computing system; distributed systems; reliability

例 2 ［引自 Electric Power Systems Research 68 (2004) ：The cascade induction machine: a reliable and controllable motor or generator］

Keywords: wire-wound rotor; commutators; squirrel cage induction machine

2. 引言

引言是文章的开头，是读者跟作者思想与写作风格实际接触的第一步。应以明快的语言从研究内容的背景、发展、需求等情况入手，阐明本文核心问题提出的原由，从而引入到正面的阐述，使读者对本文的宗旨、核心理论、核心技术和目标能较快地有所了解。从而为深入阅读、理解本文主要内容做好思想准备。引言重点是简要说明研究工作的目的、范围、相关领域的已有工作、理论和技术的空白，所提出的分析、研究设想、研究方法、实验设计、预期成果和研究意义等。引言应言简意赅，不能与摘要雷同，也不可成为摘要的注释。

引言中涉及他人的研究成果，应标明出处，用带方括号和阿拉伯数字的上标在引用处标示，并与参考文献编号相对应。

Exercises

I. Choose the best answer into the blank

1. _____ is used as coolant in light-water reactors.

    A. Gas   B. Organic compound

    C. Molten salt   D. Water

2. In a PWR, an increase of reactor power results in _____ of the coolant temperature and a corresponding _____ of the fluid density.

    A. increase, increase   B. increase, decrease

    C. decrease, decrease   D. decrease, increase

3. Nuclear steam generators are presently limited in their temperature output to about 600°F, so the thermal efficiency is usually about _____.

    A. 30%   B. 40%   C. 50%   D. 60%

4. In nuclear power plants, increases of the load demand cause _____ in the steam generator to drop.

    A. the water temperature   B. the water pressure

    C. the water level   D. the steam temperature

II. Answer the following questions according to the text

1. What functions does the coolant circuit have in a PWR?

2. What is the difference between the boiling-water reactor and the pressured-water reactor?

3. How is the reactor power controlled in a nuclear power plant with a pressured-water reactor?

4. What is the potential hazards of a nuclear power plant to the environment?

5. What is used as coolant in both light-water?

III. Translate the following into Chinese

New Energy Types for Power Generation

There are additional energy sources currently used or under development. These include the following: gas turbines, biomass, geothermal, photovoltaic, solar thermal, wind power, wastes as fuel, tidal power, ocean thermal energy conversion (OTEC), magnetohydrodynamic generation, generators driven by diesel engines, fuel cells, wave power, nuclear fusion, and the breeder reactor.

It is in the nature of some of these new sources, for example, photovoltaic and wind power, that they are of small size and widely dispersed geographically. To obtain the benefits of backup power as well as full utilization of the locally generated power, and to eliminate the need for expensive local storage schemes, these small sources may be integrated into the utility network. This poses problems for the utilities. In the past, while the load has been geographically dispersed and somewhat random in its demand, the generation has been in large plants fully under utility control. Now this new generation seems to share a property of the load; it is geographically dispersed and somewhat random in its supply. An additional feature to consider is that these smaller distributed sources may not be owned by the power utility. In this case there is need for special procedure for decentralized operation, maintenance of safety, and pricing of the energy supplies to the utility. The operation of a utility system with distributed power sources are being investigated worldwide for the time being.

gas turbine	燃气轮机
biomass	n. 生物量
geothermal	n. 地热
photovoltaic	a. 光电[池]的，光电转换的
wind power	风力发电，风力
tidal power	潮汐发电，潮汐力
ocean thermal energy conversion	海洋热能转换
magnetohydrodynamic	a. 磁流体发电的，磁流体动力的
fuel cell	燃料电池
wave power	波浪能
nuclear fusion	核聚变
breeder reactor	增殖反应

Chapter 9　Automation Control System

Section 1　Introduction

Automatic control systems permeate life in all advanced societies today. Such systems act as catalysts in promoting progress and development. They are integral components of any industrial society and are necessary for the production of goods required by an increasing world population. Technological developments have made it possible to travel to the moon and to explore outer space. The suceesful operation of space vehicles, the space shuttle, space stations, and reconfigurable flight control systems depends on the proper functioning of the large number of control systems used in such ventures.

The DC shunt motor of Fig.9-1 is an exmaple for open-loop control systems. For a given value of field current, a required value of voltage is applied to the armature to produce the desired value of motor speed. In this case the motor is the dynamic part of the system, the applied armature voltage is the input quantity, and the speed of the shaft is the output quantity. A variation of the speed from the desired value, due to a change of mechanical load on the shaft, can in no way cause a change in the value of the applied armature voltage to maintain the desired speed. Therefore, the output quantity has no influence on the input quantity.

System in which the output quantity has no effect upon the input quantity are called open-loop control systems. The example just cited is represented symbolically by a functional block diagram, as shown in Fig.9-1(b). The desired speed of the motor is the command input; the selection of the value of time on the value of voltage applied to the motor armature is represented by the reference-selector block; and the output of this block is identified as the reference input. The reference input is applied to the dynamic unit that performs the desired control function, and the output of this block is the desired output.

A person could be assigned the task of sensing the actual value of the output and comparing with the command input. If the output does not have the desired value, the person can alter the reference-selector position to achieve this value. Introducing the person provides a means through which the output is fed back and is compared with the input. Any necessary change is then

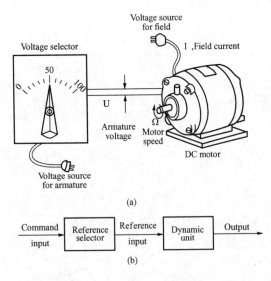

Fig.9-1　Open-loop control system

(a) electric motor;　(b) functional block diagram

made in order to cause the output to equal the desired value. The feedback action, therefore, controls the input to the dynamic unit. Systems in which the output has a direct effect upon the input quantity are called closed-loop control systems.

　　To improve the perfoemance of the closed-loop system so that the output quantity is as close as possible to the desired quantity, the person can be replaced by a mechanical, electrical, or other form of comparison unit. The functional block diagram of a single-input single-output (SISO) closed-loop control system is illustrated in Fig.9-2. Comparison be tween the reference input and the feedback signal results in an actuating signal that is the defference between these two quantities. The actuating signal acts to maintain the output at the desired value. This system is called a closed-loop control system. The designation closed-loop implies the

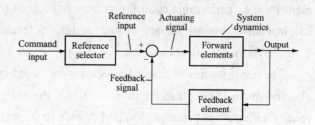

Fig.9-2　Functional block diagram of a closed-loop control system

action resulting from the comparison between the output and input quantities in order to maintain the output at the desired value. Thus, the output is controlled in order to achieve the desired value.

　　The fundamental difference between the open- and closed-loop systems is the feedback action, which may be continuous or discontinuous. Continuous control implies that the output is continuously fed back and compared with the reference input. In one form of discontinuous control the input and output quantities are periodically sampled and compared; i.e., the control action is discontinuous in time. This is commonly called a digital, discrete-data, or sampled- data feedback control system. A discrete-data control system may incorporate a digital computer, which improves the performance achievable by the system. In another form of discontinuous control system the actuating signal must reach a perscribed value before the system dynamics reacts to it; i.e., the control action is discontinuous in amplitude rather than in time. This type of discontinuous control system is commonly called an on-off or relay feedback control system. Both forms may be present in a system.

　　A signification date in the this history of automatic feedback control systems is 1934, when Hazen's paper "Theory of Servomechanisms" was published in the Journal of the Franklin Institute, marking the beginning of the very intense interest in this new field. It was in this paper that the word servomechanism originated, from the words servant (or slave) and mechanism. Black's important paper on feedback amplifiers appeared in the same year. After World War II, control theory was studied intensively and applications have proliferated. Many books and thousands of articles and technical papers have been written, and the application of control systems in the industrial and military fields has been extensive. This rapid growth of feedback control systems was accelerated by the equally rapid development and widespread use of computer.

　　The control theory developed through the late 1950s may be categorized as conventional control theory and is effectively applied to many control-design problems, especially to SISO systems. Since then, control theory has been developed for the design of more complicated systems and for multiple-input multiple-output (MIMO) systems. Space travel has become possible only because of the advent of modern control theory. Areas such as trajectory optimization and minimum-time and/or minimum-fuel problems, which are very important in space travel, can be readily handled by multivariable control theory. The introduction of micro- processors as control elements, i.e., performing control functions in contrast to being used solely as computational tools, has had an enormous impact on the design of feedback control systems that achieve desired control-system specifications.

The early studies of control systems were based on the solution of differential equations by classical means. Other than for simple systems, the analysis in this approach is tedious and does not readily indicate what changes should be made to improve system performance. Use of the Laplace transform simplifies this analysis somewhat. Nyquist's paper published in 1932 dealt with the application of steady-state frequency-response techniques to feedback amplifier design. This work was extended by Black and Bode. Hall and Harris applied frequency- response analysis in the study of feedback control systems, which furthered the development of control theory as a whole.

Another advance occurred in 1948, when Evans presented his root-locus theory. This theory affords a graphical of the stability properties of a system and permits the graphical evaluation of both the time and the frequency response. Laplace transform theory and network theory are joined in the root-locus calculation.

The Laplace transform and the principles of linear algebra are used in applying state variable methods to system analysis and design. The nth-order differential equation describing the system can be converted into a set of n first-order differential equations, expressed in terms of the state variables, that can be written in matrix notation for simpler mathematical manipulation. Matrix equations lend themselves very well to computer solution. This characteristic has enabled modern control theory to solve many problems, such as nonlinear and optimization problems, that could not be solved by conventional control theory.

Mathematical models are used in the linear analysis. Once a physical system has been described by a set of mathematical equations, they are manipulated to achieve an appropriate mathematical format. When this has been done, the subsequent method of analysis is independent of the nature of the physical system; i.e., it does not matter whether the system is electrical, mechanical, or something else. This technique helps the designer to spot similarities based upon previous experience.

The reader should recognize that no single design method is intended to be used to the exclusion of the others. Depending upon the known factors and the simplicity or complexity of a control-system problem, a designer may use one method exclusively or a combination of methods. With experience in the design of feedback control systems comes the ability to use the advantages of each method.

The modern control theory includes the method for the assignment of the complete eigenstructure, which consists of both the closed-loop eigenvalue spectrum and the associated set of eigenvectors. This method is an extension of previous methods that assigned only the closed-loop eigenvalues. The eigenvectors can be selected from identifiable subspaces that are associated with the system plant and control matrices. This method provides great potential for shaping the system output response to meet desired performance standards.

New Words and Expressions

automatic control system	自动控制系统
reconfigurable	a. 可重构的，可再构的
open-loop control system	开环控制系统
functional block diagram	功能框图
feedback	n. 反馈
closed-loop control system	闭环控制系统
single-input single-output (SISO)	单输入单输出
continuous control	连续控制
discontinuous control	断续控制
periodically	ad. 周期地
sample	n. 采样，取样，样品，试件；v. 采样
discrete-data	离散数据的
sampled-data	采样数据的
relay feedback control system	继电反馈控制系统
servomechanism	n. 伺服机构，伺服系统，随动系统
multiple-input multiple-output (MIMO)	多输入多输出
modern control theory	现代控制理论
trajectory	n. 轨迹，轨道
multivariable	多变量
differential equation	微分方程
Laplace transform	拉普拉氏变换
frequency-response	频率响应
root-locus	根轨迹
time response	时域响应
state variable	状态变量
nth-order	n. 阶
matrix	n. 矩阵
mathematical model	数学模型
eigenstructure	n. 特征结构
eigenvalue	n. 特征值
eigenvector	n. 特征向量

Notes

1. A variation of the speed from the desired value, due to a change of mechanical load on the shaft, can in no way cause a change in the value of the applied armature voltage to maintain the desired speed.

   由于轴上机械负荷的变化，转速偏离期望值，无法引起所加电枢电压的变化来维持期望转速。

2. The nth-order differential equation describing the system can be converted into a set of n first-order differential equations, expressed in terms of the state variables, that can be written in matrix notation for simpler mathematical manipulation.

   描述系统的 n 阶微分方程可转换成用状态变量表示的 n 个一阶微分方程组，它可写成矩阵形式便于数学处理。

学术论文写作（五）——正文

正文是学术论文的核心部分，占主要篇幅。其宗旨是要阐明作者研究成果或所提出理论、方法的基本内容、理论依据、正确性、实现方法、仿真或实验的验证方法及其结果分析。要求推理论证严密、论述简明准确、分析与介绍条理清晰而重点突出，全文层次清楚、结构严谨、合乎逻辑。

正文可按内容和目的划分为若干部分，每部分采用小标题，用阿拉伯数字编号；小标题下还可设子标题，其编号采用：小标题数字. 子标题数字。由于学科、专题、研究方法和实验手段等的不同，正文的结构并非千篇一律。

学术论文在体裁上属说明文。目的是解释事物，说明道理。解释事物时可以通过定义、分类、举例、比较和对比，分析其因果关系和提供数据等手段。在构思正文段落时，可以灵活地运用这些方式。

1. 定义

定义是揭示概念的内涵或者词语意义的方法。在解释事物时，往往需要对一些概念或者词语下个明确的定义。例如：

A substation is an assemblage of equipment for the purpose of switching of changing or regulating the voltage of electricity.（这一段是给 substation 下了个定义）

在下定义时，常用的词语有：be, be defined as, be known as, be called, mean, refer to, involve, deal with, be concerned with。

2. 分类

分类是把具有共同特性的有关事物分成属类。分类方法可以达到有效地组织文章的作用。例如：

Main classifications of the substations are as follow: Step-up substation, primary grid substation, secondary substation and distribution.（对变电站进行了分类）

对事物分类常用的词语有：class, group, category, kind, sort, be classified into, be classed into, be divided into, fall into, group into, be made up of。

3. 举例

举例是使用例子说明要点。它是最常见，也是最有效的一种说明方式。举例时，常用的词语有：like, an example of, such as, be illustrated by, for example, as illustrated by, for instance。

4. 比较与对比

比较是确定事物异同关系的思维过程和方法。对比是把两种不同的事物作对照，互相比较。对事物进行比较和对比时，常用的词语有：comparison, contrast, both, similar, difference, different, similarities, like, while, although, alike, same, on the other hand, in a similar way, on the contrary, however, comparing to, instead, unlike。

5. 因果分析

因果分析是用于阐述和分析某事件产生的原因和结果。解释原因和结果常用的词语有：as, because, since, accordingly, consequently, hence, therefore, thus, so, as a result, thus, so because of, account for。

Exercises

I. Choose the best answer into the blank

1. The system in which the output is controlled in order to achieve the desired value is called _____.

    A. a open-loop control system   B. a close-loop control system

    C. a sequential control system   D. an automatic control system

2. In the form of _____ the output is continuously fed back fed back and compared with the reference input.

    A. continuous control   B. discontinuous control

    C. discrete-data control   D. sampled-data control

3. "Theory of Servomechanisms" that marks the beginning of the automatic feedback control system is published in _____.

    A. 1932   B. 1934   C. 1948   D. 1950

4. The root-locus theory was presented by _____.

    A. Nyquist   B. Bode   C. Black   D. Evans

5. The state equations are _____.

    A. a set of n first-order differential equations

    B. a n-order differential equation

    C. a set of n first-order algebraic equations

    D. a n-order algebraic equation

II. Answer the following questions according to the text

1. What is the difference between the open-loop control system and the close-loop control system?

2. What is the difference between the continuous control system and the discontinuous control system?

3. What systems does conventional control theory suit to? SISO or MIMO?

4. Whose paper dealt first with the application of steady-state frequency-response techniques to feedback amplifier design?

III. Translate the following into Chinese

Practically all control systems that are implemented today are based on computer control. A computer-controlled system can be described schematically as in Fig.9-3. The output from the process $y(t)$ is a continuous-time signal. The output is converted into digital form by the analog-to-digital (A-D) converter. The A-D converter can be included in the computer or regarded as a separate unit, according to one's preference. The conversion is done at the sampling times, t_k. The computer interprets the converted signal, $\{y(t_k)\}$, as a sequence of numbers, processes the measurements using an algorithm, and gives a new sequence of numbers, $\{u(t_k)\}$. This sequence is converted to an analog signal by a digital-to-analog (D-A) converter. The events are synchronized by the real-time clock in the computer. The digital computer operates sequentially in time and each operation takes some time. The D-A converter must, however, produce a continuous-time signal. This is normally done by keeping the control signal constant between the conversions. In this case the system runs open loop in the time interval between the sampling instants because the control signal is constant irrespective of the value of the output.

The computer-controlled system contains both continuous-time signals and sampled, or discrete-time, signals. Such systems have traditionally been called *sampled-data systems*, and this term will be used here as a synonym for *computer-controlled systems*.

The mixture of different types of signals sometimes causes difficulties. In most cases it is, however, sufficient to describe the behavior of the system at the sampling instants. The signals are then of interest only at discrete times. Such systems will be called *discrete-time systems*. Discrete-time systems deal with sequences of numbers, so a natural way to represent these systems is to use difference equations.

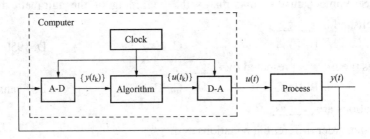

Fig.9-3　Schematic diagram of a computer-controlled system

Section 2　Determination of the Overall Transfer Function

Control systems can be represented in block-diagram form. For each block the transfer function provides the dynamic mathematical relationship between the input and output quantities. The block-diagram of a control system with negative feedback can often be simplified to the form shown in Fig.9-4, where the standard symbols and definitions used in feedback systems are indicated. In this feedback control system the output is the controlled variable C. This output is measured by a feedback element H to produce the primary feedback signal B, which is then compared with the reference input R. The difference E, between the reference input R and the feedback signal B, is the input to the controlled system G and is referred to as the actuating signal. For unity-feedback systems where $H=1$, the actuating signal is equal to the

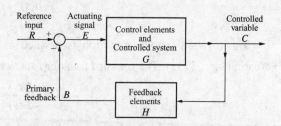

Fig.9-4　Block diagram of a feedback system

error signal, which is the difference R-C. The transfer functions of the forward and feedback components of the system are G and H, respectively.

In using the block diagram to represent a linear feedback control system where the transfer functions of the components are known, the letter symbol is capitalized, indicating that it is a transformed quantity; i.e., it is a function of the operator D, the complex parameter s, or the frequency parameter jω. This representation applies for the transfer function, where G is used to represent $G(S)$, $G(s)$, or $C(j\omega)$. Lowercase symbols are used to represent any function in the time domain. For example, the symbol c represents $c(t)$.

The important characteristic of such a system is the overall transfer function, which is the ratio of the transform of the controlled variable C to the transform of the reference input R. This ratio may be expressed in operational, Laplace transform, or frequency (phasor) form. The overall transfer function is also referred to as the control ratio.

The equations describing this system in terms of the transform variable are

$$C(s) = G(s)E(s) \tag{9-1}$$

$$B(s) = H(s)C(s) \tag{9-2}$$

$$E(s) = R(s) - B(s) \tag{9-3}$$

Combining these equations produces the control ratio, or overall transfer function

$$\frac{C(s)}{R(s)} = \frac{G(s)}{1+G(s)H(s)} \tag{9-4}$$

The characteristic equation of the closed-loop system is obtained from the denominator of the control ratio:

$$1+G(s)H(s) = 0 \tag{9-5}$$

For simplified systems where the feedback is unity, that is , $H(s)=1$, the actuating signal, given by Eq. (9-3), is now the error present in the systems, i.e., the reference input minus the controlled variable, expressed by

$$E(s) = R(s) - C(s) \tag{9-6}$$

The control ratio with unity feedback is

$$\frac{C(s)}{R(s)} = \frac{G(s)}{1+G(s)} \tag{9-7}$$

The open-loop transfer function is defined as the ratio of the output of the feedback path $B(s)$ to the actuating signal $E(s)$ for any given feedback loop. The open-loop transfer function is

$$\frac{B(s)}{E(s)} = G(s)H(s) \qquad (9\text{-}8)$$

The forward transfer function is defined as the ratio of the controlled variable $C(s)$ to the actuating signal $E(s)$. The forward transfer function is

$$\frac{C(s)}{E(s)} = G(s) \qquad (9\text{-}9)$$

In the case of unity feedback, where $H(s)=1$, the open-loop and the forward transfer functions are the same. The forward transfer function $G(s)$ may be made up not only of elements in cascade but may also contain internal, or minor, feedback loops. The algebra of combining these internal feedback loops is similar to that used previously.

It is often useful to express the actuating signal E in terms of the input R. Solving from Eq. (9-1) to Eq. (9-3) gives

$$\frac{E(s)}{R(s)} = \frac{1}{1 + G(s)H(s)} \qquad (9\text{-}10)$$

The concept of system error y_e is defined as the ideal or desired system value minus the actual system output. The ideal value establishes the desired performance of the system. For unity-feedback systems the actuating signal is an actual measure of the error and is directly proportional to the system error.

New Words and Expressions

block-diagram	框图
transfer function	传递函数
negative feedback	负反馈
error signal	误差信号
operator	n. 算子，算符，操作符，控制器
complex parameter	复数参数
frequency parameter	频率参数
time domain	时域
denominator	n. 分母
open-loop transfer function	开环传递函数
forward transfer function	前向传递函数

Notes

1. The block-diagram of a control system with negative feedback can often be simplified to the form shown in Fig.9-4, where the standard symbols and definitions used in feedback systems are indicated.

   具有负反馈的控制系统框图常可简化成图 9-4 所示形式，图中给出了用于反馈系统中的标准符号和定义。

2. In using the block diagram to represent a linear feedback control system where the transfer

functions of the components are known, the letter symbol is capitalized, indicating that it is a transformed quantity; i.e., it is a function of the operator D, the complex parameter s, or the frequency parameter $j\omega$.

在使用框图表示各组成部分传递函数已知的线性反馈控制系统中，用大写字母表示变换量，即算子 D，或复参数，或频率参数 $j\omega$ 的函数。

学术论文写作（六）——结论和参考文献

1. 结论或总结

结论是对论文的最终的、总结式的评价和提高。其宗旨是让读者对本文所介绍的精髓、意义、新思想、新方法以及验证结果有一个全貌的了解。应做到准确、完整、明确、精练。在结论中还要简单介绍研究成果可以推广的应用领域，对进一步研究提出建议、研究设想、尚需解决的问题等。

2. 参考文献

参考文献是指与论文有直接关系，在文中被引用或对研究有指导意义的文献，在论文的最后部分。一般以粗体字"References"开头，然后另起行依次列出各篇参考文献的索引条，列出的顺序一般需与其在论文中被引用的顺序一致。

根据引用参考文献的类型分别采用以下顺序编排：

（1）著作　作者．译者．书名．出版地：出版社，出版年：起～止页

（2）期刊论文　作者．题（篇）名．出版年，卷号（期号）：起～止页

（3）会议论文　作者．题（篇）名．文集名．会议名，会址，开会年：起～止页

（4）学位论文　作者．题（篇）名：[博（硕）士学位论文].授学位地：授学位学校．授学位年

（5）网上检索　网址．论文作者．论文名称

Exercises

I. Choose the best answer into the blank

1. The overall transfer function is the ratio of the transform of the controlled variable to the transform of _____.

   A. the controlled variable   B. the reference input

   C. the feedback variable   D. the output variable

2. $C(j\omega)$ indicates a function of _____.

   A. time domain   B. frequency domain

   C. s domain   D. state space

3. The open-loop transfer for the closed-loop control system shown in Fig.9-4 is _____.

   A. $G(s)$ B. $G(s)H(s)$ C. $H(s)$ D. $\dfrac{G(s)}{1+G(s)H(s)}$

4. The total transfer function for $G_1(s)$ and $G_2(s)$ in cascade is _____.

   A. $G_1(s)$ B. $G_2(s)$ C. $G_1(s)\,G_2(s)$ D. $G_1(s)+G_2(s)$

II. Answer the following questions according to the text

1. What is the transfer function?
2. How to get the characteristic equation of the closed-loop control system?
3. How to define the open-loop transfer function?
4. How to define the forward transfer function?
5. What is system error?

III. Translate the following into Chinese

Digital computers are available not only for the design of control systems, but also to perform the control function. Digital computers and microprocessors are used in many control systems, and the size and cost advantages associated with the microcomputer make its use as a controller both economical and practical. Using such a digital processor with a plant that operates in the continuous-time domain requires that its input signal be discrete, which requires the sampling of the signals used by the controller. Such sampling may be an inherent characteristic of some systems. For example, a radar tracking system supplies information on an airplane's position and motion to a digital processor at discrete periods of time. This information is therefore available as a succession of data points. When there is no inherent sampling, an analog-to-digital (A-D) converter must be incorporated in a digital or sampled- data control system. The sampling process can be performed at a constant rate or at a variable rate, or it may be random. Systems which include a digital computer are known as digital control systems. The synthesis techniques for such systems are based on representing the entire system as an equivalent sampled, discrete, or pseudo-continuous-time system.

There are various approaches that may be used in analyzing the stability and time-response characteristics of sampled-data systems. These approaches may be divided into two distinct categories: (i) direct, (ii) digitization or discrete digital control analysis techniques.

Section 3   Control–System Characteristics

Open-loop and closed-loop transfer functions have certain basic characteristics that permit transient and steady-state analyses of the feedback-controlled system. Five factors of prime importance in feedback-control systems are stability, the existence and magnitude of the steady-state error, controllability, observability, and parameter sensitivity. The stability characteristic of a linear time-invariant system is determined from the system's characteristic equation. Routh's stability criterion provides a means for determining stability without evaluating the roots of this equation. The steady-state characteristics are obtainable from the open-loop transfer function for unity-feedback systems (or equivalent unity-feedback systems), yielding figures of merit and a ready means for classifying systems.

Routh's Stability Criterion

The transfer function $F(s)$ can be expressed, in general, as the ratio of two polynomials $P(s)$

and $Q(s)$. The response transform $X_2(s)$ has the following form in Eq. (9-11). $X_1(s)$ is the driving transform

$$X_2(s) = \frac{P(s)}{Q(s)} X_1(s) = \frac{P(s)X_1(s)}{b_n s^n + b_{n-1}s^{n-1} + b_{n-2}s^{n-2} + \cdots + b_1 s + b_0} \tag{9-11}$$

Stability of the response $x_2(t)$, which is the inverse transform of $X_2(s)$, requires that all zeros of $Q(s)$ have negative real parts. Since it is usually not necessary to find the exact solution when the response is unstable, a simple procedure to determine the existence of zeros with positive real parts is needed. If such zeros of $Q(s)$ with positive real parts are found, the system is unstable and must be modified. Routh's criterion is a simple method of determining the number of zeros with positive real parts without actually solving for the zeros of $Q(s)$. Note that zeros of $Q(s)$ are poles of $X_2(s)$. The characteristic equation is

$$Q(s) = b_n s^n + b_{n-1}s^{n-1} + b_{n-2}s^{n-2} + \cdots + b_1 s + b_0 = 0 \tag{9-12}$$

If the b_0 term is zero, divided by s to obtain the equation in the form of Eq. (9-12). The b's are real coefficients, and all powers of s from s^n to s^0 must be present in the characteristic equation. A necessary but not sufficient condition for stable roots is that all the coefficients in Eq. (9-12) be positive. If any coefficients other than b_0 are zero, or if all the coefficients do not have the same sign, then there are pure imaginary roots or roots with positive real parts and the system is unstable. In that case it is unnecessary to continue if only stability or instability is to be determined. When all the coefficients are present and positive, the system may or may not be stable because there still may be roots on the imaginary axis or in the right-half s plane. Routh's criterion is mainly used to determine stability. In special situa- tions it may be necessary to determine the actual number of roots in the right-half s plane.

The coefficients of the characteristic equation are arranged in the pattern shown in the first two rows of the following Routhian array. These coefficients are then used to evaluate the rest of the constants to complete the array.

s^n	b_n	b_{n-2}	b_{n-4}	b_{n-6} $\cdots$
s^{n-1}	b_{n-1}	b_{n-3}	b_{n-5}	b_{n-7} $\cdots$
s^{n-2}	c_1	c_2	c_3	$\cdots$
s^{n-3}	d_1	d_2	$\cdots$	
	$\cdots$	$\cdots$		
s^1	j_1			
s^0	k_1			

The constants c_1, c_2, c_3, etc., in the third row are evaluated as follows

$$c_1 = \frac{b_{n-1}b_{n-2} - b_n b_{n-3}}{b_{n-1}}$$

$$c_2 = \frac{b_{n-1}b_{n-4} - b_n b_{n-5}}{b_{n-1}}$$

$$c_3 = \frac{b_{n-1}b_{n-6} - b_n b_{n-7}}{b_{n-1}}$$

This pattern is continued until the rest of the c's are all equal to zero. Then the d row is formed by using the s^{n-1} and s^{n-2} row. The constants are

$$d_1 = \frac{c_1 b_{n-3} - b_{n-1} c_2}{c_1}$$

$$d_2 = \frac{c_1 b_{n-5} - b_{n-1} c_3}{c_1}$$

$$d_3 = \frac{c_1 b_{n-7} - b_{n-1} c_4}{c_1}$$

This process is continued until no more d terms are present. The rest of the rows are formed in this way down to the s^0 row. The complete array is triangular, ending with the s^0 row. Notice that the s^1 and s^0 rows contain only one term each. Once the array has been found, Routh's criterion states that the number of roots of the characteristic equation with positive real parts is equal to the number of changes of sign of the coefficients in the first column. Therefore, the system is stable if all terms in the first column have the same sign.

Theorem 1. Division of a row. The coefficients of any row may be multiplied or divided by a positive number without changing the signs of the first column. The labor of evaluating the coefficients in Routh's array can be reduced by multiplying or dividing any row by a constant. This may result, for example, in reducing the size of the coefficients and therefore simplifying the evaluation of the remaining coefficients.

Theorem 2. A zero coefficient in the first column. When the first term in a row is zero but not all the other terms are zero, the following methods can be used:

（1） substitute $s = 1/x$ in the original equation; then solve for the roots of x with positive real parts. The number of roots x with positive real parts will be the same as the number of s roots with positive real parts.

（2） multiply the original polynomial by the factors $(s+1)$, which introduces an additional negative root. Then form the Routhian array for the new polynomial.

Theorem 3. A zero row. When all the coefficients of one row are zero, the procedure is as follows:

（1） The auxiliary equation can be formed from the preceding row, as shown below.

（2） The Routhian array can be completed by replacing the all zero row with the coefficients obtained by differentiating the auxiliary equation.

（3） The roots of the auxiliary equation are also roots of the original equation. These roots occur in pairs and are the negative of each other. Therefore, these roots may be imaginary (complex conjugates) or real (one positive and one negative),may lie in quadruplets (two pairs of complex-conjugate roots), etc..

In feedback systems, the ratio of the output to the input does not have an explicitly factored denominator. An example of such a function is

$$\frac{X_2(s)}{X_1(s)} = \frac{P(s)}{Q(s)} = \frac{K(s+2)}{s(s+5)(s^2+2s+5)+K(s+2)} \tag{9-13}$$

The value of K is an adjustable parameter in the system and may be positive or negative. The value of K determines the location of the poles and therefore the stability of the system. It is important to know the range of value of K for which the system is stable. This information must be obtained from the characteristic equation, which is

$$Q(s)=s^4+7s^3+15s^2+(25+K)s+2K=0 \qquad (9\text{-}14)$$

The coefficients must all be positive in order for the zeros of $Q(s)$ to lie in the left half of the s plane, but this condition is not sufficient for stability. The Routhian array permits evaluation of precise boundaries for K:

s^4	1	15	$2K$
s^3	7	$25+K$	
s^2	$80-K$	$14K$	
s^1	$\dfrac{(80-K)(25+K)-98K}{80-K}$		
s^0	$14K$		

The term $80\text{-}K$ for the s^2 row imposes the restriction $K<80$, and the s^0 row requires $K>0$. The numerator of the first term in the s^1 row is equal to $-K^2-43K+2000$, and this function must be positive for a stable system. By use of the quadratic formula the zeros of this function are $K=28.1$ and $K=-71.1$, and the numerator of the s^1 row is positive between these values. The combined restrictions on K for stability of the system are therefore $0<K<28.1$. For the value $K=28.1$ the characteristic equation has imaginary roots that can be evaluated by applying Theorem 3 to form the auxiliary equation. Also, for $K=0$, it can be seen from Eq. (9-13) that there is no output. It is important to note that the Routh criterion provides useful but restricted information. Another method of determining stability is Hurwitz's criterion, which establishes the necessary conditions in terms of the system determinations.

New Words and Expressions

transient   a. 暂态的，瞬态的，短暂的

steady-state error   稳态误差

controllability   n. 可控性

observability   n. 可观性

linear time-invariant system   线性时不变系统

polynomial   n.; a. 多项式（的）

response   n. 响应，答复，应答

driving   a. 驱动的

real part   实部

inverse transform   反变换

pole   n. 极，极点

necessary condition   必要条件

sufficient condition	充分条件
imaginary axis	虚轴
s plane	s 平面
triangular	a. 三角的
conjugate	n. 共轭值；a. 共轭的，共轭根的
quadruplet	n. 四件一套，四个一组
numerator	n. 分子

Notes

1. Routh's Stability Criterion　　　　劳斯稳定准则

2. Since it is usually not necessary to find the exact solution when the response is unstable, a simple procedure to determine the existence of zeros with positive real parts is needed.

因为响应不稳定通常不必求出确切的解来判断，所以需要一种确定具有正实部零点的简单方法。

句中的 zeros 是指使 $Q(s)$ 等于零的所有根。

3. Hurwitz's criterion　　　　霍尔维茨准则

电气工程及其自动化专业英文主要期刊一览表

（1）IEEE Transactions on Power Delivery　　IEEE 输电汇刊

（2）IEEE Transactions on Power　Systems　IEEE 电力系统汇刊

（3）IEEE Transactions on Industry Applications　IEEE 工业应用汇刊

（4）IEEE Power Engineering Review　IEEE 动力工程评论

（5）IEEE Transactions on Energy Conversion IEEE　能源转换汇刊

（6）IEE Proceeding-Generation Transmission and Distribution　IEEC 辑：发电、输电与配电

（7）IEEE Transactions on Circuits and Systems　电路与系统汇刊

（8）IEE Proceedings G- Circuits, Devices and Systems　IEE G 辑：电路、器件和系统

（9）IEEE Transactions on Dielectrics and Electrical Insulation, [see also IEEE Transac- tions on Electrical Insulation]　介质与电气绝缘汇刊

（10）EPRI Journal　美国电力研究会会刊

（11）Electrical World　电世界

（12）power　动力

（13）Power Engineering　动力工程

（14）Energy Policy　能源政策

（15）International Water Power and Dam Construction　水力发电与坝工建设

（16）Asian Electricity　亚洲电力

（17）Transmission and Distribution World　输电与配电世界

（18）Renewable Energy　再生能源

（19）Electric Power System Research　电力系统研究

（20）Electric Light and Power　电气照明与动力

（21）American Society of Civil Engineers Journals   美国土木工程师学会杂志

（22）ABB Review   ABB 评论

Exercises

I. Choose the best answer into the blank

1. The system's characteristic equation can be used to determine _____ of a linear time- invariant
   system.

   A. the stability   B. magnitude of the steady-state error

   C. the controllability   D. the observability

2. A system in which there are roots with positive real parts is _____.

   A. stable   B. unstable

   C. a critical state   D. decreasing periodically

3. If all the coefficients of the characteristic equation do not have the same sign, the system
   is _____.

   A. stable   B. unstable

   C. decreasing non-periodically   D. decreasing periodically

4. If the number of changes of sign of the coefficients in the first column of the Routh's array is two,
   the number of roots of the characteristic equation with positive real parts is _____.

   A. one   B. two   C. three   D. four

5. The way by which the coefficients of any row in Routhian array are multiplied by a positive
   number_____the stability of the system.

   A. may change   B. may affect   C. dose not affect   D. can enhance

II. Answer the following questions according to the text

1. What are the five factors of prime importance in feedback-control systems?

2. What advantages does Routh's stability criterion have for the system's stability ananlysis?

3. How to use Routh's criterion to determine a system's stability?

4. Which theorem should be used when the first term in a row is zero but not all the other terms are
   zero?

5. What is the characteristic equation?

III. Translate the following into Chinese

In various systems the controlled variable, labeled c, shown Fig.9-5 may have the physical
form of position, speed, temperature, rate of change of temperature, voltage, rate of flow, pressure,
etc. Once the block in the diagram are related in transfer
functions, it is immaterial to the analysis of the system
what the physical form of the controlled variable may be.
Generally , the important quantities are the controlled
quantity c, its rate of change Dc, and its second derivative
D^2, that is, the first several derivatives of c, including the

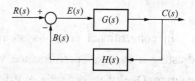

Fig.9-5   Simple feedback system

zeroth derivative. For any specific control system each of these "mathematical" functions has a definite "physical" meaning. For example, if the controlled variable c is position, then Dc is velocity and D^2c is acceleration. As a second example, if the controlled variable c is velocity, then Dc is acceleration and D^2c is the rate of change of acceleration.

Often the input signal to a system has an irregular form, such as that shown in Fig.9-6, that cannot be expressed by any simple equation. This prevents a straight-forward analysis of system response. It is noted, though, that the signal form shown in Fig.9-6 may be considered to be composed of three basic forms of known types of input signals, i.e., a step in the region cde, a ramp in the region ob, and a parabola in the region ef. Thus, if the given linear system is analyzed separately for each of these types of input signals, there is then established a fair measure of performance with the irregular input. The three standard inputs not only approximate most inputs but also provide a means for comparing the performance of different systems.

Consider that the system shown in Fig.9-5 is a position-control system. Feedback control systems are often analyzed on the basis of a unit step input signal. This system can first be analyzed on the basis that the unit step input signal $r(t)$ represents position. Since this gives only a limited idea of how the system responds to the actual input signal, the system can then be analyzed on the basis that the unit step signal represents a constant velocity $Dr(t)=u_{-1}(t)$. This in reality gives an input position signal of the form of a ramp and thus a closer idea of how the system responds to the actual input signal. In the same manner the unit step input signal can represent a constant acceleration, $D^2r(t)=u_{-1}(t)$, to obtain the system's performance to a parabolic position input signal. The curves shown in Fig.9-7 then represent acceleration, velocity and position.

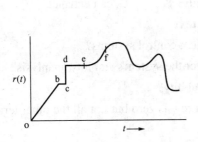

Fig.9-6   Input signal to a system

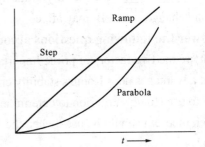

Fig.9-7   Graphical forms of step, ramp, and parabolic input functions

Section 4   Frequency Response

In conventional control-system analysis there are two basic methods for predicting and adjusting a system's performance without resorting to the solution of the system's differential equation. One of these is the root-locus method, the other is the frequency-response method. For the comprehensive study of a system by conventional methods it is necessary to use both methods of analysis. The principal advantage of the root-locus method is that the actual time response is easily obtained by means of the inverse Laplace transform because the precise root locations are known. However, it is sometimes necessary to express performance requirements in terms of the frequency response. Also, the noise, which is always present in any system, can result in poor overall performance. The frequency response of a system permits evaluation of the effect of noise. The design of a passband for the system response may exclude the noise and therefore improve the system performance as long as the dynamic performance specifications are met. The frequency response is also useful in situations for which the transfer functions of some or all of the components in a system are unknown. The frequency response can be determined experimentally for these situations, and an approximate expression for the transfer function can be obtained from the graphical plot of the experimental data. The frequency-response method is also a very powerful method for analyzing and designing a robust MIMO system with uncertain plant parameters. Thus, no particular method can be judged superior to the rest. Each has its particular use and advantage in a particular situation.

Design of control systems by state variable techniques is often based upon achieving an optimum performance according to a specified performance index PI; for example, minimizing the integral of squared error (ISE): $PI = \int_0^\infty e(t)^2 \mathrm{d}t$, where $e = r - c$. Both frequency-response and root-locus methods are valuable complementary tools for many of the techniques of modern control theory.

As pointed out earlier, solving for $c(t)$ by the classical method is laborious and impractical for synthesis purpose, especially when the input is not a simple analytical function. The use of Laplace transform theory lessens the work involved and permits the engineer to synthesize and improve a system. The root-locus method illustrates this fact.

Once the frequency response of a system has been determined, the time response can be determined by inverting the corresponding Fourier transform. The behavior in the frequency domain for a given driving function $r(t)$ can be determined by the Fourier transform as

$$R(\mathrm{j}\omega) = \int_{-\infty}^{+\infty} r(t)\mathrm{e}^{-\mathrm{j}\omega t}\mathrm{d}t \qquad (9\text{-}15)$$

For a given control system the frequency response of the controlled variable is

$$C(\mathrm{j}\omega) = \frac{G(\mathrm{j}\omega)}{1 + G(\mathrm{j}\omega)H(\mathrm{j}\omega)} R(\mathrm{j}\omega) \qquad (9\text{-}16)$$

By use of the inverse Fourier transform, which is much used in practice, the controlled variable as a function of time is

$$c(t) = \frac{1}{2\pi} \int_{-\infty}^{+\infty} C(\mathrm{j}\omega)\mathrm{e}^{\mathrm{j}\omega t}\mathrm{d}\omega \qquad (9\text{-}17)$$

If the design engineer cannot evaluate Eq. (9-17) by reference to a table of definite integrals, this equation can be evaluated by numerical or graphical integration. This is necessary if $C(\mathrm{j}\omega)$ is available only as a curve and cannot be simply expressed in analytical form, as is often the case. In addition, methods have been developed based on the Fourier transform and a step input signal, relating $C(j\omega)$ qualitatively to the time solution without actually taking the inverse Fourier transform. These methods permit the engineer to make an approximate determination of the system response through the interpretation of graphical plots in the frequency domain. This makes the design and improvement of feedback systems possible with a minimum effort.

The frequency response of a system is described as the steady-state response with a sine-wave forcing function for all values of frequency. This information is often presented graphically, using two curves. One curve shows the ratio of output amplitude to input amplitude M and the other curve shows the phase angle of the output α, where both are plotted as a function of frequency, often on a logarithmic scale. The frequency domain plots that have found great use in graphical analysis in the design of feedback control systems belong to two categories. The first category is the plot of the magnitude of the output-input ratio vs. frequency in rectangular coordinates. In logarithmic coordinates these are known as *Bode plots*. Associated with this plot is a second plot of the corresponding phase angle vs. frequency. In the second category the output-input ratio may be plotted in polar coordinates with frequency as a parameter. There are two types of polar plots, direct and inverse. Polar plots are generally used only for the open-loop response and are commonly referred to as *Nyquist plots*. The plots can be obtained experimentally or by a CAD package.

For a given sinusoidal input signal, the input and steady-state output are of the following forms:

$$r(t) = R \sin \omega t \qquad (9\text{-}18)$$

$$c(t) = C \sin(\omega t + \alpha) \qquad (9\text{-}19)$$

The closed-loop frequency response is given by

$$\frac{C(j\omega)}{R(j\omega)} = \frac{G(j\omega)}{1 + G(j\omega)H(j\omega)} = M(\omega)\angle\alpha(\omega) \qquad (9\text{-}20)$$

For each value of frequency, Eq. (9-20) yields a phasor quantity whose magnitude is M and whose phase angle α is the angle between $C(j\omega)$ and $R(j\omega)$.

An ideal system may be defined as one where $\alpha = 0°$ and $R(j\omega) = C(j\omega)$ for $0 < \omega < \infty$. (See curves 1 in Fig.9-8) However, this definition implies an instantaneous transfer of energy from the input to the output. Such a transfer cannot be achieved in practice since any physical system has some energy dissipation and some energy-storage elements. Curves 2 and 3 in Fig.9-8 represent the frequency response of practical control systems. The passband, or bandwidth, of the frequency response is defined as the range of frequencies from 0 to the frequency ω_b, where $M = 0.707$ of the value at $\omega = 0$. However, the frequency ω_m is more easily obtained than ω_b. The values M_m and ω_m are often used as figures of merit.

In any system the input signal may contain spurious noise signals in addition to the true signal input, or there may be sources of noise within the closed-loop system. This noise is generally in a band of frequencies above the dominant frequency band of the true signal. Thus, to reproduce the true signal and attenuate the noise, feedback control systems are designed to have a definite passband. In certain cases the noise frequency may exist in the same frequency band as the true signal. When this occurs, the problem of estimating the desired signal is more complicated.

Therefore, even if the ideal system were possible, it would not be desirable.

The plotting of the frequency transfer function can be systematized and simplified by using logarithmic plots. The use of semilog paper eliminates the need to take logarithms of very many numbers and also expands the low frequency range, which is of primary importance. The advantages of logarithmic plots are that (i) the mathematical operations of multiplication and division are transformed to addition and subtraction, (ii) the work of obtaining the transfer function is largely graphical instead of analytical. The basic factors of the transfer function fall into three categories, and these can easily be plotted by means of straight-line asymptotic approximations.

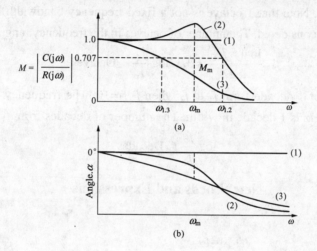

Fig.9-8   Frequency-response characteristics of $C(j\omega)/R(j\omega)$ in rectangular coordinates

In preliminary design studies the straight-line approximations are used to obtain approxi- mate performance characteristics very quickly or to check values obtained from the computer. As the design becomes more firmly specified, the straight-line curves can be corrected for greater accuracy. From these logarithmic plots enough data in the frequency range of concern can readily be obtained to determine the corresponding polar plots.

Some basic definitions of logarithmic terms follow.

Logarithm. The logarithm of a complex number is itself a complex number. The abbreviation "log" is used to indicate the logarithm to the base 10

$$\log|G(j\omega)|e^{j\phi(\omega)} = \log|G(j\omega)| + \log e^{j\phi(\omega)}$$
$$= \log|G(j\omega)| + j0.434\phi(\omega)$$

$(9\text{-}21)$

The real part is equal to the logarithm of the magnitude, $\log|G(j\omega)|$, and the imaginary part is proportional to the angle, $0.434\phi(\omega)$.

Decibel. In feedback-system work the unit commonly used for the logarithm of the magnitude is the *decibel* (dB). When logarithms of transfer functions are used, the input and output variables are not necessarily in the same units; e.g., the output may be speed in radians per second, and the input may be voltage in volts.

Log magnitude. The logarithm of the magnitude of a transfer function $G(j\omega)$ expressed in decibels is

$$20\log|G(j\omega)| \quad dB$$

This quantity is called the *log magnitude*, abbreviated Lm. Thus

$$LmG(j\omega) = 20\log|G(j\omega)| \quad dB$$

since the transfer function is a function of frequency, the Lm is also a function of frequency.

Octave and decade. Two units used to express frequency bands or frequency ratios are the octave and the decade. An octave is a frequency band from f_1 to f_2, where $f_2/f_1=2$. Thus, the frequency band from 1 to 2 Hz is 1 octave in width, and the frequency band from 17.4 to 34.8 Hz is also 1 octave in width. Note that 1 octave is not a fixed frequency bandwidth but depends on the frequency range being considered. The number of octaves in the frequency range from f_1 to f_2 is

$$\frac{\log(f_2/f_1)}{\log 2} = 3.32\log\frac{f_2}{f_1} \quad \text{Octaves}$$

There is an increase of 1 decade from f_1 to f_2 when $f_2/f_1=10$. The frequency band from 1 to 10 Hz or from 2.5 to 25 Hz is 1 decade in width. The number of decades from f_1 to f_2 is given by

$$\log\frac{f_2}{f_1} \quad \text{Decades}$$

New Words and Expressions

performance	n. 性能
frequency response	频率响应
passband	n. 通带，频带
dynamic performance	动态性能
robust	a. 强壮的，强健的，健全的，鲁棒的，坚固的
performance index	性能指标
modern control theory	现代控制理论
synthesis	n. 综合，合成
Fourier transform	傅立叶变换，傅氏变换
inverse Fourier transform	傅氏反变换
definite integral	定积分
analytical	a. 解析的，分析的，分解的
qualitatively	ad. 定性地
logarithmic	a. 对数的
rectangular coordinates	直角坐标
logarithmic coordinates	对数坐标
Bode plots	波特图
phase angle	相角
polar coordinates	极坐标
Nyquist plots	奈奎斯特图
dissipation	n. 消耗

energy-storage element	储能元件
spurious	a. 寄生的，杂散的，乱真的
attenuate	v. 衰减，减少，削弱
semilog	n. 半对数
logarithm	n. 对数
asymptotic	a. 渐近的
decibel	n. 分贝
radian	n. 弧度
octave	n. 八度，倍频程（八度）

Notes

In conventional control-system analysis there are two basic methods for predicting and adjusting a system's performance without resorting to the solution of the system's differential equation.

在传统控制分析中，有两种基本方法不用求解系统微分方程就可预测和调整系统性能。

Exercises

I. Choose the best answer into the blank

1. In the root-locus method the actual time response of a system can be obtained by means of _____.

   A. the inverse Fourier transform   B. the inverse Laplace transform

   C. the Fourier transform   D. the Laplace transform

2. The effect of noise on the performance of a system can be evaluated by means of _____.

   A. the frequency-response method   B. the root-locus method

   C. the differential equation   D. the transfer function

3. A frequency response is a function of the variable _____.

   A. s B. $j\omega$ C. D D. t

4. The plots of the magnitude of the output-input ratio vs. frequency in logarithmic coordinates are known as _____.

   A. Nyquist plots   B. Bode plots

   C. root-locus plots   D. time-response plots

5. The unit of logarithm of the magnitude of a transfer function is _____.

   A. radians per second   B. volts   C. decibel   D. octaves

II. Answer the following questions according to the text

1. What is the principal advantage of the root-locus method?

2. Is it necessary for both the root-locus method and the frequency response method to solve the system's differential equation?

3. How to determine the time response of a system when the frequency response of the system has been known?

4. What are the advantages of logarithmic plots?

5. What curves usually are used to describe the frequency response of a system?

III. Translate the following into Chinese

Controllability and Observability

The state and output equations representing a system have the form

$$X = Ax + Bu$$
$$y = Cx + Du$$

An important objective of state variable control is the design of systems that have all optimum performance. The optimal control is based on the optimization of some specific performance criterion, and the achievement of such optimal linear control systems is governed by the controllability and observability properties of the system. For example, in order to be able to relocate or reassign the open-loop plant poles to more desirable closed-loop locations in the s plane. It is necessary that the plant satisfy the controllability property. Further, these properties establish the conditions for complete equivalence between the state-variable and transfer- function representations.

Controllability. A system is said to be completely state-controllable if, for any initial time t_0, each initial state $x(t_0)$ can be transferred to any final state $x(t_f)$ in a finite time, $t_f > t_0$, by means of an unconstrained control input vector $u(t)$. An unconstrained control vector has no limit on the amplitudes of $u(t)$. This definition implies that $u(t)$ is able to affect each state variable in the state equation.

Observability. A system is said to be completely observable if every initial state $x(t_0)$ can be exactly determined from the measurements of the output $y(t)$ over the finite interval of time $t_0 \leqslant t \leqslant t_f$. This definition implies that every state of $x(t)$ affects the output $y(t)$

$$y(t) = Cx(t) = C\phi(t - t_0)x(t_0) + C\int_{t_0}^{t_1} \phi(t - \tau)Bu(\tau)d\tau$$

where the initial state $x(t_0)$ is the result of control inputs prior to t_0.

参 考 文 献

1. 阎庆甲. 科技英语翻译手册. 郑州：河南科学技术出版社，1986.

2. 卜玉坤，徐辉，张敏，等. 计算机英语. 北京：外语教学与研究出版社，2001.

3. 冯梅，刘荣强. 英汉科技翻译. 哈尔滨：哈尔滨工业大学出版社，2000.

4. 宽本. 水利水电科技英语阅读和翻译. 北京：水利出版社，1980.

5. 郑仰成. 电力英语应用文写作. 北京：中国水利水电出版社，2003.

6. Timonthy J. O'Leary, Linda I. O'Leary. 计算机专业英语（新版）. 北京：高等教育出版社，麦格劳. 希尔公司，1999.

7. June Jamrich Parsons, Dan Oja. New Perspectives on Computer Concepts .8th ed. 北京：电子工业出版社，2005.

8. 俞光昀，王炜. 计算机专业英语. 北京：电子工业出版社，2001.

9. 韩其顺，王学铭. 英汉科技翻译教程. 上海：上海外语教育出版社，1990.

10. 王泉水. 科技英语翻译技巧. 天津：天津科学技术出版社，1991.

11. 王运. 实用科技英语翻译技巧. 北京：科学技术文献出版社，1992.

12. 王秉钧，郭正行. 科技英汉、汉英翻译技巧. 天津：天津大学出版社，1999.

13. 杨泽清. 电子信息专业英语. 北京：机械工业出版社，2002.

14. Charies K. Alexander, Matthew N. O. Sadiku . 电路基础. 北京：清华大学出版社，2000.

15. William H. Hayt, Jr., Jack E. Kemmerly. Engineering Circuit Analysis .7th ed. 北京：电子工业出版社，1993.

16. D.E. Johnson, J.L. Hilburn, and J.R. Johnson. Basic Electric Circuit Analysis, 1978.

17. James Fisk. Fundamentals of circuit analysis, 1987.

18. Stephen D. Senturia, Bruce D. Wedlock. Electronic Circuits and Applications, 1975.

19. William H. Gothmann, Digital Electronics (An Introduction to Theory and Practice), 1977.

20. Warren Fenton Stubbins. Essential Electronics, 1986.

21. Donald A. Neamen. 电子电路分析与设计. 北京：清华大学出版社，2000.

22. 刘健，边康莎. 电力英语阅读与翻译. 北京：中国水力电力出版社，2000.

23. A. J. Herbert. The Structure of Technical English, 1994.

24. 能源部华北电业管理局. 电力专业英语，1994.

25. 陈雪丽，董事. 电气工程专业英语. 北京：机械工业出版社，2001.

26. Jai P. Agrawal. 电力电子系统——理论与设计. 北京：清华大学出版社，2001.

27. Prabha Kundur, Power System Control and Stability, McGraw-Hill, Inc., New York, 1994.

28. L.P. Singh, *Digital Protection-Protective Relaying from Electromechanical to Microprocessor*, John Wiley & Sons, New York, 1994.

29. Robert H. Miller, Power System Operation, McGraw-Hill Book Company, New York, 1983.

30. The Electricity Council, *Power system protection – 1 principles and components*, Peter Peregrinus Ltd., 1981.

31. L.P. Singh, *Digital Protection-Protective Relaying from Electromechanical to Microprocessor*, John Wiley & Sons,

New York, 1994.

32. T.S. Madhava Rao, *Power System Protection – Static Relays*, Tata McGraw-Hill Publishing Company Limited, 1979.

33. A.R. Bergen, *Power System Analysis*, Prentice-Hall Inc., New Jersey, 1986.

34. Theodore Wildi, Elcctrical Machines, Drives, and Power Systems, Prentice-Hall Inc., New Jersey, 2002.

35. Arthur R. Bergen, Power Systems Analysis, Prentice-Hall, Inc., New Jersey, 1970.

36. Vincent Del Toro, Electric Power Systems, Prentice-Hall, Inc., New Jersey, 1992.

37. Theodore Wildi, Electrical Machines, Drives, and Power Systems, Pearson Education, 2002.

38. John J.D'azzo, Constantine H.Houpis. Linear Control System Analysis and Design (Fourth Edition). McGraw-Hill, 2000.

39. Karl J.Astrom, Bjorn Wittenmark. Computer-controlled systems theory and design (Third Edition).